Library of
Davidson College

ATLA Monograph Series
edited by Dr. Kenneth E. Rowe

1. Ronald L. Grimes. *The Divine Imagination: William Blake's Major Prophetic Visions.* 1972.

2. George D. Kelsey. *Social Ethics Among Southern Baptists, 1917-1969.* 1973.

3. Hilda Adam Kring. *The Harmonists: A Folk-Cultural Approach.* 1973.

4. J. Steven O'Malley. *Pilgrimage of Faith: The Legacy of the Otterbeins.* 1973.

5. Charles Edwin Jones. *Perfectionist Persuasion: The Holiness Movement and American Methodism, 1867-1936.* 1974.

6. Donald E. Byrne, Jr. *No Foot of Land: Folklore of American Methodist Itinerants.* 1975.

7. Milton C. Sernett. *Black Religion and American Evangelicalism: White Protestants, Plantation Missions, and the Flowering of Negro Christianity, 1787-1865.* 1975.

8. Eva Fleischner. *Judaism in German Christian Theology Since 1945: Christianity and Israel Considered in Terms of Mission.* 1975.

9. Walter James Lowe. *Mystery & The Unconscious: A Study on the Thought of Paul Ricoeur.* 1977.

10. Norris Magnuson. *Salvation in the Slums: Evangelical Social Welfare Work, 1865-1920.* 1977.

11. William Sherman Minor. *Creativity in Henry Nelson Wieman.* 1977.

CREATIVITY IN HENRY NELSON WIEMAN

by
William Sherman Minor

with a Foreword by
Bernard E. Meland

ATLA Monograph Series, No. 11

The Scarecrow Press, Inc.
and
The American Theological Library Association
Metuchen, N.J. & London
1977

230
W646xm

Library of Congress Cataloging in Publication Data

Minor, William Sherman, 1900-
  Creativity in Henry Nelson Wieman.

  (ATLA monograph series ; no. 11)
  Bibliography: p.
  Includes index.
  1. Wieman, Henry Nelson, 1884-   I. Title.
II. Series: American Theological Library Association.
ATLA monograph series ; no. 11.
BX4827.W45M55   1977   230'.092'4   77-8087
ISBN 0-8108-1041-7

Copyright © 1977 by William Sherman Minor

Manufactured in the United States of America

80-1014

EDITOR'S NOTE

Since 1972 the American Theological Library Association has undertaken responsibility for a modest dissertation publishing program in the field of religious studies. Our aim in this monograph series is to publish in serviceable format and at reasonable cost at least two dissertations of quality each year. Titles are selected from studies in the several religious and theological disciplines nominated by graduate school deans or directors of graduate studies in religion. We are pleased to publish William Minor's fine study of creativity in Henry Nelson Wieman as number 11 in our series.

Professor William Sherman Minor is a native of Western Pennsylvania. Following undergraduate studies at Washington and Jefferson College, he studied philosophy and theology at the University of Chicago where he also took the doctorate in 1971. In addition to his post as associate to the dean of the Rockefeller Memorial Chapel at the University of Chicago, he also served as a teaching fellow. Since then Dr. Minor has taught in the School of Religion at the University of Missouri, Columbia; Earlham College; and West Virginia University, Morgantown. More recently he has served as director of the Foundation for Creative Philosophy, Carbondale, Ill. In addition to articles and reviews in professional journals Dr. Minor has co-authored five books and edited a sixth.

We are indebted to Professor Bernard E. Meland for his helpful Foreword.

Kenneth E. Rowe
Series Editor

Drew University Library
Madison, N.J.   07940

TABLE OF CONTENTS

Editor's Note	iii
Foreword (Bernard E. Meland)	ix
Acknowledgments	xiii
Preface	xvii

I. INTRODUCTION: HENRY NELSON WIEMAN'S
COMMITMENT TO CREATIVITY IN CONTEXT ... 1

Wieman's Commitment to Creativity	1
Wieman's Commitment in Context to 1915	2
Wieman's Commitment in Context, 1915-1917, and Thereafter	4

II. CREATIVITY IN WIEMAN AS A RESPONSE TO
PERRY'S INTEREST THEORY OF VALUE ... 8

Some Affirmations by Wieman of Perry's Interest Theory of Value	8
Wieman's Criticism of "Harmonious Happiness" As Perry's Principle for the Organization of Interests	10
As Presented in the Harvard Dissertation	10
As Presented in Wieman's Later Writings	14
Creative Tension in Wieman	19

III. CREATIVITY IN WIEMAN AS A RESPONSE TO
HOCKING'S RELIGIOUS PHILOSOPHY ... 22

Wieman's Response to Hocking in Context	23
Wieman's Response to Creativity in Hocking	29
Wieman's Response to Hocking's Delineation of Acts of God Through Personal Experience	30

vi / Table of Contents

Wieman's response to revelation in Hocking	30
Wieman's response to creative event in Hocking	37
Wieman's response to prophetic consciousness in Hocking	42
Wieman's Response to Hocking's Delineation of Providence as an Act of God Through Over-Individual Experience	48

IV. CREATIVITY IN WIEMAN AS A RESPONSE TO BERGSON'S AND WHITEHEAD'S ORGANISMIC PHILOSOPHY ... 71

Wieman's Response to Bergson's Organismic Philosophy of Creativity ... 72

Wieman's Response to Whitehead's Organismic Philosophy of Creativity ... 86

- Relativity and Societism ... 90
- Process Philosophy and Becoming ... 94
- Atomism and Actual Entities ... 96
- Empiricism and Thought ... 98
- Subjectivism and Experience ... 100
- Feeling and Prehension ... 103
- Creativity and God ... 105

V. CREATIVITY IN WIEMAN AS A RESPONSE TO JAMES' AND DEWEY'S REALISTIC AND EMPIRICAL PHILOSOPHIES ... 118

On the Early Formation of Empiricism in the Philosophies of James and Dewey ... 119

Dewey's Philosophy of Instrumentalism: a Self-facilitating Creative Process ... 122

Creative Experience in Dewey and Wieman's Response ... 125

Dewey's Reaction to the Theistic Import of His Own Religious Philosophy As Expressed by Wieman: Consequent Communications and Wieman's Responses ... 135

- Dewey Reviews *Is There a God?* and Wieman Responds ... 136
- Meland's letter to Dewey and Dewey's response ... 141

Table of Contents / vii

    Wieman's response   145

    Wieman Reviews <u>A Common Faith</u>: Consequent
        Communications and Wieman's Responses   148
        Aubrey's letter to Dewey and Wieman:
            responses from Dewey and Wieman   152
        Relevant correspondence between Jacobson
            and Dewey   161
        Wieman's 1961 and 1970 responses to Dewey   163

Clarification of Dewey's Concepts: Ideal, Natural
    Forces and Conditions, and Imagination in the
    Context of Creative Interchange   170

Import of James for Creativity in Dewey and Wieman   178

VI.   SUMMARY AND CONCLUSION   185

Chapter Notes   193

Bibliography   216

Index   225

FOREWORD

Henry Nelson Wieman was a theologian of the American experience in much the same sense that John Dewey has been described as a philosopher of the American experience. Toward the end of his life, on looking back over his years of writing and reflecting, Wieman remarked that, in retrospect, he could see that he had had more in common with Dewey than with any other thinker of modern times. In saying this, Wieman had in mind not only their common empirical orientation, but their common concern in focusing upon value and motivation within human experience, and the range of issues they brought to such inquiry: a format peculiarly adapted to reflecting upon the American experience. Thus with Wieman's death on June 19, 1975, at age ninety, one has the sense of a half century of theological Americana coming sharply into focus.

At the close of his career the impact of Wieman's thought was more evident among social scientists, psychologists, and educators than among theologians; though, interestingly enough, during the sixties and early seventies younger minds, alerted to problems of the ministry in their revolutionary social context, found Wieman's recent writing on "creative interchange" as stimulating and exciting as religious thinkers and ministers throughout the Midwest and Southwest had found his philosophy of religion during the twenties and thirties.

Until recent years little attention was given to the historical context of Wieman's thought and the philosophical influences which had shaped his distinctive mode of religious thought. To be sure, there was awareness of his early interest in Bergson, Dewey, and Whitehead, but to what extent, in what sense, or to what end were not always clear. Wieman, himself, had acknowledged an early acquaintance with the philosophy of Josiah Royce, and had made frequent references to his indebtedness to William Ernest Hocking, but his comments regarding them seemed more in the mood of nostalgia than by way of pointing to formative influences. He offered hints of such influences in autobiographical essays, as in "Theocentric Religion" [in Contemporary American Theology: Theological Biographies, first series, edited by Virgilius Ferm; 1932], and in his "Intellectual Autobiography" in The Empirical Theology of Henry Nelson Wieman [edited by Robert W. Bretall; New York: Macmillan, 1963]--but these, again, were reminiscent and impressionistic, with little critical probing into the sources of his thought. Not until Charles Rich's doctoral dissertation on "Henry Nelson Wieman's Functional Theism as Transcending Event" (1962) was a sustained effort made to explore specific strands of influence which had shaped Wieman's thinking.

The present work undertakes an even more sustained and probing effort to explore Wieman's thought in relation to that of philosophical mentors who influenced him, notably Ralph Barton Perry, William James, John Dewey, William Ernest Hocking, Henri Bergson, and Alfred North Whitehead. Minor's book is more than a background study: It is an insightful inquiry into the interplay between Wieman's empirical, realistic thinking and reflection upon specific insights of each of his philosophic mentors. What is distinctive about Minor's treatment in this book is the graphic and penetrating way he relates various turns of thought in Wieman's own philosophy of religion to comparable notions expressed in the writings of his mentors, enabling one to see not just affinities between them in their use of ideas or in ways of addressing issues, but subtle turns in Wieman's own thought, reflecting the way he either appropriates, or veers away from, their ways of stating an issue, or of formulating a working idea. This process of interchange is made particularly vivid in relating Wieman's thought to Hocking's notion of "creative event," or his "prophetic consciousness," or Hocking's "principle of alternation." In every instance a genuine interchange of meaning is demonstrated, indicating an assimilation of what Hocking had set forth, yet with a selective and critical reformulation of Hocking's notions within the context of Wieman's own thought, rendering them at once related, yet novel in what they purport. In a similar way, Minor demonstrates an interchange between Wieman and other mentors mentioned, citing specific legacies within their thought which have influenced his formulation of the notion of creativity. On Wieman's own admission, Hocking exerted a more sustained influence upon him over the years than any other philosopher. And when one reads Minor's account of the way the two men address themselves to the same or similar issues in philosophy, one can see that Hocking's influence was profound and substantive, more so even than that of Dewey's. It was Dewey's specific focus of issues and his empirical rigor in method of inquiry that attracted Wieman, but it was the vision and depth of Hocking's probing and range of inquiry that made his influence the lodestar of Wieman's intellectual and religious pilgrimage.

In focusing upon the notion of creativity, relating its development in Wieman's thinking exclusively to that of philosophers who had influenced him, Minor's study would seem to represent him exclusively in the role of philosopher. This comment is made, not to counter what Professor Minor has done in this definitive work, exploring the sources of Wieman's reflections upon creativity; but to define the limits of its inquiry, and to point to the source of its significance. There can be no understanding of the theological dimension of Professor Wieman's thought without an adequate understanding of the deeply philosophical context in which his theological quest was pursued. William S. Minor has vividly disclosed that context. Having this fascinating "creative interchange" between Professor Wieman and major philosophical thinkers of the modern era recounted and documented is an achievement for which one must be grateful. It is a contribution that can only enhance the legacy of the one being interpreted.

Bernard E. Meland

Chicago
January 1976

ACKNOWLEDGMENTS

I wish to acknowledge the assistance and guidance of my dissertation advisor, Bernard Eugene Meland, especially for his contagious interest in analyzing philosophic and theological strands within the history of Wieman's thought; for his contribution to the understanding of creativity in William James; for his sensitivity to the limitations and possibilities of problematic issues within the processes of research; for his forthright criticisms which invite creative interchange; and for his suggestions in improving linguistic expression.

I wish to acknowledge the contributions of The University of Chicago and its Divinity School for providing the services of Bernard Eugene Meland as my advisor, and Schubert M. Ogden and Joseph Sittler as readers; and also the services of other members of the regular and visiting faculty who have made significant contributions to the development of my research in philosophy of creativity, including: Shailer Mathews' language analysis of terms in the history of theology; Edwin Ewart Aubrey's analysis of theological issues; Thaddeus Ames' and Edmund S. Conklin's distinctions between pathological and creative religious behavior; Charles W. Gilkey's sponsoring my organizing and conducting an interdisciplinary seminar of graduate students for study of philosophy of creativity, which continued for a period of two years, and for the opportunity to present innovating contributions in conducting university chapel worship services; Alfred North Whitehead's, Charles Hartshorne's, and Henry Nelson Wieman's contributions to philosophy of creativity through lectures and seminars, especially Wieman's, whose early writings on philosophy of creativity I first read in the 1920's, and which determined my decision to register in The University of Chicago as a graduate student and consequently to continue research on creativity.

I wish to acknowledge the leave of absence given me during 1964-1965 by West Virginia University for research on creativity.

My former students at the University of Missouri, Earlham College, and West Virginia University, especially my assistants in the department of philosophy, and those who have been awarded doctorates, have served as a source of stimulation for rethinking and extending my research on creativity.

For Charles Mark Rich's doctoral dissertation, entitled "Henry Nelson Wieman's Functional Theism as Transcending Event," and for personal conferences with him, both of which have made a significant contribution to my research, especially in seeing more clearly the presence of Wieman's epistemological neo-realism in his philosophy and its import for his theology, I am deeply grateful.

I acknowledge the cooperation of the American Philosophical Association in launching in 1952 a research program on creativity in the context of the Association and in developing it through the Society for Philosophy of Creativity sponsored by the Foundation for Creative Philosophy, incorporated in 1957. In this context I acknowledge contributions to research on creativity in Whitehead, Mead, James, Bergson, Dewey, Hartshorne, and Wieman by Charles D. Tenney, David L. Miller, Bernard E. Meland, Joseph S. Wu, Robert L. Holmes, Lewis E. Hahn, and Daniel D. Williams, respectively, in the national meetings with groups of critics and discussants.

I acknowledge the contributions to research and to research planning by the consultants, and especially by the co-directors of the Foundation, John W. Davis, Howard L. Parsons, Lewis E. Hahn, and Galia M. Minor.

Finally, I acknowledge the cooperative services rendered by Southern Illinois University, including the Southern Illinois University Foundation for its assistance in the advancement of research on creativity, and especially in developing the 1969 National Conference for Philosophy of Creativity; Central Publications for its assistance in publishing and distributing research materials on creativity; the John Dewey Center for its research and publications; and the University Library as recipient of the Henry Nelson Wieman Archives.

I acknowledge the following permissions for reprinting copyrighted material:

Excerpts from Religious Inquiry by Henry Nelson

Wieman; copyright © 1968 by Henry Nelson Wieman; reprinted by permission of Beacon Press.

Excerpts from The Christian Century (February 8, March 1, March 22, April 5, and May 31, 1933; November 14 and December 5, 1934); copyright © 1933, 1934 by The Christian Century Foundation and reprinted by permission of the Foundation.

Excerpts from Realms of Value by Ralph Barton Perry; copyright © 1954, by Harvard University Press; reprinted by permission of Harvard University Press.

Excerpts from Creative Evolution by Henri Bergson, translated by Arthur Mitchell; copyright © 1911, 1939 by Holt, Rinehart and Winston; reprinted by permission of Holt, Rinehart, and Winston, and of Macmillan Administration (Basingstoke) Ltd.

Excerpts from Human Nature and Conduct by John Dewey; copyright © 1922 by Henry Holt & Co., reprinted by permission of Holt, Rinehart and Winston.

Excerpts from Process and Reality by Alfred North Whitehead; copyright © 1929 by Macmillan Publishing Co., renewed 1957 by Evelyn Whitehead. Reprinted by permission of Macmillan and of Cambridge University Press.

Excerpts from Philosophy, Religion, and the Coming World Civilization: Essays in Honor of William Ernest Hocking, edited by Leroy S. Rouner; copyright © 1966 by Martinus Nijhoff, reprinted by permission of Martinus Nijhoff, publishers.

Excerpts from Experience and Nature by John Dewey; copyright © 1929, 1925 by Open Court Publishing Co.; reprinted by permission of Open Court Publishing Co.

Excerpts from Intellectual Foundation of Faith by Henry Nelson Wieman; copyright © 1961 by Philosophical Library, Inc.; reprinted by permission of Philosophical Library, Inc.

Excerpts from Art As Experience by John Dewey; copyright © 1934 by John Dewey, renewed; reprinted by permission of G. P. Putnam's Sons.

Excerpts from The Source of Human Good, Religious Experience and Scientific Method, and Man's Ultimate Commitment, all by Henry Nelson Wieman. Copyright © 1946 by Southern Illinois University Press; copyright © 1926 by The Macmillan Company, renewed 1954 by Henry Nelson Wieman; copyright © 1958 by Southern Illinois University Press, respectively. Reprinted by permission of Southern Illinois University Press.

Excerpts from The Meaning of God in Human Experience by William Ernest Hocking; copyright © 1912 by Yale University Press; reprinted by permission of Yale University Press.

William Sherman Minor

PREFACE

The object of this study is to make some further contribution toward understanding the nature of creativity operative in the religious philosophy of Henry Nelson Wieman. The method of procedure is primarily internal analysis of main sources reconceived by Wieman in developing his own philosophy of creativity, with further analysis of Wieman's responses. These sources include especially contributions to a philosophy of creativity by Ralph Barton Perry, William Ernest Hocking, Henri Bergson, Alfred North Whitehead, William James, and John Dewey. The thesis which is defended is that there is a continuing tension in Wieman's religious philosophy of creativity, expressed with variable insights into the basic problem which generates this tension. The general context of the problem is Wieman's life commitment to religious inquiry. His formulation of the central problem in religious inquiry takes the form of the following question:

> What operates in human life with such character and power that it will transform man as he cannot transform himself, saving him from evil and leading him to the best that human life can ever reach provided that he meet the required conditions?[1]*

In its early stages, this basic concern for Wieman took the form of an inquiry into the problem of value. In effect, that context was never completely abandoned, even after he entered upon a cosmological and theological discussion of the issues. And more recently, with Wieman's increasing attention to problems of inter-relationship and response within the human community, this earlier focus of the problem seems to have reappeared in his writing. From the mid-twenties through the forties and on into the fifties, however, the basic problem for Wieman centered in formulating

---

*Notes to the Preface and chapters I-VI begin on page 193.

what he called "a working conception of God," which, in effect, amounted to stating in definitive and functional terms how the "Supreme" or "Ultimate" Value was to be conceived so as to provide explicit directives for living that could, in turn, provide conditions which would be creative of value in human experience. The meaning of God for Wieman always took the form of an experienceable event: <u>the meaning of God in human experience</u>, as Hocking, one of Wieman's early and beloved teachers, was to formulate the inquiry.

No other formulation of the problem of God interested Wieman; hence, while he was attentive at various times to cosmological and ontological dimensions of the inquiry, he was quick to abandon them when he sensed that they became a detour in his thinking from the experiential arena of value and creativity. To understand Wieman, one must take this experiential focus of ontological, cosmological, and mystical inquiries seriously. In all of the sources of thought which he studied, probed, and pondered through the years, he sought light on this basic inquiry, and related what he found there to his own basic inquiry into an experiential view of value as creativity.

The fact, however, that value and creativity could never be understood by Wieman as being solely a datum of human experience, isolated from what James had called the MORE, meant that such inquiry into value and creativity as experienced was always in juxtaposition with a penumbra of unmanageable occurrences of cosmic dimensions which precluded translating the religious inquiry into one of value, and creativity into a purely axiological or sociological inquiry, however much such inquiry might throw light on the problem. Creativity for Wieman was this experiential datum and MORE. Retaining awareness of this unmanageable penumbra of the reality of God that is "more than we can think," was for Wieman indispensable as an orientation in which to pursue the problem of value and creativity; yet to veer from the experiential base of the inquiry into absorption in this supervening depth of mystery, either as mystic or metaphysician, was to pursue a course that was equally rejected by Wieman. Thus we discover that the specific problem which generates the continuing tension is found in the following statement on religious inquiry into the nature of human creativity:

> Human creativity consists in bringing together these two sides of discovery, open awareness on the one hand and theorizing on the other--with its

analysis, discrimination, definition and experimentation. When these two are united and rightly balanced, human life leaps forward like an open spillway or a hound unleashed. Life becomes suddenly and marvelously abundant. When these two are brought into fruitful interaction, the richness of the world and the fertility of life is shown to be amazing. The artist, the prophet, the moral and social reformer, the scientific genius, the religious seer, all rise up in numbers and power when awareness of the wide, rich, novel fullness of concrete experience can be combined with the scientific method. But wide open mystic awareness flounders helplessly and blindly when unassisted by scientific method. And scientific method becomes a barren definition of concepts without yielding anything to enrich life when not supported by open awareness. [2]

Therefore, the problem in this study is "bringing together these two sides of discovery." From this study we point to the further import of creativity in Wieman.

Chapter I

INTRODUCTION: HENRY NELSON WIEMAN'S COMMITMENT TO CREATIVITY IN CONTEXT

WIEMAN'S COMMITMENT TO CREATIVITY

In closing his unpublished "Intellectual Autobiography" written in 1957, Mr. Wieman says: "My religious thinking, as I see it, can best be traced by examining the problem on which I have been working and explaining what I have done with it."[1] The problem stated by him in this paper is presented in the form of a question:

> What operates in human life with such character and power that it will transform man as he cannot transform himself, saving him from evil and leading him to the best that human life can ever reach, provided that he meet the required conditions?[2]

To this question, whether simply stated or stated more analytically as in the quotation given, whether answered directly or indirectly and inductively, and in whatever linguistic form, Wieman's answer has always been "God." Wieman then asks: "... to what should we refer when we use the word 'God'?"[3] In reply he says:

> We should refer to that kind of doing which is ascribed to God, namely, the doing of creation; the doing of salvation; the doing which keeps history going and judges history, the doing revealed in Jesus Christ; and, finally, the doing which occurs in the church when it is faithful to its mission.[4]

Creativity is the abstract form which is the "knowable aspect" of God.[5] During recent years the language Wieman uses to refer to this "knowable aspect" of God is "creative interchange." His choice of the phrase, "creative interchange," is for the sake of clarity. He says,

> this kind of doing, in all five of the different forms, is the doing of a kind of communication. This kind

1

of communication occurs to some degree between persons all the time. Without it we would not be human. But to be radically creative, transforming and saving, it must rise to a high level of dominance over counter processes which in ordinary life suppress and obstruct it. When the required conditions are present, however, it does rise to a level of power endowing human life with all its great values.6

We find that Wieman's firm and explicit commitment to creativity is expressed as early as 1917 in his doctoral dissertation, "The Organization of Interests," in which he says: "... cast all fortunes, for destruction or eternal life, on the side of creativity."7 Wieman's basic problem, expressed in the form of his analytic question quoted above, is the basis for this study of the role of creativity in his religious philosophy of living.

WIEMAN'S COMMITMENT IN CONTEXT TO 1915

Wieman's 1957 formulation of his main question was fifty years in the making. He began, in a general way, to formulate the basis for this question in the spring of 1907 when he was an undergraduate in Park College. At this time there was a dramatic change in his vocational direction. This change is vividly described by him:

> Throughout high school and up to the month of April in my senior year at College I was very sure that I should be a journalist. My mother's brother was editor of a small paper and in that unspoken way of hers my mother's expectations for me had become my expectations for myself. I would follow in the footsteps of my uncle. But one evening six weeks before my graduation I came to my room after the evening meal and sat alone looking at the sunset over the Missouri River. Suddenly it came over me that I should devote my life to the problems of religious inquiry. I never had a more ecstatic experience. I could not sleep all night and walked in that ecstasy for several days.8

This devotion of Wieman's life "to the problems of religious inquiry" was the beginning for the formation of the question stated analytically fifty years later as the central problem of his vocational career. The context of his devotion clarifies his commitment. His home was the manse of the Presbyterian church in which his father was minister. He says:

> My mother was a woman of profound piety and great power of religious devotion. She shaped the minds of her children in ways religious not by verbal instruction but by the encompassing might of her faith. This faith seemed to envelop our lives. She influenced others in the same way. Until she was past eighty a company of women some thirty in number came regularly to her home for worship and study every week. 9

In the Calvinistic Presbyterian tradition of Park College, Wieman participated as a college student in the college church, required chapel, daily morning worship, and many courses in Bible and religious thought. It was in Park, says Wieman, under the instruction of Ernest McAfee, teacher of "comparative religions," and Silas Evans, teacher of philosophy and college preacher, that he was first awakened "to the imperative urgency of the intellectual problem involved in the conduct of religious living."10 He was introduced to the philosophy of Josiah Royce by Silas Evans who "spent one entire course interpreting The World and the Individual,"11 Royce's Gifford Lectures, in two volumes, delivered in the University of Aberdeen during the years 1899 and 1900. Through Wieman's study of this work, he was also introduced to contributions from the philosophy of Charles Sanders Peirce, which through Royce's later development and clarification, proved to be influential in the formation of Wieman's concept of creative interchange.

Upon completing his college work, Wieman knew of no place to pursue his study of the religious problem except theological seminaries, so he entered the San Francisco Theological Seminary, a Presbyterian institution, where he remained for three years. At graduation he was awarded the traveling fellowship to study for a year in Germany. After working in philosophy of religion with Rudolf Eucken in Jena, and Windelband and Troeltsch in Heidelberg, he returned to the United States and served as a Presbyterian minister for four years. We can conclude our brief survey of the first thirty years of Wieman's life by saying that his pursuit of the problems of religious inquiry up to that time was strongly conditioned by his context in the environment of Calvinistic Presbyterian supernaturalism as an expression of the Christian tradition. And it was in this Calvinistic context that he assimilated influences from his study of Royce, Eucken, Windelband and others.

The second dramatic experience in Wieman's pursuit of the problems of religious inquiry occurred in the closing period of his pastorate in Davis, California, where he carried responsibility for education in religion of students in the State Farm School of the University of California. Of this experience Wieman says:

> I read Bergson and found him exciting. Bergson gave to my thinking a direction which deflected the influence of Harvard and caused me to reinterpret my teachers as I would not otherwise have done. Ever since those days of private study in Davis my thinking has been deeply influenced by Bergson's idea of Creativity, although my interpretation is somewhat different from his.[12]

WIEMAN'S COMMITMENT IN CONTEXT, 1915-1917, AND THEREAFTER

In leaving his pastorate in California to work for his doctorate in the Department of Philosophy at Harvard, Wieman observed that "one cannot effectively reach the students in an institution of higher learning unless one is himself a part of the institution as a member of the faculty or otherwise connected officially."[13] His enthusiastic response to Harvard as an institution where he could study the problems of religious inquiry led him to say fifty years after receiving his doctorate there in 1917 that "Harvard was the most stimulating and intellectually transforming experience of my life up to that time. It seemed to open up a new world and wide free ranges of thought."[14]

During the summer following Wieman's first year in the graduate school at Harvard, Josiah Royce died, but Wieman's early interest in the philosophy of Royce was carried forward and enriched by his work with William Ernest Hocking, whom Wieman discovered to be "another devoted follower of Royce."[15] In 1957 Wieman says: "The religious thinking of Professor Hocking has become an enduring part of my life."[16] Again in 1966, in reflecting on his work at Harvard, he says of Hocking's The Meaning of God in Human Experience: "... this book has nurtured my religious thinking more than any other book.... This book is the one I studied more devotedly than any other...."[17] He found Hocking to be "carrying further the changes initiated by Royce whereby idealism was becoming increasingly a kind of interpersonal creativity."[18] Wieman responds by identifying his own direction with these changes in Royce and Hocking: "This is the direction in which I myself have been moving to the point where my idea of creative interchange can no longer be called idealism in the sense in which Hegel intended."[19] However, he states a significant qualification regarding this identification by saying: "Bergson had already intervened to turn me away from the metaphysics of idealism...."[20]

In addition to Hocking there was another who most influenced Wieman at Harvard. This man was Ralph Barton Perry.[21] When Wieman arrived at Harvard, Perry, at thirty-nine, had taught philosophy for fifteen years, thirteen of them on the Harvard faculty, beginning there as an instructor and becoming in 1913 a full professor. Hocking was forty-two. He had been awarded his doctorate in philosophy at Harvard in 1904. After teaching in other institutions, including two years at Andover Theological Seminary, two years at the University of California, and five years at Yale, where he wrote The Meaning of God in Human Experience, published in 1912, Hocking was called to a professorship in Harvard in 1914. So, Hocking had been on the Harvard faculty for only a year when Wieman arrived. Perry was then working on his interest theory of value, which was to assume published form as The General Theory of Value in 1926. His Gifford Lectures, published as Realms of Value in 1954, summarized and developed his theory as presented in the earlier volume. It was this theory in its early stage of development which challenged Wieman as he continued to become more deeply involved in his study of the problems of religious inquiry. And it was these two philosophers, Perry and Hocking, both distinguished as teachers and for their writings, especially in the value disciplines, both having received their doctorates from Harvard, both in their early forties, who became most influential in Wieman's context as a graduate student in Harvard.[22]

Although the notion of creativity came to the fore in the development of Wieman's thought when he was reading Bergson's Creative Evolution just before he went to Harvard, we suggest that the birth of his philosophy of creativity occurred during the writing of his Harvard dissertation, in which we find four main strands of philosophic influence that were determining factors in making creativity focal in Wieman's philosophy: (1) Ralph Barton Perry's interest theory of value; (2) Josiah Royce's theory of interpretation--significantly, a response to interpretation in Charles Sanders Peirce--and William Ernest Hocking's theory of the Absolute; (3) Henri Bergson's philosophy of creativity with critical support and development from the works of Leonard Trelawney Hobhouse, and later from the works of Alfred North Whitehead; (4) William James and John Dewey, especially in their emphasis on the empirical, instrumental method of inquiry for understanding and improving the human situation. There was also significant influence from psychologists and social scientists, including E. B. Holt, C. A. Elwood and C. H. Cooley during the Harvard period, and others in later years including Harry Stack Sullivan, Peter Drucker and Kenneth Boulding, to mention only a few of them. Furthermore, we must be ever mindful of the fact that these intermingled strands of influence have their context in Wieman's earlier conditioning by a Calvinistic interpretation of the Judeo-Christian tradition.

In delineating these strands of influence, and their consequent development through critical interaction with other influences encountered during five more decades, we are beginning with Wieman's doctoral dissertation because we find that it is his first analytic and systematic expression of his religious philosophy of creativity. It is a unique dissertation in that it not only fulfills the commonly accepted requirement of focusing attention on the main issue, namely, "The Organization of Interests," but also it affords its author the opportunity to express and to organize his own interests in the development of his own systematic philosophy up to that time. We have discovered, with special significance for this study of creativity in Wieman, that his dissertation does express analytically and systematically both the form and content of his philosophy of creativity, not only at that time but also for its consequent development during the following five decades of his life and more. However, this observation does not refute the claim that Wieman's philosophy of creativity during the past fifty years has undergone continuous and significant change. In fact, his philosophy may well be characterized as a persisting structure of creativity within which we observe continuous expression of novelty. Therefore, we are giving special attention to the formation of his philosophy of creativity as expressed in his Harvard dissertation. From the four main strands of influence found in it, and these in the context of his earlier Calvinistic conditioning, we use this early formative structuring as significant for studying the further emergence of his philosophy of creativity.

Chapter II

CREATIVITY IN WIEMAN AS A RESPONSE TO PERRY'S INTEREST THEORY OF VALUE

Henry Nelson Wieman's dissertation, "The Organization of Interests," was written under the direction of Ralph Barton Perry, but this was nearly a decade before the publication of Perry's The General Theory of Value, and nearly thirty-five years prior to publication of Perry's Realms of Value. However, Wieman discovered in his working with Perry, during those years of 1915 to 1917, that Perry's "interest theory of value" was sufficiently challenging to cause him to write his dissertation as a critical response to it. The "problem" of his dissertation, as stated by him, is "to discover that organization of human interests which is most conducive to their maximum fulfilment." His "thesis is that all interests should be so organized as to function as one; and that one should be creative interest." The "principle of organization" which he affirms is "creativity." The "object" of his "quest" is "the greatest good."[1]

SOME AFFIRMATIONS BY WIEMAN OF PERRY'S INTEREST THEORY OF VALUE

Wieman listed six of Perry's writings in the bibliography of his dissertation. One was an essay on "The Definition of Value" in which Perry says that "value consists in the fulfillment of interest as such."[2] Perry treats interest as an attitude, a tendency toward action. The fulfillment of the interest is the fulfillment of a specific attitudinal interest in its patterned guidance of action. On this basis Perry makes clear the fact that his theory of value is in direct opposition to those theories, such as G. E. Moore's, which claim that value is indefinable. Perry says that "the attitude of interest either constitutes values or it cognizes them."[3] His claim is that this attitude of interest does constitute value but it does not cognize value. Since this attitudinal interest constitutes values, "the cognition of value lies in the observation, comparison, recording, and systematic description of interests in their relations to their objects and to one another."[4] Furthermore, he says that "the Judgment of Value is the judgment about interests, and is otherwise like any other judgment."[5]

In contrast to his own approach, Perry observes that if one claims that "the interest cognizes values, then values themselves are not matters of interest at all, but qualities of objects for which interest furnishes simply the requisite sensibility."[6] Perry then says: "If we accept this alternative we are thrown back upon Moore's contention that value is indefinable."[7]

It is evident from Wieman's response in his dissertation that his acquaintance with the development of Perry's theory went beyond what he found in the article, "The Definition of Value." Further knowledge of Perry's theory came from work on other writings by Perry listed in Wieman's bibliography, and also from courses and personal conferences with Perry, himself.

Wieman affirms Perry's theory of value in the sense that in his dissertation he begins to deal with his problems of religious inquiry by turning to "interests" as basic data to be examined. Wieman says that an interest is "a tendency to act in a certain way," which indicates that he accepts Perry's claim that an interest is an attitude, a tendency toward action. Wieman further says that "to carry out the tendency is to satisfy the interest."[8] On this basis Wieman derives his conception of "the ultimate unit of good," which is "satisfaction of interest."[9] These affirmations indicate that Wieman discovers the locus of value as such to be in an attitudinal interest and the locus of the ultimate unit of good to be in "satisfaction of interest." Furthermore, Wieman affirms that these designated meanings for "value" and "good" are abstractions attained by excluding the effects and ignoring "all ... future consequences" so that "the accomplishing of the act is a good so far as it fulfils that single interest under consideration."[10] Wieman then goes further to clarify his use of the term, "interest," by indicating how comprehensive it is, in that "interest" includes "all the activities of a physical organism," including "motor attitudes."[11] Interest is the "response of the organism to its environment."[12] These specific affirmations by Wieman indicate that he is following Perry's approach to value thus far. This he acknowledges.[13]

WIEMAN'S CRITICISM OF "HARMONIOUS HAPPINESS" AS PERRY'S PRINCIPLE FOR THE ORGANIZATION OF INTERESTS

... As Presented in the Harvard Dissertation

Clarification of Wieman's criticism of Perry's principle of "harmonious happiness" will be served, we believe, by placing Wieman's main affirmations on "interest," "good," "greatest good," "God," etc., in the context of his vocational commitment, i.e., to "problems of religious inquiry." The "greatest good" in the dissertation is "maximum fulfilment of interest," or "some massing of the ultimate units of good." In this immediate context he suggests that "We cannot know God's will except as we somehow find it in ourselves."[14] From this suggestion it seems that he is assuming that God is "the greatest good" which is found "in ourselves." Since, for Wieman, the "ultimate units of good" are determined by "fulfilment of interest," and since the "maximum fulfilment of interest" as "greatest good" is determined by "some massing of the ultimate units of good" as interests being fulfilled, we can see how Wieman's main problem in his dissertation emerges as "the massing" or organization of interests. However, there is more to his problem than mere organization. It is "to discover that organization of human interests which is most conducive to their maximum fulfilment." If we question the significance of such a discovery, we find Wieman's answer to this question in what he designates as the "object of his quest," namely, "greatest good." We observe that this "quest for greatest good" is his quest for understanding the nature of God in ourselves by discovering that kind of organization of interests which makes for their maximum fulfillment. The root meaning of his dissertation, from the very beginning of it, is clarified as basically theological, a study within the area of "problems of religious inquiry," which was the object of his vocational commitment as a college student. This kind of quest is not evident in Perry's interest theory of value. Wieman senses this deeply. This is why he becomes profoundly critical of it.

Wieman discovers that Perry's principle of organization of interests for their maximum fulfillment is the principle of coordination and harmonization.[15] This is what Wieman specifically rejects. Wieman says that the principle of organization is "creativity." The "thesis" which he sets forth and defends in his dissertation is that "all interests should be so organized as to function as one, and that one should be creative interest."[16]

Both Perry and Wieman agree that increase of value in human life requires organization of interests. This is not the issue between them, for Perry says: "The organized fulfillment of a self is better than the disorderly indulgence of its several impulses, on the ground that the fulfillment of interests as such is good, and therefore the more the better."[17] Perry goes further by supporting organization of interests, not only of the self as an individual, but also in the community. He says:

> Similarly, collective interest, as the fulfillment of the demand of community of interest signifies a greater measurement of fulfillment than does a private interest.[18]

Therefore, we see that Wieman's basic criticism of Perry is directed at the kind of principle of organization of interests which Perry supports.

Perry's principle of the harmonization of interests, which he later calls "harmonious happiness" in Realms of Value, is not stated explicitly as a theistic principle, but neither is it set forth explicitly as a non-theistic principle. In Perry's article, entitled "Contemporary Philosophies of Religion,"[19] he identifies his approach in philosophy of religion with what he calls "progressivism," illustrated in Development and Purpose by L. T. Hobhouse, rather than with mystical idealism, illustrated by The Meaning of God in Human Experience by William Ernest Hocking. Perry concludes this article by saying: "A philosophy of religion, in short, should devote itself to the construction, not of the most hopeful belief, but of the most credible hope."[20]

Perry's empirical emphasis suggested here, as opposed to mystical idealism, is reinforced later in Realms of Value. It is this empirical approach which determines Perry's moral theory of value. His "first principle," "harmonious happiness," emerges from this context. It is "that organization of interests in which each enjoys the non-interference and support of the others, whether within the personal life or the life of society."[21]

Perry then asks: How is this principle of organization to be proved? He replies by saying:

> Moral knowledge possesses the same general characteristics, and is subject to the same dis-

cipline, as all knowledge. It is true or false according to the evidence. It must avoid contradiction. It must invent and verify hypotheses. It must be faithful to the specific purpose of knowing, despite all temptation to the contrary. It must be self-denying, and accept the verdict pronounced by the facts or necessities of its subject matter. It must define its terms. These and all other formal criteria, or maxims, which are applicable to knowledge in general, are applicable to moral knowledge in particular, and in the same sense.[22]

With this clear-cut and uncompromising empirical method, Perry proceeds to use it in the following way in his effort to offer proof for verification of the principle of "harmonious happiness" for the organization of interests. First, he distinguishes "two kinds of moral knowledge, derivative and basic." Basic knowledge is attained by tracing derivative knowledge in the form of premises back to the ultimate or first premise. Perry presents "harmonious happiness" as the first premise of his moral theory of value. He supports it not only as a first premise but also as a first principle to be tested in governing human conduct. He says:

> If harmonious happiness can be truly affirmed to be the moral standard, it must so agree with human nature and the circumstances of human life that men can adopt it by education, persuasion, and choice; and, having adopted it, can govern their conduct in accordance with its requirements.[23]

The actual proof or evidence that the principle of harmonious happiness will satisfy the requirements for guiding human conduct "will be found," says Perry, "in the fact that it is so adopted and employed."[24] Furthermore, he says it is applicable. Since interest as such generates good and a harmonious relation of interests constitutes moral good and "since the principle of harmonious happiness deals with the nature of interest in general and with its types of relationship, it is applicable to all interests and persons."[25] Finally, Perry claims that

> harmonious happiness ... is the only norm which is capable of appealing to all men not only severally but jointly. It is the only norm which promises benefits to each interest together with all other interests. It does not rob Peter to pay Paul, but

limits Peter in order to pay both Peter and Paul. ...26

So, for Perry, "harmonious happiness" is the ultimate principle for the "organization of life by which conflict is escaped and by which cooperation is achieved...."27

Wieman, with rugged determination, disclaims the validity of this principle of "harmonious happiness" for the organization of human interests, the principle which Perry as his advisor for the dissertation has so firmly set forth. Wieman's acceptance of empiricism in Perry's theory of knowledge clears the ground for coming directly to the basic issue in question. For Wieman, creativity expressed in creative interest is the one valid principle for organizing human interests in the process of guiding human conduct. Wieman's commitment to creativity is prompted not merely by the fact that it is expressed in human interests, but that creativity is the ultimate principle of organization from which creative human interests are derived. It is a theistic religious principle for Wieman and not merely a moral ideal which, according to Perry, is the status of "harmonious happiness."28

Wieman's classification of human interests is based on their functioning under a system of organization. The degree of their satisfaction is determined by the manner of their correlation. The types of interest as classified are evaluated on the basis of their satisfaction or maximum fulfillment. The three categories in Wieman's classification are: (1) "automatic," which refers to interests expressed in innate reflexes and routine habits with no thought of consequences (their function is to adapt the organism to its environment in a process of sustained adaptation); (2) "instrumental," or those interests whose function is to form new combinations of adaptive reactions with ultimate satisfaction in adaptation (these instrumental interests are unstable in that they move toward becoming either automatic or creative, more often automatic); and (3) "creative interests," or paradoxical interests which are "satisfied by dissatisfaction." They are fulfilled by uncoordinated interests. They feed on dissatisfaction with adaptive interests. In creative interest there is increase of the range, complexity, and intensity of the consciousness of reality. "It is the increasing concreteness of reality which is the sole satisfaction of creative interest." Wieman's basic claim is that maximum satisfaction of interest is attained only by commitment to creativity.29

Wieman's rejection of Perry's "harmonization of interests" as ideal is based on his observation that this ideal is an outcome of the empirical human situation. For Wieman, this ideal is unrealistic because human conflict is an inevitable and realistic fact of life which is not to be discounted by any ideal of harmonization or coordination. Human conflict is to be accepted for "Friction between persons is necessary in order that there be any mutual interpretation of minds."[30] The real issue is how to deal with conflicting human interests. For Wieman, they can be dealt with either destructively or creatively. Creative interest makes use of conflicting interests. This is so in "humor, art, friendship, and the relations of the individual to society."[31] Creative organization of conflicting interests produces the "most remarkable effect" with a peculiar acceleration, exuberance, and development of self-consciousness, the growth of which "is what we mean by creativity."[32] "It is the antagonism of other minds," says Wieman, "which, more than anything else, stimulates the processes" of what he calls "secondary" or self consciousness.[33] For Wieman, the study of creativity is centered in the interaction of minds in society. This area is, for him, the most pormising field for such study because we find in it the "mutual creativity of minds, which is of highest worth."[34] But we also find opposite tendencies as necessary conditions. Therefore, our actual society cannot be organized into an ideal society of coordinated and harmonious interests as presented by Perry. His essential principles of social organization of interests are distinctly different from Wieman's mode of organization, which is creative. Wieman's claim at this point is based on his classification of interests. There is a quality and pattern of creativity in creative interests which is not found in either automatic or instrumental interests. This quality and order of creativity for Wieman is religious. It is only at this level of organization of interests that the basic conflicts in society can be dealt with creatively.[35]

... As Presented in Wieman's Later Writings

Forty years later, Wieman was to return to his critical response to Perry's theory of value. He acknowledged that is was Perry who introduced him to the philosophical study of the problem of value, which he says has been for him "a central concern ... ever since, although I have departed from Perry's treatment of it."[36] In <u>Man's Ultimate Commitment</u>, published in 1958, he was to address himself directly and extensively to Perry's theory of value as one of nine sources of moral confusion.[37] Here he calls it "liberal harmony." As an introduction to his main criticism of it, he makes five statements about it. First, he says that it is "the most popular" of all the nine norms. Secondly, he says that this norm of liberal harmony "has been identified with Western democracy." Thirdly, he claims that this norm "is most congenial to our way of thinking." Fourthly, he says that because of these conditions, "it is difficult to see the danger in it." Fifthly, he points to the need for exposing this danger by "further criticism" of it.[38]

Wieman's summary criticism of Perry's liberal harmony is that it is a trap in which we have been caught. The conditions that have brought about this predicament are as follow: (1)

> When judgments of better and worse are made by many people these value judgments cannot be readily ordered into a liberal harmony if they are judgments made by the total self in all the uniqueness of its individuality.[39]

For Wieman, it is not what men have in common but rather the uniqueness of their individuality, insofar as they can function as whole selves, which makes it so difficult to order their value judgments into a liberal harmony. The fact of novelty which renders individual human life unique is taken seriously. This quality of novelty in the individual is appreciated as essential to creative activity and is not to be obstructed or suppressed by mass conformity. But this is just what happens when men are caught in the trap of liberal harmony as the basic norm in value theory. Further clarification is needed to show how this occurs. (2) The second condition is an outcome of the first. The effort to harmonize value judgments of total selves in their novel expression requires sacrifice of the wholeness of self attained, so that less and less of the total self can be expressed. Consequently, value judgments expressed by partial selves are not open judgments of the authentic self, but partial and distorted judgments. (3) "These value judgments of the partial self can become pernicious when they do not generate conflict between associated individuals."[40] This is a further direct reference to Wieman's acceptance of conflict as an essential and empirical basis of his value theory. Not the ideal of liberal harmonization of human conflict, yielding mass conformity with sacrifice of individuality and personal integrity, but instead, the open sharing of personal and interpersonal conflict dealt with creatively, through mutual interpretation of conflicting interests, is Wieman's way. (4) Wieman observes that when a collective judgment is formed under the ideal of liberal harmonization of interests, with the consequent outcome of mass conformity, it is

> exceedingly difficult for any individual or small minority to break through the crust of conformity thus imposed. Especially is this true if the mass agreement is about a matter mistakenly held to be of supreme importance for the nation or the total culture or, as it might be, for all humanity. In this way men are caught in a trap of collective judgment and driven to seek evil under the illusion that it is good. [41]

In this more recent work, Wieman offers further criticism of tragic errors he discovers in Perry's theory. Two of these are significant for special analysis and interpretation. His criticism of these two errors is based on his observation that Perry's theory of value is one form of utilitarianism that begins with inquiry into "the thronging concrete fulness of life," in terms of what man "now likes and dislikes and into all which he can imagine himself liking and disliking in the consequences flowing from the alternatives before him."[42] This is not only an individual but also a social approach, for it should include all that man "is now able to approve and disapprove in the interests of other people throughout the expanse of humanity and history so far as his imagination can extend." From this context one

> should choose the alternative which yields the greater balance of what he favors and approves as over against what he disfavors and disapproves. In this way he seeks the most inclusive, liberal harmony of all interests. "Liberal" in this context means that each individual should be free to choose what his own unique individuality demands so long as it does not hinder like privileges of others. [43]

These two criticisms, based on a balanced harmonization of personal and social likings experienced now, and also as imagined possible likings, are expressed in the first, in terms of "enjoyment" and in the second, in terms of "pleasant feeling," both as existing within the process of Perry's "likings."

The first criticism holds that what one, and others, now enjoy, and also imagine or anticipate that they can enjoy, offers no reliable indication of their future enjoyments, since "more experience and more knowledge ... with progressive reorganization of ... personality" through interchange with others may make a radical difference in what is or is not later enjoyed. Therefore, for one to choose in terms of present and anticipated enjoyments for one's self and others "is to choose in a way that is doomed to error and disappointment," not so much for short-range choices but more especially for long-range "decisions which determine national and social policy" and "life commitment ... in trust that it will make for the greatest possible good for himself and for all men in all times."[44]

For Wieman, this criticism means that all present and anticipated enjoyments should be experienced and enjoyed subject to radical transformation, because of possible emergence of novel experiences which cannot possibly be experienced, known, predicted, or even imagined "prior to their occurrence." This criticism claims that, if man orders his life solely in terms of what he presently likes, enjoys, and can imagine, he shuts himself off from the grace of creative interchange, and then finds himself imprisoned by his own zeal for maximum order and efficiency. Wieman concludes this criticism by saying:

> From observation of others and from the records of history, literature, and psychological studies, the happy life is most likely to result from new enjoyments arising unexpectedly, which could not be anticipated except in the sense of knowing that if one lives in such a way as to expand and deepen his capacity for appreciation such glad surprises will occur. But this cannot be accomplished by way of any calculus of specific favorings now accessible to knowledge and imagination.[45]

The second of these two criticisms points to the tragic consequence of a theory of value which centers attention on likings as pleasant feelings and the harmonization of them, rather than on the causes of likings and pleasant feelings. If one's attention is diverted from the causes, such as a ball-game, a friend, or a sunset in order to evaluate the pleasant feelings experienced, the pleasant feelings or enjoyments in such instances fade out. Wieman concludes this criticism with the following statement:

> ... to find the greater good one needs to forget his own preferences and feelings of enjoyment and devote himself to what creates progressively in his own person and in his associates the capacity to appreciate a wider range and diversity of entities even though at the time he cannot imagine what these entities might be, and is totally unable to enjoy them until after the capacity to enjoy them has been created in him.[46]

At this point Wieman's faith in further creative novel emergence of value, prior to any knowledge or imagination of its occurrence, is more sharply focused. There is a mystical trust in this kind of faith in that values will be created beyond anything we can now know or imagine. However, the mysticism in it may well be characterized as empirical and realistic in that the faith is in an actuality and not in a mere possibility. Nor is it in an impossibility as something which never can become actual. The actuality is creativity itself operative within the actual world of human experience. From this context we can now see more clearly why Wieman finally opposed Perry's liberal harmony as the ideal for mankind. Wieman calls it "that non-existent impossibility that never can be."[47] He then points to the fact that "many an aesthete and lover of art, and others," including Perry, "have been eloquent on this point."[48]

With a summary perspective on Wieman's later criticisms of Perry's theory of value, offered after he wrote his Harvard dissertation, we see that they are not only an outgrowth of those offered in his dissertation but are also consistent with them. In each of these later criticisms, Wieman sees creative organization of conflicting human interests through mutual interpretation of them as the basic corrective for Perry's norm of liberal harmony of interests. This approach of creative organization will make possible: (1) growth of appreciation for the emergence of novel human behavior with creative organization and preservation of it, as opposed to liberal harmonization requiring sacrifice of novelty in human individuality with consequent mass conformity and prevention of wholeness of expresssion of human selves; (2) personal and social guidance of human behavior by emerging novelty creatively organized, as opposed to organization of merely present and imagined likings which is a trap for all who fail to open the way for creative emergence of novel behavior prior to its actual occurrence; (3) more objective centering of attention on what one is interested in and on what one likes, with growing understanding of and appreciation for the causal conditions and consequences of interests and likings, as opposed to centering attention sentimentally on the subjective abstraction of feelings from what is felt, of likings from what is liked, and of enjoyments from what is enjoyed, which yields a fading of value from the creative causal conditions and consequences, impoverishing the meaning of life itself.

CREATIVE TENSION IN WIEMAN

In concluding this chapter we wish to emphasize that however cognizant we have become of Wieman's adverse criticisms of Perry's theory of value, we are no less aware of Perry's positive contributions to Wieman's philosophy of creativity. We have said earlier that Perry's empirical theory of inquiry was accepted by Wieman for study of the problems of value. In Wieman's first book he says: "For introduction to the spirit of scientific method, and enthusiastic appreciation of it, I owe most to Professor Ralph Barton Perry."[49] In Chapter VI, entitled "Scientific Method," Wieman clarifies what he means by it. He draws from Perry what Wieman calls "a most excellent statement" of it:

> Scientific description, then, is governed by two motives, on the one hand, unity, parsimony, or simplicity, the reduction of variety and change to as few terms as possible; and, on the other hand, exact formulation. When a scientific description, satisfying these conditions is experimentally verified, it is said to be a law....[50]

Wieman proceeds further by using from Perry an illustration of scientific method, and also Perry's interpretation of the illustration.[51] The main issue which impressed Wieman from this context of study with Perry was not the operation of scientific method as such, after granting its basic significance as a valid mode of inquiry, but the question as "to the central motive of scientific investigation, the index of its great value and the mark of its severe limitations."[52] The tension between its great value and its severe limitations was felt and carried forward by Wieman down through the years. He, like many others, has found that a fair balance of emphasis on the values and the limitations has been difficult to maintain. Wieman sees that "the scientist isolates certain portions of the world and deals with them to the exclusion of all else." He sees these portions as fine threads of correlation.[53] This, like Perry's, is Wieman's accepted mode of inquiry to gain knowledge. But this restricted mode of inquiry does not reveal the rich and massive fullness of value which may enter human awareness of the world even though this awareness does not of itself constitute knowledge. Out of this tension between the values and limitations of science, initiated and intensified by his work with Perry, Wieman formulates his perception of human creativity by saying:

> Human creativity consists in bringing together those two sides of discovery, open awareness on the one hand and theorizing on the other--with its analysis, discrimination, definition and experimentation. When these two are united and rightly balanced, human life leaps forward like an open spillway or a hound unleashed. Life becomes suddenly and marvelously abundant. When these two are brought into fruitful interaction, the richness of the world and the fertility of life is shown to be amazing. The artist, the prophet, the moral and social reformer, the scientific genius, the religious seer, all rise up in numbers and power when awareness of the wide, rich, novel fullness of concrete experience can be combined with the scientific method. But wide open mystic awareness flounders helplessly and blindly when unassisted by scientific method. And scientific method becomes a barren definition of concepts without yielding anything to enrich life when not supported by open awareness.[54]

That concern with open awareness of the concrete fullness of reality was not derived from Wieman's study of Perry's theory of value, but from others, especially by the one other professor at Harvard who influenced Wieman most, William Ernest Hocking. The tension between open mystical awareness of reality richly present in Hocking, and empirical scientific analysis of issues in the context of epistemological neo-realism, highly developed in Perry, was personalized and dramatized by these two men for Wieman at Harvard. Perhaps it is not far afield to suggest that this tension is a major source of his own creativity.

We have seen that Wieman's criticisms of Perry's theory of value, based on the ideal of liberal harmonization of human conflict, calls for creative organization of human conflict by means of mutual interpretation of interests. Therefore, our study of creativity in Wieman will proceed by investigating those sources which have centered attention on mutual interpretation and which have been used by Wieman. These are mainly works of Josiah Royce, including his response to Charles Sanders Peirce on this issue, and of William Ernest Hocking. Since the birth of Wieman's philosophy of creativity occurred at Harvard, with his study focused mainly in work with Perry and Hocking, our study may well turn now to Wieman's response to Hocking, treating these other influences, including Royce and Peirce, in this context.

Chapter III

CREATIVITY IN WIEMAN AS A RESPONSE TO HOCKING'S RELIGIOUS PHILOSOPHY

William Ernest Hocking's religious philosophy had four main components to which Wieman was to respond, namely: mysticism, realism, pragmatism, and metaphysical idealism. These components are often treated as philosophic schools. For Hocking, they were functionally related. Each contributed something significant to religious philosophy. In this context Hocking saw idealism as being fulfilled. In his Preface to The Meaning of God in Human Experience, Hocking described his philosophic attitude in summary form by saying:

> It is the finished pragmatist who best knows the need of the absolute. It is the finished mystic who best knows the need of active life and its mediation. It is the finished idealist who best knows the need of the realistic elements of experience; the mystical and authoritative elements of faith. I know not what name to give to this point of convergence, nor does name much matter: it is realism, it is mysticism, it is idealism also, its identity, I believe, not broken. [1]

At this point Hocking became specific in stating what he meant by idealism:

> For in so far as idealism announces the liberty of thought, the spirituality of the world, idealism is but another name for philosophy--all philosophy is idealism. [2]

This is radical idealism, for Hocking says:

> It is only the radical idealist who is able to give full credit to the realistic, the naturalistic, even the materialistic aspects of the world he lives in. [3]

Wieman's response to Hocking, expressed first in his Harvard dissertation, continued through the years with both appreciative and critical analyses of main principles, until finally in responding to the invitation to contribute to the Hocking Festschrift, Wieman accepted as an opportunity to show, as he said, "how my empirical philosophy of religion has developed out of his but has taken a different form."[4]

Wieman had differed not only from Perry on Perry's interest theory of value and the liberal harmonization of values,[5] but also from Hocking, mainly on Hocking's metaphysical idealism.[6] Wieman describes his confrontation with Hocking at the close of his oral examination for the doctorate at Harvard, as follows:

> As I left the room after receiving the judgment of the examining faculty, Professor Hocking stood at the door as I went out. In his courtly way he extended his hand to me and said, 'Some day we'll have a good fight together.'[7]

Wieman's full response to this challenge did not come until nearly fifty years after this event. It is expressed systematically in the same courtly way, as if by extended hand, in his chapter, "Empiricism in Religious Philosophy."[8] But first we shall look at Hocking's religious philosophy in context.

WIEMAN'S RESPONSE TO HOCKING IN CONTEXT

Our contextual survey of the Hocking influence, and through Hocking the salient influences from Royce, Peirce, and James, seems significant in order to deepen and vivify our range of perspectives for our further and more specific study of Wieman's response to creativity in Hocking.

We shall see that both Hocking's and Wieman's religious philosophies of creativity are at root philosophies of creative communication. This fact will become increasingly evident as we proceed to explore the Hocking context, the influence of Hocking on Wieman, and Wieman's response.

Hocking's mystical, empirically realistic, pragmatic, and idealistic strands in his philosophy are especially influenced by Josiah Royce and William James, two of Hocking's Harvard professors whom he described as "my honored masters in these matters, the groundwork of my thinking."[9]

In observing the strand of empiricism in Hocking's philosophy, we find that he was first introduced to writings of William James, radical empiricist, while he was an undergraduate civil engineering student in the State College at Ames, Iowa. James' *Principles of Psychology*, which he read at that time, was the determining factor in his decision to go to Harvard to study with James.[10] Leaving Ames before finishing for his degree in engineering, he taught school for several years to earn enough to go on to Harvard. There he was influenced not only by James, distinguished for his pioneering radical empiricism and pragmatism, but also by Royce, whom James had brought to Harvard and who was increasingly influenced by James. Furthermore, through Hocking's work, first with Royce, and later with James, his empiricism and pragmatism were also influenced by Charles Sanders Peirce. In the beginning of Hocking's work with Royce, Royce was working on possible contributions of Peirce's mathematical logic to problems regarding the reality, perfection, and infinite nature of the absolute. Aristotle had claimed that "the infinite cannot be real or actual, because an infinite series cannot be 'run through' to its last term."[11] Francis Herbert Bradley, in his *Appearance and Reality* (1893), had argued "that since the actual infinite is unending it is imperfect and therefore irrational."[12] Royce had published his Gifford Lectures, entitled "The World and the Individual" (1899-1901), to refute Bradley's "denying to the human mind genuine knowledge of the individual."[13] In these Gifford Lectures, Royce was defending

> the actual infinite and thus of attempting to show how genuine individuals can be the subject of a metaphysical dialectic ... pointing out how a formula that expresses a general purpose and requires an infinite series of terms for its complete expression is the model of the actual infinite.[14]

Royce thought he had found in Peirce's infinite "an ideal logical model for the formal characteristics of the absolute,"[15] for Peirce had suggested "that a real or actual infinite is not irrational, but a perfect order."[16] Supplementing Peirce's contribution, Royce accepted the mathematician, Dedekind's definition of the infinite, "not as an unending series, but rather as a definite type of 'system.'" Then Royce added his own claim that "the infinite system is purposive."[17]

From this context Royce reasoned that the relating of things such as numbers in a series involves something more than the things to be related. "It involves the thought which relates them." The relation is therefore not "dyadic" but "triadic." From this he developed his theory of interpretation, "the key to all reality," which is "the process of the present interpreting the past to the future." Royce saw this as a social process of the scientific community as a whole including the work of individuals. This process he called "the absolute." It is the basis of his philosophy of communication. For Royce, in Rouner's terms,

> The interpreting work of each individual is a self-representation of the work of the absolute, which is the actual, purposive, infinite structure of the world.[18]

While Hocking found significance in Royce's theory of interpretation, he did not find in it what he was searching for, namely, direct empirical knowledge of ourselves and of other minds. This, for Hocking, seemed essential for a justifiable philosophy of communication. Hocking was interested in the complete defeat of solipsism,[19] for it was the subjectivism within the tradition of idealism which, according to both Royce and Hocking, was self-defeating.[20] And it was their moving toward epistemological realism and empirical pragmatic methods of knowing that was most appreciated by and acceptable to Wieman.

Hocking's empiricism as influenced by direct contact with William James did not occur until after he had worked with Royce at Harvard, since James had been on leave to deliver the Gifford Lectures in Scotland. When James returned to the campus with his manuscript of The Varieties of Religious Experience, Hocking, appreciatively oriented in the philosophy of Royce, was critical of James as having a "lack of method." But after studying the varieties of mystical religious experience reported and interpreted by James, Hocking began to appreciate James' interpretation of religious mysticism. James was saying that there is a genius in the religious experience of the mystics and that this is not to be confused with the symptoms of nervous instability and abberation, for they have experienced the "original source" of ordinary, conventional religion. Hocking accepted this general thesis and used it in The Meaning of God, claiming that "the 'true mystic' is the one most acutely aware of the 'original sources' of Everyman's knowledge of God."[21]

In *The Varieties of Religious Experience* James defines experience, as opposed to the reduction of experience to the philosophical ideas of the absolute idealists, "as being the real backbone of the world's religious life."[22]

Rouner, with his characteristic conciseness, summarizes Hocking's response:

> Hocking's metaphysics argues that the mystic is a radical empiricist, dealing with the stuff of experience in its most profound dimension. His theology argues, in opposition to the usual contrast between mysticism and prophecy, that the mystic is both the 'true worshipper' and the 'true Prophet.' He is the one who combines the most perceptive religious insight with the most effective religious activity in the world.[23]

In our delineation of Hocking's religious mysticism as the "original source" of man's knowledge of God, we shall see the profound influence of James, for Hocking's analysis of the creative acts of God stems from this "original source" of the mystics. This is the context for Hocking's experience of the creativity of God. Furthermore, we shall see that Wieman accepted this empirical mysticism of the James-Hocking legacy as basic to the development of his own philosophy of creativity.

However, Hocking is both appreciative and adversely critical of the pragmatic method of knowing. He distinguishes positive from negative pragmatism. For him, negative pragmatism based on the claim that "That which does not work is not true," is "invaluable as a guide" to truth. It is "an effective instrument of knowledge." It is especially "significant ... in the field of religious knowledge." Of this he says:

> It is the function of the pragmatic test (as of pain and discomfort generally) to point out something wrong; the work of discovering what is right must be done by other means.[24]

For Hocking, on the other hand, positive pragmatism "as a positive builder ... has little to recommend it."[25] It places the responsibility for attaining knowledge on the subjectivity of human will and human value rather than on the objective realism of superpersonal will and value on which man is dependent for whatever he tries to create. Human creativity is derived from divine creativity, which is the criterion of reality.[26]

We find in Wieman's The Source of Human Good, Chapter VII, "Truth," and Chapter VIII, "Knowledge," evidence for Wieman's support of Hocking's realism in knowing divine creativity, and in countering subjectivism in the merely human effort to know and to create. We believe that Wieman's basic criticism of non-theistic pragmatism is that the creativity upheld is "that of the human mind, not a creativity working antecedently to the mind, creating it along with its world."[27]

Neither Hocking's emphasis on objective realism and individuality nor his own individuality was sacrificed in his working appreciatively with his "honored masters." He expressed dissent from the view of both Royce and James.

> I have differed freely from both, in the spirit of their own instruction, but not without the result of finding myself at one with both in greater measure than I would once have thought possible--or logically proper![28]

While maintaining his individuality, perhaps it was Hocking's open and sensitive feeling of awareness of the conflicting philosophic currents around him that stimulated in him a growing philosophic interest in creative communication. We suggest that Wieman's deep and lasting concern for learning how to deal creatively with human conflict, without loss of individuality, through mutual interpretation and creative communication can be better understood by knowing his religious philosophy in the context of Hocking, Royce, and James.

Hocking's unpublished Harvard dissertation, "The Elementary Experience of Other Conscious Being in Its Relations to the Elementary Experience of Physical and Reflexive Objects,"[29] is a treatise on philosophy of communication. "A note above the title describes it as 'Philosophy of Communication, Part I,'" according to Richard C. Gilman,[30] quoted by D. S. Robinson in "Hocking's Contribution to Metaphysical Idealism."[31] Gilman suggests that Hocking's note not only announces the central theme of Hocking's dissertation, but also indicates "the author's further plans for research and publication on that topic."[32] Furthermore Gilman says:

> The main thesis of this work, which might be restated as 'How We Know Other Minds,' is the original statement of Chapters XVII to XX of The Meaning of God in Human Experience.[33]

In addition to this clarification of the formal title of Hocking's dissertation, Robinson informs us that the dissertation is an outgrowth of an essay which Hocking had written[34] and submitted to Royce while having a course in metaphysics with him during his last graduate year in Harvard, 1903-1904. In Hocking's Preface to Marcel's volume on Royce, we find significant content for our further study of the emerging experience of creative communication in Hocking's religious philosophy. It is here that Hocking says that he "ventured to differ from one of his [Royce's] central doctrines." Hocking says:

> I was expecting a radical criticism from my revered professor. Instead, when Royce handed my essay back, he pointed out the dissenting passage with the comment, 'this is your insight: you must adhere to that!' Without assenting to my view, he had given me his blessing for its development.[35]

Royce's central doctrine from which Hocking dissented is expressed by Hocking as follows:

> ... we have no direct knowledge either of our own minds or of other minds. For, as he held, selves are individual; and individuals are beings such that, for each one, there can be in the whole universe no other precisely like it; this is what we mean by our individual attachments. Such uniqueness can be no matter of empirical knowledge: it is rather a matter of will: 'it is thus ... that the mother says, "There shall be no child like my child"' (The World and the Individual, 458-460) ergo no possible substitution, no recompense for loss.[36]

In dissenting from this "central doctrine" in Royce, Hocking says:

> I reported an experience in which, as I read it, I was directly aware of another mind and my own as co-knowers of an 'It.' So far as feeling was involved, that feeling was cognitive, not simply an I-will: we must extend the conception of empirical

knowledge, and so admit an element of realism within the ideal totality.[37]

This further development of realism and empiricism in Hocking's religious philosophy, which began during the period of his graduate work in Harvard, and continued in later years, especially observable, as Gilman says, in The Meaning of God in Human Experience, is the direction in Hocking which was accepted by Wieman.

WIEMAN'S RESPONSE TO CREATIVITY IN HOCKING

We find in Hocking's works, but more especially in The Meaning of God in Human Experience, many specific contributions from his understanding of creativity. In The Meaning of God, Hocking says: "... what is more to be wished for than insight into creativity?"[38] In his four closing chapters, PART IV, "The Fruits of Religion," we find the climactic development of this classic in religious philosophy. We observe here a systematic treatment of what Hocking means by "creativity." The "fruits" are the "results" of religion. The "results" are acts of God: for that is an act of God which cannot happen without turning the mind to God."[39] The locus of these results is the worship of God: "... we must recognize in worship the very process through which religion becomes historically fertile."[40] Hocking's classification of these results is similar to his classification of ethics, namely, personal and social. There are acts of God through personal or individual experience and there are acts of God through social or "over-individual" experience. The creative acts of God through personal experience are of three types: (1) revelation, (2) the creativity of religion: inspiration or the creative event,[41] and (3) the prophetic consciousness, treated in Chapters XXX, XXXI, and XXXII, respectively. The creative acts of God through social or over-individual experience (Chapter XXXIII) which appear in "the structure of the social environment, ... the general movement of history," are the expressions of "providence."[42] These creative acts of God are clarified by Hocking by his placing them in the context of mysticism, that "original source" of conventional religion to which William James directed attention.

From Wieman's earliest work on his Harvard dissertation, in which he claims that the creativity of God expressed through worship is the source of creative communication as an alternative way to deal most effectively with human conflict, as opposed to Perry's ideal liberal harmonization of interests, and on through his later major writings, Wieman never loses sight of what he learned from this analysis by Hocking of the creative acts of God. From this context Wieman develops his claim that the creativity of God expressed in his acts within both personal and social experience is the source of human good, the salvation of man.

Wieman's Response to Hocking's Delineation of Acts of God through Personal Experience

Wieman's response to revelation in Hocking

For Hocking, the original and elemental stage of the mystic is revelation, "that <u>knowledge</u> which is the especial product or by-product of religion." Revelation is distinguished from the creative event (inspiration or religious creativity) in that "the contents of 'revelation' are twofold":

> There is first the certainty and praise of God, and of the mystic's relation to God; this knowledge moves within its own circle, and has no apparent fruit nor progress, being to an external view self-absorbed and empty, not much else than certainty of certainty. But secondly, there is the positive contribution of the mystic and prophet to the concrete spiritual wealth of mankind, a creativity to which we can discern no limit. [43]

Here then in Hocking we have the ground of creativity in the reality of God actually known, not in any scientific sense, but through the revelation of God which is an act of God connecting God and man through mystical, sensitive and receptive immediate feeling awareness of the individual worshiper of God. Hocking sees this feeling awareness as properly limited to a bare revelation of God. Its content is not analytic. It is vague and unclear, however certain it may be. Even though this bare revelation carries the possibilities for the birth of ideas of God, the mystic's feeling awareness of the reality yields only a knowledge which belongs to a primitive but essentially human and reliable religious certainty. From this source there emerges, in the experience of man, the unpredictable and seemingly unparented creative event. For Hocking, this is the second of the four creative acts of God which are experienced in the worship of God.

We discover in Wieman this mystic certainty of the reality of God which Hocking calls revelation.

> Never once throughout my life have I doubted the reality of God, whatever the revolutionary changes in my ideas about what, in truth, does have the character and power to transform man after the manner indicated. 44

The "manner indicated" is clarified in his next sentence.

> These changes in my religious thinking never dimmed my awareness of the reality that man is subject to transformation from the worse to the better in ways which he cannot himself determine, except in the sense of meeting certain required conditions. 45

We offer the following observations on these statements in relation to Hocking's revelation as the initial fundamental act of God experienced by man through mystical worship of God.

First, we see clearly the determining epistemological neo-realism which is common to both Hocking and Wieman. It was present in Royce. Hocking had received Royce's blessing for him to carry it further. 46 For Wieman, the reality of God is distinct from any ideas which may be abstracted through analytic intellectual inquiry concerning the nature of that reality. Through Wieman's epistemological neo-realism, the reality that God is stands as objectively distinct from what the analytic abstract nature of God is.

> ... [T]he object of religious experience is just as indubitably an object, independent of human fancies, as is the United States. Just what it is, we cannot be sure; but that it is, we cannot doubt. 47

Second, the reality of God is certain. Abstract ideas of the nature of that reality are less than certain, but the experience of "the unique datum" is "indubitable."

> The religious datum is given; and it is more certain than the seemingly verified concepts of science. In this sense the religious symbol most certainly does not represent an illusion or a dream. 48

We observe in our quotation from Hocking[49] that he

emphasizes certainty as the mystic's response to the revelation of God, "even not much else than certainty of certainty" for one whose view of the revelation is merely external.

Third, we observe that Wieman specifies by means of denotative definitions what this "awareness of the reality" points to. The problem, stated by him as best for examining his thinking through the years, [50] includes this kind of denotative definition of the reality of God. Earlier denotative definitions of this kind are similar in content.

> Whatever else the word God may mean, it is a term used to designate that Something upon which human life is most dependent for its security, welfare and increasing abundance.... The mere fact that human life happens, and continues to happen, proves that this Something, however unknown, does certainly exist. [51]

Then again, he says that this awareness is

> awareness of the reality that man is subject to transformation from the worse to the better in ways which he cannot himself determine, except in the sense of meeting certain required conditions. [52]

Even though these definitions of this reality are sophisticated analytic formulations born of intellectual inquiry, it is necessary that we distinguish sharply the awareness of the reality, _qua_ reality, from all later efforts to formulate designatively the awareness of it. The designation itself is a designation of the goodness of the reality. It is something which the mystic, at best, experiences in the context of worship.

Hocking has many comments on the nature of the mystic's worship of the reality of God which claim that the reality is not only distinct from the mystic's ideas about it, but also is the source of human good. Furthermore, the mystic tries to protect his revelatory experience of reality from any ideas which may obstruct or interfere with it.

> No matter how true an idea of God religion may hand on, the true _idea_ may constitute a wall which keeps God out, if it is adopted as an idea simply, --that is to say, as a repetition of other men's insights, as a universal idea. [53]

We observe that it is the mystic's feeling awareness of the <u>goodness</u> of the reality of God, as distinct from any ideas which may obstruct the connection of this goodness with his experience of it, that is of primary concern. Hocking supports our observation.

> God, who is truly said to explain man to himself, must explain <u>me to myself</u>. What I require to find in a god is that 'This is what I have wanted; this is what I have been meaning all the time; the world as I now see it is a world in which I as a primitive, various, infinitely discontented will can completely live and breathe.'[54]

So this reality for the mystic does mean something ultimately good, found good through worshipful experience of it as an act of God.

Fourth, we observe that Wieman's denotative definitions of the reality of God as that basic goodness capable of transforming the life of man "from the worse to the better in ways he cannot himself determine, except in the sense of meeting certain required conditions," imply a dependence of man on God as the source of goodness which man himself cannot determine. It appears, therefore, that the awareness of the reality of God as good is an awareness of the grace of God from which the basic goodness of man is derived.

From these observations we discover, through worshipful awareness of the reality, a massive depth of qualitative richness which makes it possible for the mystic, in Hocking's terms, to "completely live and breathe."

In a consummatory expression, Hocking says that "the chief burden" of the mystic's revelation "is that religion must exist as experience and not as idea only."[55] Wieman, as a radical neo-realist, would omit the "only." Having pointed with Hocking to the massive reality yielding the grace of God's goodness for man, the certain awareness of this reality, however satisfying for many mystics, is not the end but a prelude for a new beginning. This, for Wieman, is directed to understanding the nature of God by the methodology commonly described as scientific. In Hocking's terms, it is the understanding of "a creativity to which we can discern no limit."[56]

In concluding our treatment of Wieman's response to

revelation in Hocking, we find that Hocking has claimed that through immediate feeling awareness the mystic receives actual knowledge of the reality of God. Its context is religious worship.[57] Neither the experience nor certain knowledge of it by denotative definition is denied by Wieman, but such experience and denotative knowledge of it must not be confused with analytic knowledge of the nature of the reality of God. To do so sacrifices credibility in the knowing process. Wieman wants to distinguish more clearly than Hocking has done the mystical primitive awareness of the reality of God from the abstract analytic knowledge of the nature of God which yields evidence gained by the methodology of the sciences.

Wieman claims for the reality of God a certainty which scientific knowledge does not have. Furthermore, he claims for it a basic importance, since without the reality of God, no religious experience is possible. Certainty of the reality of God precedes scientific interpretation of the nature of that reality. Here again we see the force of Wieman's radical epistemological neo-realism.

Hocking calls Wieman back to the primitive feeling experience of the reality and then tries to reinforce this experience with the poetry of hope. Wieman turns instead to intellectual religious inquiry in order to give to religion the credibility and respect it needs. Hocking was aware of this difference when he wrote his review of <u>Is There a God?</u>[58] Hocking queries

> ... why ... so little use of those strands of religious experience which unite sophisticated modernity with its original sources.... Given the indispensable critical sense, determined, in Mr. Wieman's vigorous words, to 'extricate the existence of God from all the crudity, fallibility, and folly of our beliefs about God' we can with the more assurance gain from elemental belief its endless instruction.[59]

Hocking seems to feel more akin to our primitive ancestors in religion, saying, "... the question, Is there a God? is ... a matter of experience, but of the simple and primitive sort." He calls the experience "an immediate sense of God." This immediate sense is derived from continuous interaction with Nature which is deeper than occasional interaction with one's fellows. It is focused in the self-consciousness of "being acted upon," and "being made."

> This is the merest beginning of the knowledge of God ... but it has in it the germ, the primitive affirmation, upon which further experimental knowledge can grow. To this center, all the various 'approaches' bring their contributions; on it build the visions of the prophets and the mediators.[60]

However, Hocking recognizes that this mystic knowledge "mingles in the course of history an abundance of human error and subjective illusions," but the choice is not between these illusions and "no God at all." The choice is

> between an imperfect God and the true God--between a God who is the shadow of our infirmities, cast on the clouds of the nether deep, and the God whose voice is the speech of the world's hope.[61]

From this context the issue becomes clear. Wieman is not dissenting from Hocking's affirmation of denotative knowledge based on immediate sense of the reality of God. But he is dissenting from the confusion of poetic romantic expressions about the reality of God with immediate awareness of God based on denotative definition of God as the good which is merely the identification of the reality of God as the good. Wieman's "immediate awareness" as a radical mode of neo-realism to identify the reality of God as the good, makes use of "awareness" in the context in which Ralph Barton Perry and G. E. Moore used it.

> ... [T]he object of a sensation is not the sensation itself. In order that a sensation shall be an object, it is necessary to introduce yet another awareness, such as introspection, which is not at all essential to the meaning of the sensation itself. And 'the existence of a table in space is related to my experience of it in precisely the same way as the existence of my own experience is related to my experience of that.' In both cases awareness is evidently a 'distinct and unique relation,' 'of such a nature that its object, when we are aware of it, is precisely what it would be, if one were not aware.'[62]

Wieman's mode of immediate awareness of the good took the form in his Harvard dissertation of the quest for the greatest good: "The object of our quest is the greatest good."[63] The principle of the greatest good is creativity.

The functioning of this principle of creativity within human experience takes the form of creative interest. The principle for organizing conflicting human interests is the principle of creativity expressed as creative interest. [64]

Wieman began his quest for knowing descriptively the nature of the good, as the greatest good, where G. E. Moore left off. Wieman with Moore defined denotatively "the good" by pointing with certainty to it. Moore was sure that "the good" could not be defined descriptively. Wieman's life quest has been to define descriptively the nature of "the good" as "the greatest good." Finally, Wieman sees "the greatest good" as "the creative good," distinct from the multiplicity of "created goods."[65]

For Wieman, mere affirmation of knowledge of the reality of God based on immediate sense or awareness, however fundamental as the indispensable and original source of knowledge, is a less sufficient condition for continuity of the world's hope than Hocking assumes. Man needs to know more about the nature of God in order to minimize illusion in religious experience and eliminate increasingly from religious experience its evil practices. If God is to be known as the basis of the world's hope, it must be, for Wieman, as Perry has said, a hope that is credible. [66]

For Wieman, the nature of all events, God or otherwise, is known descriptively by intellectual abstraction, or selection, from the massive context of reality. These intellectual abstractions are slender threads of knowledge subject to correction and refinement by the rational, observational and experimental methodology of the sciences, but these threads, however slender and however subject to further correction and refinement, constitute the evidence as distinguished from beliefs based on mere hope and wish-fulfillment. It is the evidence that gives to all kinds of intellectual inquiry, including religious inquiry, the kind of integrity and consequent respect it sorely needs. [67]

We have observed in Wieman a sharp distinction between immediate awareness of the reality of God and intellectual analysis of that reality as creative good or creative event, a distinction which is comparable but not identical with Hocking's distinction between immediate mystical sense of revelation as an act of God and knowledge of the creative event and other specified events, as acts of God. Therefore, we shall proceed by analyzing Hocking's second act of God, the creative event, classified by him as expressed through individual personal experience, and Wieman's response to it.

Wieman's response to creative event in Hocking

Hocking, in his essay on the second of the four fundamental acts of God, as he sees them, entitles his chapter, "The Creativity of Religion: Theory of Inspiration."[68] In this essay he is clarifying what he means by "creative event," including illustrations. He says:

> It is our purpose now to enter as we can into the logic and meaning of the creative event, and to sketch its reechoings in life generally.[69]

We recall immediately that Wieman uses this same term, especially in The Source of Human Good,[70] to symbolize what he means by creativity as creative good operative within human experience. It is now our purpose to analyze and to compare critically both Hocking's and Wieman's use of this term, "creative event," in order to clarify Wieman's response to creative event in Hocking.

Hocking's claim that there is a logic of the creative event is based on his observation that revelation as the act of God is the source from which the succeeding acts of God emerge. The locus and condition of their fullest and freest emergence is man's worship of God.

> For creativity has its method and logic; not such as binds it or predetermines it, but such as gives it root, lodgement, and effect.[71]

Reality is its root. Worship is its lodgment. The acts of God are its effects.

Hocking identifies the creative event with the emergence of novelty in human experience. It is present to some degree in everyone, but there are dramatic examples which may best illustrate it:

> ... every soul of man that lives and works in the world is creating at every moment of his life some infinitesmal rill of novelty. We need then only such examples of creativity as may bring us to consciousness of what goes on in ourselves.[72]

Hocking finds significant illustrations from Aylmer Maude's Life of Tolstoy. Tolstoy tells in his educational journal of a boy, in his experimental peasant-school, whom he had punished for stealing by hanging a placard on his back. Then Tolstoy says:

> I glanced at the face of the punished boy which had become yet paler, more suffering, and harder than before, and I thought of convicts; and suddenly I felt so ashamed and disgusted that I tore the stupid card off him, told him to go where he liked, and became convinced--and convinced not by reason, but by my whole nature--that I had no right to torment that unfortunate boy; and that it was not in my power to make of him what I and the innkeeper's son wanted to make of him. I became convinced that there are secrets of the soul hidden from us on which life may act, but which precepts and punishments do not reach. [73]

Hocking cites other illustrations from Tolstoy. One is based on his witnessing an execution in Paris:

> When I saw the head separate from the body, and how they both thumped into the box at the same moment, I understood, not with my mind, but with my whole being, that no theory of the reasonableness of any present progress can justify this deed; and that though everybody from the creation of the world on whatever theory had held it to be necessary, I knew it to be unnecessary and bad. [74]

Another refers to those

> who prayed in the churches for the success of our arms; and the teachers of the faith acknowledged killing to be an act resulting from the faith. -- It was impossible not to see that killing is an evil, repugnant to the principles of any faith. [75]

There is one more, again with the central theme of punishment, the deliberate effort to hurt, wound, or annihilate someone or some group. This one on self-punishment is a confession from Tolstoy.

> One can only go on living when one is intoxicated

with life; as soon as one is sober, it is <u>impossible</u> <u>not</u> <u>to</u> <u>see</u> <u>that</u> <u>it</u> <u>is</u> <u>all</u> <u>a</u> <u>mere</u> fraud.... Sooner or later my deeds will be forgotten, and I shall not exist. Then why go on making any effort.... How can men fail to see this?

I now see that if I did not kill myself, it was due to some dim consciousness of the invalidity of my thoughts. I, my reason, has acknowledged life to be unreasonable. But how can reason, which (for me) is the creator of life, and (in reality) the child of life, deny life? <u>There</u> <u>is</u> <u>something</u> <u>wrong</u> <u>here</u>.

Then I turned my gaze upon myself, on what went on within me, and I remembered that I only lived at those times when I believed in God. As it was before, so it was now: I need only be aware of God to live; I need only forget him or disbelieve in him, and I die.... 'What more do you seek?' exclaimed a voice within me. '<u>This</u> <u>is</u> <u>he</u>. He is that without which one cannot live. To know God and to live is one and the same thing!'... and the light did not again abandon me. 76

What quality, what character, what depth does Hocking discern in these illustrations which he presents so extensively? All of them have the background theme of nihilistic punishment including school-boy punishment, capital punishment, military punishment in war, and finally self-punishment and suicide. Then in each case, punishment is rejected with the emerging of a new insight, perspective or idea. Is this the mode of experience in which the creative event emerges? Is there some indication from these illustrations that Hocking sees nihilism operative in human experience as the antithesis of creativity? Is rejection of the former a favorable condition for realization of the latter?

We shall find that the moments of creation are moments in which the old is not less, but more, intensely present to consciousness; it is grasped as a whole, and <u>realized</u>, as for the first time; and in that realization we shall see emerging a dogma of rejection, 'This (old position) cannot be the truth,' 'This cannot be so.' Which negative dogma will make way for a positive dogma--equally unparented so far as that moment discerns-- 'This contrasting thing must be so,' and herewith the new idea has its footing in the world, both as something <u>necessary</u>--having therefore a parentage though as yet unnameable, a parentage which we may be able to make evident. [77]

Depth of contrast between nihilism and creativity is evident, the one old, the other ever new. The creative event emerges in the transition from the old rejected, to the new accepted. The old is "freshly realized" and "freshly connected with reality." It is "made a conscious part" of one's own "literal and present world."

And this old idea, in being realized, is at the same time repudiated; repudiated, not with any pure and blank negation, but in favor of some positive thing which in time will make itself known. In this realizing and repudiating, the new thing is already asserting itself, and doing conscious work. ... [I]t is when some deep-set love of life and reality reaches a point of wrath and habit-breaking, or in other moods, of wholly joyful inertia-killing; it is in such moments that creation takes place. [78]

With these illustrations, Hocking concludes that "we need look no further for instances of creative event" since "these may be typical of all, whether in art or morals or science or religion."[79]

For Wieman, the creative event refers not merely to an emerging novel idea, as in Hocking, but to the whole process of divine creation. It refers to the same reality as does the term, God. Like other events, it is largely unknown; but also like other events, it has a structure by means of which it can be at least partially known. Its structure, or formative pattern, is creativity, which makes creativity an abstraction from the creative event, but creativity is that character of the creative event which is indissolubly connected with it, and which makes it possible for the creative event to be known. The creative event is imbedded in the mysteries of massive reality, experienced by man in his immediate feeling awareness of reality and through this awareness identifiable as certainly existing, ultimately the source of human good. [80]

In Hocking, the referent for creative event is not the encompassing whole of divine creation. The creative event is one specific act of God, the second among four fundamental and logically ordered creative acts which can be identified. Hocking's creative event is, for Wieman, the first subevent among the four subevents which constitute the creative event.

For Wieman, one, by selective abstraction, can observe, for example, in the process of creative communication in human existence in which learning takes place, the emerging of new perspectives, insights, or ideas. The emerging of these perspectives cannot be forced, managed or manipulated by man. However, if one has some understanding of the kinds of contexts which are more favorable for their emergence, then one can, at best, provide some of these favorable conditions. The most favorable condition is the worship of God. Wieman and Hocking are in agreement on this fact. It is a long-time agreement. Wieman expresses it in the closing of his Harvard dissertation,[81] and in developing his understanding of worship in successive volumes, until in his most recent one, Religious Inquiry: Some Explorations,[82] he distinguishes two levels of worshipful commitment and shows how they are combined to bring fear and anxiety under creative control as opposed to expressing them in nihilistic destructive conflict. New insights and perspectives are necessary conditions for creative control.

We have found in Hocking that it is mystical feeling awareness in worship through which man receives the ultimate revelatory act of God. Feeling, itself, carries a cognitive content. It is idea in the process of being born: "... there is no idea apart from feeling, as there is no feeling apart from idea."[83] The worshiper, receptive to the revelatory act, experiences the connection between this first act of God and the creative event, as the second act of God, through reflection.

> It is through alliance with the Absolute that man is able to reflect: it is through his reflexion that he becomes creative of novelty, system-destroying novelty.[84]

Wieman uses the term "contemplation" instead of Hocking's "reflexion" to account for the mode of connection between these two acts of God in human experience. His early definition of worship which appears in his first book is clarifying: "Worship at its best is that contemplation which is finely balanced between thinking and mysticism, and fulfills itself in action."[85]

With these similarities and differences in mind between Hocking's analysis of the four fundamental acts of God and Wieman's four-fold analysis of the creative event, we shall proceed by examining "prophetic consciousness" in Hocking, as the third act and similarly, the second and third subevents of the creative event in Wieman.

Wieman's response to prophetic consciousness in Hocking

Hocking sees the prophetic consciousness as that act of God which confers on man the "power and freedom to create."[86] This power and this freedom are not of ourselves as the Stoics would have it, nor are they products of altruism.[87] In the prophetic consciousness Hocking links man's attitude of humility toward God with man's pride of individual creatorship.

> The pride of creatorship, ... the highest prerogative of our individual selfhood, may turn to the veriest curse at the moment when the goods in our hands appear to us as nothing but our own creations.[88]

In accounting for this linkage, Hocking says:

> In some degree ... every soul of us knows the whole, and feels in his own limbs the thud and the impulse of the engines of reality: it must be possible, then, for our wills, to the same degree, to contain the will of the universe.[89]

When the prophetic consciousness as an act of God is received by man into his own experience, man reaches a kind of maturity in respect to God himself and is

> ready to assume the burden not only of omniscience--as we continually do--but also of omnipotence, with regard to some fragment, however minute, of the historical work of the universe.[90]

When, in this way, man shares with God the work of the universe, man becomes "completely real." His reality is shared with divine reality.

> In such a moment the act which we should utter would be known as a completely real act; and since

we cannot separate our own reality from the reality either of our objects, or of our deeds--we too become for the first time completely real.⁹¹

This is the context from which man receives the prophetic consciousness as an act of God, and expresses power and freedom to create. With this power and this freedom man attains a knowledge that his acts, as real, "succeed and hold" their "place in history." Hocking says there are those who reject this attainment, claiming either that the prophetic consciousness is an impossibility or that it

> is associated in theory with the ruthless, the violent, the competitive, the relentlessly self-assertive, as in the philosophies of Hobbes and Nietzsche.⁹²

In reply to these rejections, Hocking asks:

> ... may it not be that this instinctive love of power which is in every human creature needs only to be raised to the dignity of prophecy to lose both its cruelty and its incredibility? May it not be that these philosophers of the Wille zur Macht have but labored to preserve to us our confidence in the chief moral element of our nature?⁹³

Then acknowledging the existence of false prophets, Hocking defines man in the following terms:

> A man is he who can infallibly exercise or acquire a certain minimum of assured power over facts, in work and speech and habit; man is defined by a certain high level of assumable power.⁹⁴

This assumable power in prophets with mature self-knowledge is well defined, including limited consciousness of power, yet they may be "so convinced of ... necessary acceptance of their idea that they are willing to persist in uttering it in face of universal repudiation...." In the prophet there is a love for truth as he finds it and a love for others. In this assurance and this love, his "prophecy reaches its summit in the most presumptuous of all commands, 'Follow me.'" His love "discounts all obstacles in advance, and instates itself in unquestioning command of life and body." These commands are world-making and history-making. They are perfected in the presence of God. Born of a "total and universal meaning," and imposed on the course of things, the prophet and others suffer and excite wrath. With a "fierce joy in the power to perfect," the prophet renounces, demonstrates, denies, and opposes to move a "huge segment of sluggish, inert earth." In this context,

> we find re-entering into our souls those lost virtues of war and asceticism--virtues which can never be artificially fostered or reclaimed. 95

Using insights from Maeterlinck's <u>Wisdom and Destiny</u>, Hocking sees in the acts of prophetic consciousness adventures and heroism, but these pass.

> ... '[W]hen Jesus Christ met the Samaritan, met a few children, an adulterous woman, then did humanity rise three times in succession to the level of God.' This is that 'consciousness of self' which 'with the greatest of men implies consciousness up to a point of their star or their destiny'; and not alone because 'they know in advance how events will be received in their soul,' but because in addition to this they also know <u>what they will do with these events</u>, and what stamp history will carry as it falls back from that encounter. 96

Hocking then asks: "Shall we not acknowledge, then, that the prophetic consciousness is a wholly credible experience... ?" If so, "... history can never become wholly alien to us."

Hocking inquires: How do these acts, these experiences come to the prophet? Do they come by laying "aside the attitude of humility, ... with the swing of his own arm?" In reply, and in closing this chapter on the prophetic consciousness, Hocking's prose sings with creativity and power.

> My answer is that the prophetic consciousness is possible in the same way that reflexion is possible, in the same way that a total present judgment upon the world is possible.... The prophet is but the mystic in control of the forces of history, declaring their necessary outcome: the mystic in action is the prophet.... Prophetic power is the final evidence to each individual that

he is right and real; it is his assurance of salvation; it is his share of divinity; it is his anticipation of all attainment.... There are no deeds more permanent than those of Buddha, of Mohammed, of Jesus.... The deeds of the mystics constitute the hard parts of history; the rest has its day and passes.
The mystic is precisely the timeless and unhistorical being.... If he is a true creator he addresses history itself, with all its accidents.
The next swing of the alternation of mind brings the scientist, who is the mystic confronting the fact with his absolute. Objectivity of mind is the most germane fruit of religion; and science becomes possible only through long discipline of worship....
It is only the developed spirit that can bear the fact in its nakedness.
...[F]aith is but the love of God, the prophetic consciousness, confronted by the particulars of history.
There is such a thing as losing one's soul: and that is, rejecting one's call to prophesy. [97]

Wieman's Harvard dissertation reflects in many of its parts the strong influence of Hocking, but we find this direct quotation from Hocking in it: "In whatever sense God is to triumph in history, in that same sense must I triumph also."[98] In this closing paragraph of his dissertation, Wieman sees in the prophetic consciousness the repudiation of subjectivism in religion: "We can be satisfied only in achievement which reaches beyond our own subjective disposition."[99] With this anticipated satisfaction and achievement, Wieman's neo-realism at work in his own prophetic consciousness makes it possible for him to say: "We must be able to change the world beyond ourselves in some significant and eternal manner."[100] Neither is the power of the prophet absent from his thinking: "The good which we desire is the power to so achieve...."[101]

Going back much farther than the Harvard years when the young Wieman as a prospective sophomore applied for admission to Park College, one of the questions in the application form was: "What is your object in seeking an education?" He replied by writing in the blank space one single word: "Power."[102] Power as the educational objective of this adolescent youth, as an individual, has not faded during succeeding decades of his life, but rather has it been an evolving and maturing experience, a realization of power in prophetic consciousness.

This realization of power is evidenced by the kind of teaching which Wieman has done through the years. It has been basically the teaching of his own religious philosophy. We are not saying that his own books and articles were required reading for his students. He seldom, if ever, did that. But the source materials selected and used for special study were analyzed not only with faithful commitment to the ideal of reporting objectively their content, but also with his own personal power of prophetic consciousness in criticizing the sources.[103]

Wieman's analytic response to Hocking's prophetic consciousness as an act of God is found mainly in what he says about the nature of the second and third subevents of the creative event, for the creative acts in both of these subevents are combined in what Hocking refers to as prophetic consciousness.

For Wieman, there is a distinction to be made within the functioning of the prophetic consciousness between the creative <u>integrating</u> of insights and ideas which emerge within the mind of man in the process of communication, and the <u>expanding</u> of one's appreciative consciousness of his world. These are distinctly different subevents within the on-going creativity of the creative event, yet they are indissolubly connected, not only as these two events are connected, but also with the other two of the four subevents. The integrating of new perspectives or ideas is a cohesive and unifying process yielding individuality and integrity for the prophetic consciousness, giving it strength and power.

> The individual becomes more of a personality when these meanings derived from others are integrated with what he already has. His thoughts and feelings are enriched and deepened.[104]

The expanding of one's appreciative consciousness of his world is a creative diversification of personal experience.

> There is a range and variety of events, a richness of quality, and a reach of ideal possibility which were not there prior to this transformation.[105]

This extending and expanding of the senses so that one can

see and hear and feel beyond his previous limits releases one from narrow ego-centric interests, parochialism, partisanship, nationalism, and sectarianism. It is an experience of new freedom born of the emerging of new insights and the integrating of them due to the creative functioning experienced in the first and second subevents combined.

Wieman's distinction between the integrating of new perspectives and the expanding of the appreciative world of the individual permits centering of attention on each of these functions of the creative event so that not only growth of understanding of each of these functions may be facilitated, but also problems of discovering and providing the necessary conditions for further integrating and expanding of these functions can be studied more objectively.

We see that the creation of new perspectives and their emergence in the life of the individual person are only frustrating until they have undergone creative integration in the individual self. Emphasis on the necessary connection between the first and second subevents, in order that the creative event may function as creative, is evidence for this. The second subevent has a creative function which is continuity of the creative process as opposed to the obstruction of creativity at a given juncture, making it uncreative. Wieman says:

> These newly communicated meanings must be integrated with meanings previously acquired or natively developed if the creative event is to occur.[106]

There is tragedy in receiving floods of new insights, new perspectives, and new ideas or dissociated meanings which are not undergoing creative integration with previous meanings.

> This integrating does not occur in every case of communicated meaning, since there is much noncreative communication in our modern world by way of radio, television, movies, newspapers, and casual interchange between individuals.[107]

There is also tragedy at the juncture of mere expansion of one's appreciable world apart from the fourth subevent, the widening and deepening of community among men.

> ... [T]his expanding of the appreciable world may

> make a man more unhappy and more lonely than he was before; for now he knows that there is a greatness of good which might be the possession of man but is not actually achieved.
> ... Such loneliness indicates a vast emptiness which love between men might fill. This lonliness might become so deep and so intense that a man could not endure it unless he were permitted to die upon a cross for love; he might then fill an emptiness no actual love can fill by a sacrificial expression of love. This seeking for a love that is never fulfilled might become so deep and so intense that a man would spend all his life preaching the principles of a kingdom of love that would sound like the beatitudes of madness in a world like this.[108]

At this high level of sensitivity and receptivity to the creative acts of God, the sense of tragedy is intensified, as symbolized by the Christian Cross, because of the fact that the creative event is being experienced richly but not in the fulness of its actuality. This tragic sense can be used either destructively or creatively: destructively if the way of creativity is closed, creatively if the way of creativity is kept open. If kept open, creativity is experienced as providence unifying history, for Hocking and as "widening and deepening community between those who participate in the total creative event," for Wieman.

Wieman's Response to Hocking's Delineation of Providence as an Act of God Through Over-Individual Experience

Providence, the fourth fundamental act of God, as Hocking sees it, is an over-individual or social act expressed through prophetic consciousness in the unifying of history.

> ... [T]he whole race of prophets and world-builders stands helpless in the presence of a wider agency whose name is either Fate or Providence. Without the cooperation of an environment not less than infinite, the best prophet comes at last to zero--... beside the work of God which we have been tracing in the individual mind, there is a supplementary work of God in the world beyond the human will.... Thus the theory of religion rests

back upon ... the philosophy of a wider history for its final justification.[109]

The prophetic attitude is not justified without an environment which "faithfully conserves values." It is the function of the prophet either to find or to create "in the current of history a unity corresponding to the unity in the physical universe...." It is through providence at work in the worshipful will of the prophet that brings about the unification of history and the conservation of values. Hocking sees the prophetic attitude as expressed in worship to be reinforced by its social contagion: "No human attitude is more socially contagious...." The first work of the prophetic attitude is its social contagion: "... it begins to crystallize its environment, that is, to organize the social world upon its own principle."[110]

The principle of providence is that it is a creative act of God. Its spirit is irresistible. Through the prophet it creates a new environment. It organizes the religious institution as a historic body with work to perform. It makes history possible. It is an "irruption of the divine into history." Detaching itself from the national life, "it begins a universal propaganda," and "refers itself and its adherents to some distinctive historic object as the beginning of its temporal undertaking."[111]

The locus of the religious institution in history is

> between the creative individual will and that unordered, or unstably ordered, human social mass, before whose free mobility and passion that will is indeed in a hopeless plight.[112]

This worshiping institution of the providence of God "defies the clash and decay of the political attempts of men...." It is the ultimate critic of all established institutions and their only hope. In it individual worship is fulfilled in social worship, including not only present participants, but also the prophets of the past and those who will arise in the future to continue to ensure a common spirit and a common faith in unifying history. It is an educating body with singleness of mind and purpose yielding a sense of responsibility for the worth and freedom of individual persons. It is through this agency that salvation of man is won and the forgiveness of sin.[113]

Wieman's response to providence in Hocking is the fourth subevent in the creative event: creating a "widening and deepening community"[114] ... "among those who participate in this total creative event of intercommunication."[115] The range of functioning of the creative event extends from intimate participation in the human mind to society, and on into the indeterminate processes of history. The creativity in the creative event is a new structure of creative interrelatedness, "whereby events are discriminated and related in a manner not before possible." These interrelations are meaningful connections yielding "an abundance of quality that events could not have had without this new creation." This new creation which works through creative communication has something in common with prior creation on the subhuman level, namely, creativity; but the structure of creativity is itself creative with distinguishable levels of creativity. Worshipful commitment to the creative event, functioning at the level of what Wieman more recently calls creative interchange through human communication, is a commitment which does not deny the history of creation, nor would it commit the genetic fallacy by worship of some earlier form of historic creation as opposed to its present level of creativity including further creative possibilities. Wieman says:

> It is true that there is a creative process that has worked through many centuries to bring forth the kind of organism that can participate in the creative event of human communication.[116]

Recognition of this fact is an acknowledgment of the indefinite range of creativity in history, but there is also a recognition of the continuity of creativity in history now working at its highest known level through creative communication, yielding creative community among men. At this level we <u>know</u> a "new creation" which is the creative structure of the creative event.

This knowledge and the increase of it through reliable religious inquiry is necessary in order to provide analytically and critically disciplined minds with an equally analytic and critical religious discipline for basic criticism of human participation in history. Without such a discipline relevant to present technological advance in civilization, divine providence is not sufficiently clear and vivid to make its offering acceptable for the guidance of man in history. Wieman's deep and active concern for the advance of religious inquiry has not abated, even under the impact of Hocking's sharp criticism of it as not sufficiently balanced by return to worship of the wholeness of reality through primitive mystical awareness.[117] However, Wieman does keenly recognize the limitations of man's knowledge regarding any event or events, including the creative event. With his continued use of epistemological neorealism, he sees only a

> thin layer of structure characterizing events knowable to the human mind by way of linguistic specification ... compared to that massive, infinitely complex structure of events, rich with quality, discriminated by the non-cognitive feeling of associated organisms human and nonhuman.[118]

If the thin layer of structures knowable by intellectual formulation is to retain depth and richness of quality, it must be seen as

> conjunct and integral with this deep complex structure of quality built up through countless ages before even the human mind appeared and now accessible to the feeling-reactions of the human organism.[119]

For Wieman, worship of God as the creative event includes its known consummatory functioning of widening and deepening creative community, but the creative event is recognized as inestimably *more* than the "thin layer" of known creative structure.

> ... [W]hen the human mind in its pride tries to rear its knowable structures as supreme goals of human endeavor, impoverishment, destruction, conflict, and frustration begin because these structures are then cut off from the rich matrix of quality found in organic, non-intellectual reactions.[120]

Yet knowledge of God as reliably specified structure is precious for Wieman, however limited it may be, because knowledge is useful in intelligent as opposed to elusive and illusory service of God. With growth in knowledge of God, man can live more meaningfully and creatively in creative community if depth and range of perspective on the limitations of knowledge in relation to its massive matrix is not lost. When man lives in this way,

> he experiences an uncomprehended depth and

richness which give content to the abstractions of rationally comprehended structures. When he does not, life loses quality and value.[121]

We find that Wieman is aware that his vocational commitment to religious inquiry to attain reliable knowledge of God may appear to others to be his ultimate commitment, but this is not so. His ultimate commitment is not given to human knowledge, nor to human interests, desires, ideas, ideals, beliefs, or philosophic systems, but only to "the deeper matrix of value.... We live in and by and for it."[122]

From this deeper matrix of creation, as a continuous process, community is being created. According to Wieman, two main kinds of goods are given to the community through this matrix by the creative event:

> (1) Created intrinsic good ... is the appreciable world made richer with quality and meaning by this creative event. It is culture. (2) Instrumental good ... is a structure pertaining to events wherein the qualities of the events are not relevant to the value of the structure. It is civilization or technology, in contrast to culture.[123]

We believe that any attitude toward or overt treatment of these goods as properly abstracted or bifurcated from the rich matrix of the creative event, except for mere analysis, is a deep tragedy with loss of value for creative community. Furthermore, obstruction to creative interchange between culture and technological civilization is further tragic loss of value. The outcome of improper or final abstraction is the disintegration of created goods including technological civilization and culture.

We shall restate these perspectives in relation to history: When there is any obstruction to creative interchange between goods treated basically as created instrumental goods on the one hand, and created intrinsic goods on the other, deep tragedy occurs in the loss of value in history; for goods treated in this way apart from the creative process are no longer integral with this process and thereby lose their creative quality. This is the root tragedy which obstructs creative community.

Created goods belong to the rich matrix in the creative process. From this perspective no good is a pure waste: from dust to paper boxes, glass, and all commonly called garbage and sewage, to plants, subhuman animals, men, their civilizations and cultures. These events, in continuous transformation, exist for service of the creative event which creates community. It is the basic office of man to provide every possible condition for this transformation and service. Intelligent service of this office is based on reverence for creativity in the rich matrix of ecological systems. We believe that there is a wealth of creative structure discoverable in these systems and that the ecological sciences, as basic for all the sciences, are at root theological.

From these perspectives, it would appear that Wieman's response to providence in Hocking, and also the further import of Wieman's philosophy of creativity which we have stated here, is not only consistent with, but also a reconception of Hocking's fundamental insight into religion as the mother of the arts and the sciences. [124]

The sins of man and his consequent suffering are an outcome of the dissociation of goods from their creative context. Physical and organic reassociation and reconciliation of created goods with their creative matrix may seem impossible, in which case the creative event would be limited to lower levels of creative interchange, but creativity at work in the ecology of nature is a basic support to which men may awaken, serve with increasing intelligence, and thereby provide conditions necessary for human salvation through further release of creative interchange.

Hocking stakes his faith in the prophetic consciousness present in the attitude of Jesus Christ, whose power in providence penetrates and creates community.

> The founder of a popular religion held up to the minds of a spell-bound multitude, as his own original revelation, a God who 'maketh his sun to rise on the evil and the good, and sendeth rain on the just and the unjust.' Upon this basis he defined the 'perfection' of God, and summoned men to the same perfection, the same absolute bearing. Thereby he defined an attitude of mind which was indeed new in that world, an attitude of equal treatment toward friend and enemy, toward good and bad ... the only radically creative attitude yet known to humanity. [125]

Both Hocking and Wieman see that man struggles and suffers in his limited effort to express this attitude and to be guided by it in community, but "Each individual by proper action," according to Wieman, "can become a participant" in creative community and history. "To undertake such action is the decision required of us."[126]

Proper action for both Hocking and Wieman is appreciative reception of the acts of God in human experience. In Hocking the just and loving power of providence is the creative guide in community and history. In Wieman we experience "widening and deepening community between those who participate in the total creative event." Proper action or participation involves mutual interpretation through a specific kind of communication guided by the total creative event as creative interchange.

Again, may we be reminded that Wieman, throughout his professional career, says that this kind of communication accepts human conflict as opposed to the effort to harmonize it, as Perry aimed to do.[127] This kind of communication internalizes conflict so that each communicant can feel what the other person feels, see what he sees, hear what he hears, and think what he thinks, so that the insights and ideas and meanings of each are integrated into the life of the other. Only by acceptance of human conflict and by communication of it in this way can one serve creative interchange, come to know realistically what is going on in the life of the other as an original person, and be free from the masks which alienate one from another. One may discover in the other not only approval, appreciation and genuine love, but also denials, repudiations, bitterness and other negative responses. All of these are

> a form of understanding and community. ... They [the negative responses] may contribute as much to the scope and richness of one's mind, to one's appreciable world, and to the depth of one's community with others as perspectives which we affirm and with which we agree.[128]

In this kind of communication, the good produced by creative interchange

> brings increase in suffering as well as increase in joy; community brings a burden as well as a release. Those who cannot endure suffering cannot

endure the increase of human good. Refusal to take suffering is perhaps the chief obstacle to increase in the good of human existence.[129]

In concluding our study of Wieman's response to creativity in Hocking's religious philosophy, we shall distinguish Wieman's acceptance of the empirical nature of creativity in the metaphysics of Hocking's Absolute from his rejection of other non-empirical aspects of this metaphysics. We have found that creativity, as defined by Wieman, is clearly identified with the empirical nature of Hocking's Absolute. Wieman's definition of the metaphysical nature of creativity is as follows:

> It is what makes possible the widest range of diversity and the freest, fullest expression of unique individuality, but providing such relations between these diversities that they are mutually sustaining rather than mutually annihilating or frustrating, as they would be without such relations to one another.[130]

This definition seems to be clear and comprehensive in stating briefly the essential metaphysical nature of creativity as Wieman sees it. He says:

> The Absolute is precisely this very creativity which is necessary to human existence.... That is what Hocking means by the 'Absolute' and that is what I mean by it, although we interpret the word in different ways.[131]

These "different ways" of interpreting the "Absolute" in Hocking, for Wieman, are empirically metaphysical as opposed to conceptually metaphysical interpretations. Wieman accepts the former and rejects the latter. The locus of the empirically metaphysical interpretation in Hocking is illustrated, according to Wieman, by Hocking's "statements about the 'empirical route to an absolute goal.'"[132]

We find this "route" to be the way Hocking's four fundamental acts of God enter human experience. There is sufficient epistemological neo-realism in Hocking for him to see rather objectively that these acts do enter human experience, and there is also sufficient empiricism in Hocking for him to see that having entered human experience, these creative acts function empirically en route to their "absolute goal."

The absolute goal is the "whole idea," but the "work of the whole idea" which Wieman refers to, is the work en route to Hocking's absolute goal. This is, for Wieman, the empirical work of creativity: "I call it creativity, or the continuous creation of coherence by way of creative interchange between individuals and peoples."[133]

Wieman explains what he means by creation of coherence:

> Stated in the simplest possible form, this absolute goal is the creation of coherence, the recovery of coherence when it is disrupted, and the extension of coherence by absorbing new insights, when conditions make this possible.[134]

We find that Wieman's use of the term "coherence"--in order to bring out the nature of creativity as empirical--is clarifying.

> Coherence is integration of social and cultural elements based on a consistent pattern of values and a congruous set of ideological principles.[135]

The empirical nature of creativity operating as creation of coherence is emphasized in Wieman's saying:

> The actual empirical reality which we find occurring in human life is creativity operating to create coherence in the forms of language and logic, in the forms of science and art, in the forms of love, friendship and community of minds, in the forms of coherent culture and the continuity of history. We can further establish empirically that this creation of coherence operates in human life in the form of a kind of interchange which I have called creative, and have discussed at length in other writings.[136]

Wieman affirms an absolute goal in his own empirical metaphysics. It is creativity. Its functioning in human existence is continuously empirical, creating coherence. Hocking's absolute goal is different in that there is an empirical route to it, but the absolute goal itself is merely conceptual in two respects, as Wieman sees it: (1) It "is a final and completed form." (2) It "eternally comprehends all reality."[137]

For Wieman, the absolute goal is absolute because it

is a goal intrinsic to human existence of such sort that human beings could not exist without it. It is absolute in the sense that the very continuance of human life requires it.[138]

Furthermore, Wieman rejects the absolute goal as a final and completed form. Wieman's metaphysics is a process metaphysics, but Hocking's is only a semi-process one because Hocking affirms an empirical route to the absolute goal, but the route ends in a goal which is final and complete. This is Hocking's perfectionism involving completion and finality. For Hocking, any goal which is not perfect in this sense is a finite or limited goal and therefore not absolute. Hocking makes a clear statement about God as finite in his concluding analysis and evaluation of McTaggart's views on the nature of God.

It will not be amiss to emphasize in conclusion the entire justice of McTaggart's contention that the finite God is of no worth.[139]

Within the perspectives of empirical process metaphysics, Hocking's characterization of the nature of God as absolute goal in terms of completion and perfection becomes an affirmation of God as finite because this conception requires that divine creativity be a finished and complete process, in which case there is no further process, no further creativity since creativity requires continuity in order to be creative. From these perspectives, it is clear that Hocking's semi-process metaphysics is inconsistent: Its creative process route to his absolute goal is inconsistent with the finality and completeness of the goal itself.

Wieman's rejection of finality and completeness in his empirical process metaphysics of creativity is an affirmation of continuity as characteristic of creativity, which suggests that creativity has an infinite and eternal quality unless creativity were in some way eliminated from all levels of existence. In brief, the quality of the infinite belongs to the existence of creativity.

With regard to the second respect in which Wieman rejects Hocking's conceptual, semi-process metaphysics of the absolute goal, Wieman suggests that we have no empirical evidence that Hocking's Absolute of his absolute goal "eternally comprehends all reality." Since Hocking says that whatever else God may be, God must be the all-comprehending Absolute which we know as God,[140] Wieman's rejection is of Hocking's claim that the Absolute Mind of God eternally comprehends all reality.

> A 'mind' which 'knows' by instantaneous intuition the total cosmos across vast spaces requiring a ray of light millions of years to traverse, is not 'mind' and is not 'knowing' as these words apply to human beings. The difference in what is designated is so radical that 'mind' in the one case is a different word from 'mind' in the other case, even though the spelling and the pronunciation are the same. Also 'knowing' in the one case is an entirely different word from 'knowing' in the other case. Consequently there can be no all-knower. There can only be an all-X....[141]

We suggest that the "all-X" in Hocking, according to Wieman, is a merely conceptual object which falls within Hocking's merely conceptualistic metaphysics rather than his empirical metaphysics of the Absolute.

Furthermore, since we have found in Wieman's creative process metaphysics that God is intrinsically creative, both as the formal structure of God which we know, and also as the empirical creative process of the creative event, it would be presumptuous to claim that God eternally comprehends <u>all</u> reality since reality is in process of being created.

However, we can well understand the basis of Hocking's belief that God eternally comprehends all reality. It is a part, if not the root, of his conceptualistic metaphysics of idealism, retained after extensive incorporation into his philosophy of contributions from realism, empiricism, and pragmatism.

> In the first place an idea must be permanent, whereas feeling is essentially transient. An idea may guide a feeling to its goal and its cessation;

but as the experience passes, the idea does not cease to exist.... 142

It is the conceptualistic nature of Hocking's Absolute as the "whole idea" which determines a radical difference between Wieman and Hocking regarding the nature of evil as obstructing creativity.

> Wherever consciousness enters we have to combine the scientific reaction with another, one which involves turning away from the defect and asserting in effect that the evil is less-than-real, that the real is the good. 143

Hocking goes further by identifying "less-than-real" with appearance.

> For life is but a certain consciousness of the Absolute, in process of application; and the application of this Idea is the substance of all positive worth, conferring upon 'contents' what quality they have. Attachment to life is simply attachment to the source of value; and that which appears evil does so appear because the Real cannot be recognized in it.... 144

In contrast to Hocking's view of evil, Wieman affirms that evil is not less-than-real but real, as real as the good, and not mere appearance. Wieman clarifies what he means by evil by first distinguishing two kinds of evil: (1) obstructive evil is that which obstructs the absolutely and intrinsically creative good; (2) destructive evil is that which destroys created goods. Of these two kinds of evil, the obstructive is most deadly because it obstructs the very source of human good which is creative good, even though "creative good cannot be destroyed." For Wieman, obstructive evil is ultimately real and "absolute on four counts: it is universal, unqualified, ultimate, and unconfined."145

We shall state what Wieman means by characterizing evil as absolute on each of these four counts:

(1) By "universal," he means that the evil is absolute

> everywhere and under all circumstances. Its evil is not relative to time and place and person, to interest, need, social situation, or culture. 146

(2) By "unqualified," he means that the evil is absolute

> from every standpoint. Whether one takes the viewpoint of the cosmic whole or the view of some part; whether one views it from eternity or from time, as a condition promoting freedom and moral responsibility or any other alleged end, from every angle of vision it is evil to obstruct creative good. It only magnifies the evil to try to interpret opposition to creativity as somehow from some view not really evil after all.[147]

(3) By "ultimate," he means that the evil is absolute in that

> it neither originates nor ends in goods necessarily. It is not an episode of time rounded out by eternity that is perfect in its goodness.[148]
>
> ... Evil is not truly evil if it is predetermined to be overruled or if it is bounded above, below, before, and after by an eternity of perfect good. If this is true, then our war against evil becomes a kind of sardonic joke.[149]

(4) By "unconfined," he means that the evil is absolute in that

> it is not necessarily bound to any limits. How completely it is kept down, how closely it will be confined, how narrowly restricted, will depend on the fortunes of the great struggle. The outcome is not predetermined by the nature of reality....
> ... Evil is not a domesticated animal, kept inside a pen by a power which holds it under control. Evil is a wild thing; it wanders abroad because the creative power of good has not been able to confine it or annihilate it. All other views represent evil as kept by the Almighty in a pen to do what the power of good may require of it, until the time comes when it shall be slaughtered. When we say that evil is absolute in this last sense, we mean to contradict this view of evil as inclosed within bounds beyond which we can be sure that it cannot pass.[150]

This difference between Wieman and Hocking in their treatment of evil is relevant to the conditions which may be provided for releasing creativity in human existence in the interest of the salvation of man from sin and other forms of evil. We have found that both agree that the basic condition to be provided is worship. But, pray, What is worship? This, we believe, is the crucial issue for Hocking, and also for Wieman in responding to creativity in Hocking's religious philosophy.

Hocking's principle of alternation between work and worship is the structural form of the basic conditions which he regards as necessary for the salvation of man. Neither work alone nor worship alone is adequate for attainment of this objective.

> The effort of work ... provides for its own arrest. Work, simply as a voluntary application of ideas, does gradually disintegrate those values for which alone work exists. In all literalness life ceases to be worth living, and death in some shape will be sought.[151]
>
> For worship cannot last; it also has its type of self-defeat and death. The worshipper who persists in his contemplation of the whole, thinking to establish himself permanently in the immediate presence of God, becomes an automaton, precisely as the determined worker becomes a machine.[152]

The rhythmic alternation suggested is really between duty and religion.

> Duty has no right over men apart from their religious experience. On the other hand, religion has no right apart from its descent into the world of effort.[153]

However, we observe that Hocking is not fully satisfied with his principle of alternation between work and worship as a means for the salvation of man.

> In reality, in the logical and eternal order of things, these two phases of experience belong together, and in time also are always finding their way together: but in psychological order, in the natural history of the mind, they fall apart, and must be pursued separately.
> Any given moment of life must choose between two goods, psychologically incompatible.... But

there is a better choice: namely, the choice of both. For the life of each is that it may lose itself, from time to time, in the life of the other. And this, which is obvious in things partial, is true--and even chiefly true--in things total.[154]

So, we find that Hocking's dissatisfaction with the principle of alternation he has set forth is due to the fact that he has had some insight regarding relations between work and worship which indicate that they not only fall apart, but may, from time to time, fall together as one process. Yet, Hocking proceeds to develop his religious philosophy in our common life of space-time on the basis of the principle of alternation. Work as duty, though derived from worship, and, at best, supported by the theory and practice of the sciences, is distinctly different and apart from worship.

We find that Wieman has not only reconceived Hocking's principle of alternation, but he has also reconstructed it. The result is a different structure. Only recently has he stated this difference systematically and in bold relief. We find, first, that the basis for this difference is in Wieman's rejection of Hocking's non-process, conceptualistic interpretation of "absolute goal," and secondly, in Wieman's rejection of Hocking's equally conceptualistic belief that God "eternally comprehends all reality."[155] Wieman begins his systematic reconception by saying:

Hocking has studied extensively the practice of worship and some of his most valuable insights pertain to it. There is a practice of worship, says Hocking, yielding an experience wherein the striving for unattained goals ceases for the time being as one becomes aware of their final attainment in God. This enables one to return to striving after these goals with a confidence and a courage which cannot be daunted, because the worshipper knows that the ultimate outcome is eternally in being. In worship one rises above the conflicts and unsolved problems because he is aware that they are ultimately solved in the being of God. In worship the alienation between oneself and other persons, also the alienation between oneself and nature, are overcome because in God these seeming oppositions are reconciled. Preeminently the mystic worshipper has this experience.[156]

Wieman concludes this account of worship as Hocking developed it, by saying that "it is one of the most highly valued parts" of Hocking's philosophy of religion, and that he agrees with Hocking "that worship does yield an experience which can be interpreted in this way"; but Wieman then proceeds to introduce his empirical approach to worship in contrast to Hocking's basically conceptual approach by asking the following questions:

> What empirical reality do we actually experience in worship? Is it the eternal coherence of all reality? Or is it the profound awareness that there is a creativity operating to create wider and deeper coherence when we meet the required conditions and when we commit ourselves to it?[157]

In response to these questions, Wieman states four contrasting interpretations of worship, indicating in each case how his own interpretation differs from that of Hocking:

(1) According to Hocking,

> worship enables us to apprehend the final solution of all our problems.

According to Wieman,

> worship puts us more completely into the power and keeping of the creativity which operates to solve our problems by generating insights and deepening appreciative understanding and community between persons and peoples and between human beings and the rest of nature.

(2) According to Hocking,

> worship is an outreach to what comprehends all reality.

According to Wieman,

> worship is an inreach to what expands our vision indefinitely, when we meet the required conditions.

(3) According to Hocking,

> worship gives us the anticipation of final attainment.

According to Wieman,

> worship yields the experience of 'being born' again into that creativity which, from infancy on through life, creates the appreciative consciousness in community with others and in community with nature.

(4) According to Hocking,

> worship gives us the end result of human life.

According to Wieman,

> worship gives us the ever renewed creative origins of human life.[158]

We believe that Wieman not only agrees with Hocking in that Hocking's principle of alternation between worship and work is not wholly satisfactory for guidance in religious living, but he also makes an effort to overcome this dissatisfaction by developing what he calls the two-level commitment.

In distinguishing two levels of worshipful commitment, Wieman refers to the one as the ultimate, the deepest or the bottom level; and to the other as the upper or top level commitment. These two levels of commitment operate together as the basic condition for creative worshipful control of human anxiety and destructive human conflict, and thereby open the way for the emerging of novel perspectives and insights in human experience as the first subevent of the four-fold creative event. The deepest level commitment is

> to whatever does in truth operate in human life to make life better, even before one knows what it is and before one knows what the greater good might be.[159]

This deepest level commitment is based on recognition of the fact that human knowledge of whatsoever kind, including knowledge of God, is limited, limited in ourselves, limited even in the wisest of men. It is a common human problem to eliminate or even minimize the bias and endure the consequent anxiety in order to face this fact. Insofar as man is able to sense his own limitations and accept this fact, he is then "open to further insights" which may correct and transform his present beliefs and practices. This sense of limitation and this openness are conditions favorable to this deepest level commitment wherein the individual commits himself without reservation or qualification and without doubt to what does create, sustain, and transform human life toward the greater good when required conditions are present, and he does this no matter how mistaken his present beliefs about it may be.[160]

It is this deepest level commitment shrouded in mystery, which "does, in truth, create, sustain, save, and expand the appreciative consciousness of man."[161]

However, this deepest level commitment "can give no guidance, no direction, unless supplemented by commitment" to the upper level which operates through religious inquiry.

Therefore one searches until one finds what evidence seems to indicate does operate in human life to transform toward the greater good.... But his <u>ultimate</u> commitment will not be to this, even though he is ready to die for it, fail for it, suffer for it, and live for it.[162]

The ultimate commitment, which is both the basic commitment and also the primary or initial commitment, must be supported by increasing knowledge of the nature of the reality to which the commitment is made if the reality is to be served intelligently and efficiently, for we observe that it is the lack of growing understanding of the nature of the ultimate reality to which one is committed that is indeed the ultimate source of human anxiety and frustration. This tragic lack of understanding has two sources. One is the failure to attain and/or maintain sufficient human sensitivity to become clearly aware of and completely committed to the source of human good. The other is failure to develop a methodology of knowing to make possible an increasingly intelligent and efficient upper or consequent commitment to this reality. Therefore, it seems evident to Wieman that the combining of the two-levels in worshipful commitment is a favorable condition for: (1) control of anxiety; (2) freedom from nihilism; and (3) growth in knowledge of the <u>nature</u> of the reality of God.

Since creativity is precisely the source of innovating insights, commitment to it is the only possible way by which the truth can ever be attained or approximated. Therefore, commitment to this creativity is identical with the two-level

> commitment. The top level is what we now believe
> this creativity to be; the bottom level is what does,
> in truth, create, sustain, save, and expand the ap-
> preciative consciousness of man. But this fuller
> truth can only be gained by insights emerging by
> way of the creativity, because creativity as used
> here means the emerging of insights which expand
> and deepen the knowledge and value accessible to
> the human mind.... In any case, the two levels
> of religious commitment are combined when we
> commit ourselves to this creativity.[163]

Wieman's two-level commitment does not alternate between worship and work as does Hocking's principle. Hocking turns <u>from</u> worship <u>to</u> dutiful work which is not worship. Worship, for Hocking is not practiced from a sense of duty, but from appreciative experience and reception of the revelatory acts of God as good. However, dutiful work, at best, is in some way derived from worship. Yet this relating of duty to worship seems paradoxical to Hocking, for duty and work must not be confused with worship based on the love of God. This paradox seems to be a significant factor in the need for alternation.

In Wieman's reconstructed principle of worship, one does not turn within the worship experience, from worship, but rather moves through one level of worship to another level of worship. It is a moving through ultimate commitment to that reality of God who certainly exists as good, as denotatively defined, to that same reality further defined, but in this case, descriptively and experimentally, with the profound conviction that any assumed understanding of the nature of God must be held subject to further analysis, criticism, and correction by further experience of God. In the instance of critical correction of the descriptive nature of God, one's commitment to God with these attributes is released, but with retention of one's ultimate commitment. According to Wieman, man

> does this by bringing his total self, with all re-
> sources, into action in service of his faith. With
> this kind of commitment one finds a way to tri-
> umph in defeat. In this manner he finds a way
> to exercise wisdom when admitting himself to be
> human. With such a commitment he finds a path
> leading beyond the dead end of tragedy into the
> continuity of history.[164]

Wieman is aware that some may think that this two-level commitment is also paradoxical in that "we should commit ourselves to this creativity and at the same time seek a better understanding of what calls for our most complete commitment." But, he says, "this is precisely what is meant by the two-level commitment," and that: "It is not self-contradictory."[165] He points to the fact that there is a valid and consistent two-level commitment to created goods which is analogous to the two-level commitment to creative good.

> The parent who cannot combine devotion to his child with continuous endeavor to obtain a better understanding of the child is not fit to be a parent. A husband or wife who is unable to combine devotion with continually striving to understand the values of the other person, is not fit to enter marriage. A political leader who is unable to combine a full commitment to serving the people he leads with continual striving to acquire a better understanding of the needs and values of the people to whom he is committed, is not fit to be a political leader. An individual who cannot combine, in the conduct of his life, both a commitment to the best that his life can yield and also a continual striving to discover what that best may be, is not fit to live the human life. Human life should be distinguished by a continual creating of expanding perspective, beginning with the early days of infancy and ending when the individual ceases to show the distinguishing characteristics of human life.[166]

The distinguishing of these two levels of worship and the alternation from the top, descriptive and experimental level in case of error, to ultimate dependence on the deepest level alone, and then on into further description by experimental effort to gain further understanding in the worship of God, do not separate these two levels, for they operate as an interdependent process in which creative interchange functions between these two levels within human experience when creativity is not obstructed. In this form of worshipful living, a creative act, classified as work, is a functionally meaningful act in worshipful problem-solving. It is not a futile, meaningless act alien to the source of human good. From this context a creative vocation has a functionally meaningful relation to God. Through worship the profane is transformed and becomes sacred.

The further dimension in Hocking's principle of alternation which is basically objectionable to Wieman is not only Hocking's description of the nature of God as intrinsically complete, as opposed to being intrinsically creative, but also Hocking's description of God as eternally comprehending all reality, which would be an impossibility for any mind as we use the term, since reality in Wieman's creative process metaphysics is both in its actuality, and in its possibilities, in-the-making.

In Hocking's alternation between worship and work, he finds it necessary to turn away from work because work apart from the source of human good in futile. So he turns to the worship of God in order to be rearmed with the spirit of God so that he can return to secular work with a renewed spirit. But continued involvement in the secular world only leads to a further sense of futility of work itself. Apart from worship, work becomes mechanical, lacking the richness of qualitative meaning. Furthermore, continuous worship, Hocking says, makes a person an "automaton," which condition, we believe, would be, for Hocking, a loss of personal autonomy. So turning to work apart from worship provides the condition for autonomous expression. Therefore, the principle of alternation, for Hocking, is to prevent one from becoming the secular world's mechanic on the one hand, and on the other hand, God's automaton. But Hocking finds this principle unsatisfactory because "these two phases of experience belong together." Yet Hocking finds no way to bring them together, even though, "from time to time,"[167] they do occur together.

We suggest that Wieman has not only found the cause of this unsatisfactory paradox in Hocking's principle of alternation, but that he has also analyzed and presented in his two-level commitment the conditions for removing this paradox.

In reconceiving Hocking's principle, we observe that worship of God as commitment to a final and completed form and commitment to one who eternally comprehends all reality, makes the worshiper a victim of perfectionism whose worship denies the creativity of God, since creativity is intrinsically continuous, never final or complete. This perfectionistic worship of God as final and complete in form and in knowledge infects man with an inevitable and incurable desire to become perfect. This kind of worship is indeed satiating for it prevents man from becoming creative in his work.

Work performed in the interest of perfection is inevitably a failure since the events of the world, both the created events and the creative event are not things as finished, self-enclosed independent objects.

In Wieman, we work worshipfully as creative coworkers with God with no sense of absolute finality or completion ever. So work, insofar as it can be done creatively with God, and not done perfectionistically, is never futile. This destroys the paradox of worship and work, the alternation between satiating worship of God as final and completely perfect, and of the necessary failure and futility of the imperfect work of man.

We observe that insofar as man is bound personally and in his cultural situation to live with this paradox, that both he and his culture suffer alike from sense of failure, frustration, and the futility of perfectionistically conceived impractical ideals striven for in work. Man is then driven, in order to renew hope, back to worship of the perfect God, in an effort to renew life and continue his work. This analysis plumbs the depth of schizophrenic divisiveness in men and their culture insofar as they try to live by practicing this paradoxical form of worship. We suggest that Hocking's dissatisfaction with it and his vision of seeing it removed "from time to time," together with Wieman's further corrective, are memorable events in the history of creative religious philosophy, but the following questions arise: (1) In Wieman's two-level commitment to God as the creative event, does tension[168] remain between on the one hand the deepest or ultimate mystical commitment so strongly emphasized by Hocking as the valid and primitive source of religion, and on the other the analytic, abstract, cognitive commitment so strongly emphasized by Perry as necessary to intelligent commitment to any object or event? (2) If tension remains, does it necessarily obstruct worship of God as creative event? (3) If tension does not remain, is it possible to worship God as creative event? We shall keep these questions before us in our continuing study.

Having recognized the significance of the contributions of both Hocking and Wieman to the philosophy of creative worship, including Wieman's rejection of Hocking's commitment to God as a final and completed form and as one who eternally comprehends all reality, we are yet cognizant of the fact that there remains, in Wieman, a two-level structure of commitment different from Hocking's. We believe that this difference is to be accounted for, initially, by Wieman's earlier study of and appreciation for the organismic metaphysics of creativity in Henri Bergson's Creative Evolution,[169] for we have found that Wieman says, in referring to the enduring influence of Hocking: "Bergson had already intervened to turn me away from the metaphysics of idealism ...."[170] Therefore, we believe that further understanding of Wieman's two-level commitment may be attained by examination of the influence on Wieman of Bergson's organismic metaphysics of creativity. Furthermore, having found that Whitehead's organismic metaphysics of creativity is a significant but later influence in the development of Wieman's philosophy of creativity, we shall examine both of these related sources of influence in the following chapter.

Chapter IV

CREATIVITY IN WIEMAN AS A RESPONSE TO BERGSON'S
AND WHITEHEAD'S ORGANISMIC PHILOSOPHY

In a chapter in American Philosophies of Religion, written jointly by Bernard Eugene Meland and Wieman, they say:

> Since the publication of Bergson's Creative Evolution in 1911, ... modern philosophy has been turning more and more to an organic conception of reality.... [A] trend of thought emphasizing this organic character of the world ... has been designated organismic philosophy.... Among the important contributions to this trend is ... Whitehead's great work, Process and Reality. [1]

Wieman has made many direct references to Whitehead in his writings, and comparatively few to Bergson, but these, however brief, indicate that Bergson's philosophy of creativity, as well as Whitehead's, has had a profound influence on Wieman in developing his own philosophy of creativity.

That Wieman found Creative Evolution exciting when he read it during those four years of his pastorate, 1911-1915, before he went to Harvard, is significant for three reasons: (1) Wieman's study of Creative Evolution at that time was his introduction to the new bio-mystical process philosophy of creativity, which proved to be a continuing influence. (2) Of Bergson's influence, we have found that Wieman says: "[He] gave to my thinking a direction which deflected the influences of Harvard and caused me to reinterpret my teachers as I would not otherwise have done."[2] (3) Wieman's study of Bergson was done several years before Wieman began to read Whitehead, for he says:

> Very shortly after leaving Harvard, while teaching at Occidental College in Los Angeles, I began

reading avidly his [Whitehead's] books as they appeared. Later, when teaching on the faculty of the Divinity School at the University of Chicago, I received his <u>Process and Reality</u> in page proof and read it through three times before it came off the press.[3]

Not only has Wieman read Whitehead and many of his followers extensively, but he has also responded to their writings. From his first book in 1926 to his most recent one in 1968, he has made references to Whiteheadian philosophy including significant essays in which he expresses not only deep appreciation, but also adverse criticism.

Since Wieman was profoundly influenced by both Bergson and Whitehead, especially by their organismic metaphysics of creativity, it seems fitting to bring them together in this study.

WIEMAN'S RESPONSE TO BERGSON'S ORGANISMIC PHILOSOPHY OF CREATIVITY

"Duration" is the term most frequently used by Bergson to designate what he believed to be the ultimate nature of reality, but he used other terms for this purpose, including "time," and "creativity." He brings these concepts together by saying:

> The universe <u>endures</u>. The more we study the nature of time, the more we shall comprehend that duration means invention, the creation of forms, the continual elaboration of the absolutely new.[4]

The enduring quality of time is emphasized. It is continuous. The quality of continuity and creation is undivided, for he says that "'real duration' signifies both undivided continuity and creation."[5] Bergson distinguishes <u>real</u> or concrete time from what he calls <u>abstract</u> time. Real time is duration itself. In the continuity of real time "There is no instant immediately before another instant;..."[6] as there is in mathematical time, which Bergson describes as "artificial," but which we interpret as "timing," rather than time. By timing, we mean the scientific process of measuring the quality called duration, or time. It is done by abstracting a structural unit or event from duration, by giving it a name such as "day," and by inventing a mathematical means of counting days, such as a calendar year. Scientific measurement of a quality is a process of abstraction. As abstracted, it is, in a sense, artificial, as Bergson says, but the measured quality has been, to some extent, objectified. The objectified quality, as measured, is rendered intelligible. It then belongs to the life of the abstract intellect. It becomes a useful tool in practical work-a-day living. In abstraction, it is far removed from its rich context: the enduring flow of duration, as undifferentiated quality, which is real. We believe that Bergson's clear-cut philosophic aim is to awaken man to a realization of his basic office: to live in the context of the real, and not merely in the abstract and artificial life of the intellect. A consummative observation on Bergson's metaphysics might be that duration is the locus of creativity: "Duration means invention, the creation of forms, the continual elaboration of the absolutely new."[7]

We, therefore, do not interpret Bergson's metaphysics as being anti-intellectual. Its purpose is to fulfill the life of the intellect by realization of the necessary relation of the functioning of intellectual life to its rich qualitied source in the real and continuous flow of time which is duration: "the creation of forms, the continual elaboration of the absolutely new." Yet, we can understand why many Bergson scholars intepret Bergson's analysis of the role of the intellect in relation to intuition of the real as anti-intellectual, for Bergson does affirm opposition between intellect and intuition. It is, in fact, an affirmation of conflict between intellect and intuition. But with the maintenance of the realization of the necessary relation of intuition as the creative source of intellect, the scientific work of the intellect is transformed. This yields a new perception of scientific endeavor in the context of creativity which is real. We do not interpret Bergson as meaning that the opposition, as conflict, is destroyed or made harmonious; but rather that the transformation is a creative treatment of the conflict, issuing from the fact that there is now a new positive relation with the real that is creativity. This interpretation is our reconception of what Bergson says:

> Let us try to see, no longer with the eyes of the intellect alone, which grasps only the already made and which looks from the outside, but with the spirit....[8] To intellect, in short, there will be added intuition.... In our hypothesis, ... science and metaphysics are two opposed although comple-

mentary ways of knowing, the first retaining only moments, that is to say, that which does not endure, the second bearing on duration itself.[9]

The creative transformation of the opposition between the abstract analytic way of scientific knowing and the metaphysical way of intuition renders the relationship that of complementariness or mutual dependence, each way supplementing the other without eliminating the opposition.

In the transformed situation, the mind would renounce its most cherished habits.

> It is within becoming that it would have transported us by an effort of sympathy. We should no longer be asking where a moving body will be, what shape a system will take, through what state a change will pass at a given moment: the moments of time, which are only arrests of our attention, would no longer exist; it is the flow of time, it is the very flux of the real that we should be trying to follow.[10]

Yet Bergson sees that there are advantages in attaining and using scientific knowledge: It enables us "to foresee the future," and makes "us in some measure, masters of events.... It symbolizes the real and transposes it into the human...," but it is intuitional knowledge which "expresses" the real.

Bergson then tries to clarify what he means by expression of the real, first by saying what intuitional expression will not do, and then by saying what it will do. Intuitional knowledge,

> if it is possible, is practically useless, it will not extend our empire over nature, it will even go against certain natural aspirations of the intellect; but, if it succeeds, it is reality itself that it will hold in a firm and final embrace. Not only may we thus complete the intellect and its knowledge of matter by accustoming it to install itself within the moving, but by developing also another faculty, complementary to the intellect, we may open a perspective on the other half of the real. For, as soon as we are confronted with true duration, we see that it means creation, and that if that which is being unmade endures, it can only be because it is inseparably bound to what is making itself.[11]

By "making itself," we interpret Bergson as meaning self-facilitating. This reveals the union between creativity and continuity which Bergson affirms.[12] It is what we mean by saying that creativity is intrinsically creative. Without continuity, or duration, there is no creativity.

Bergson then suggests that the import of his metaphysics really is for revealing the growth of the universe and for the creative evolution of life within it.

> Thus will appear the necessity of a continual growth of the universe. I should say of a _life_ of the real. And thus will be seen in a new _light_ the life which we find on the surface of our planet, a life directed the same way as that of the universe, and inverse of materiality.[13]

Bergson sees the inorganic within nature, not as animated, but rather characterized by inertia. In this respect there is a dualism of opposing forces between movement and inertia in his metaphysics. It is the inorganic domain which has been the basic concern of the sciences and which has determined their traditional methodology. Insofar as creativity is released within the domain of organic life, it struggles with the inertia of materiality. Seen in this context, organic life suffers limitations in participating in creative evolution. The _distinguishing_ _mark_ _of_ _man_ _in_ _contrast_ _with_ _the_ _lower_ _levels_ _of_ _organic_ _life_, _is_ _the_ _creative_ _expanding_ _of_ _man's_ _consciousness_. This is the spirit of man. This is the expression of the real in man, the continuity of creativity in time without "dilution of eternity."

Bergson is most concerned that human consciousness be freed from the life of mere intellect for expression in creative evolution of consciousness.

> It is this freedom that the human form registers. Everywhere but in man, consciousness has had to come to a stand; in man alone it has kept on its way. Man, then, continues the vital movement indefinitely, although he does not draw along with him all that life carries within itself.[14]

Crucial in this freeing of human consciousness for its indefinite expansion is human communication; for it is through sympathetic communication, established by our intuition of real duration as creativity, that the way is opened for this indefinite expansion

> by the sympathetic communication which it [intuition] establishes between us and the rest of the living, by the expansion of our consciousness which it [intuition] brings about, it [intuition] introduces us into life's own domain, which is reciprocal interpretation, endlessly continued creation.[15]

However, in Bergson, intelligence is not separate from intuitional creative communication: "... though it [intuition] transcends intelligence, it is from intelligence that has come the push that has made it [intuition] rise to the point it has reached."[16]

Bergson goes further to suggest just how human consciousness really expands through creative communication with its source in the intuition of real duration. He asks: "But do we ever think true duration?" He replies:

> It is no use trying to approach duration: we must install ourselves within it straight away. This is what the intellect generally refuses to do, accustomed as it is to think the moving by means of the immovable.[17]

By installing ourselves straight away, we interpret Bergson as meaning our becoming forthrightly involved and committed as participants in the felt flow of qualified creative duration.

In this new transforming situation in which human consciousness is undergoing creative expansion through reciprocal interpretation,[18] both causality on which scientific analysis is based with its consequent multiplicity of scientific facts, and also finality with its import of completion in the one, are indeed transcended. Bergson expresses this consummatory insight in different ways.

> Thus, intuition may bring the intellect to recognize that life does not quite go into the category of the many nor yet into that of the one; that neither mechanical causality nor finality can give a sufficient interpretation of the vital process.[19]

Then, in clarifying the meaning of creative evolution in individuals and in society, Bergson expresses the same principle of transcendence of the many and the one.

Hence, throughout the whole realm of life, a

balancing between individuation and association. Individuals join together into a society; but the society, as soon as formed, tends to melt the associated individuals into a new organism, so as to become itself an individual, able in its turn to be part and parcel of a new association.[20]

Yet Bergson is deeply aware of the tragic limitations of "new association" through creative evolution. He says:

> In the humanity of which we are a part, intuition is, in fact, almost completely sacrificed to intellect.... [C]onsciousness has had to exhaust the best part of its power. This conquest ... has required that consciousness should adapt itself to the habits of matter.... Intuition is there, however, but vague and above all discontinuous. It is a lamp almost extinguished, which only glimmers now and then, for a few moments at most. But it glimmers wherever a vital interest is at stake. On our personality, on our liberty, on the place we occupy in the whole of nature, on our origin and perhaps also on our destiny, it throws a light feeble and vacillating, but which none the less pierces the darkness of the night in which the intellect leaves us.[21]

Wieman's response to Bergson is not only comprehensive in that it encompasses the whole range of Bergson's metaphysics, theory of knowing, and theory of valuation, but it is also penetrating in that the depth of Bergson's creative process philosophy is reconceived, and in significant respects reconstructed. The organizational structure of Wieman's Harvard dissertation which we have found to be basically formative for his whole philosophy of creativity is a reconception, and with significant originality, a restructuring of Bergson's metaphysics of creative evolution. This deep and comprehensive response to Bergson documents Wieman's statement regarding the influence of Bergson on his response to what he received from his teachers at Harvard. The statement was that Bergson gave to Wieman's thinking a direction which deflected the influences of Harvard and caused him to reinterpret his teachers as he would not otherwise have done.[22] His dissertation, entitled "The Organization of Interests," is presented in four parts. Part I is "An Interpretation of Human Interests in Three Categories." The categories, as listed in the title of Chapter II, are "Adaptive, Instrumental, and Creative Interests."[23] We see these categories to be basically Bergsonian in that they are a critical reinterpretation of Bergson's general analysis of the organismic nature of creative evolution which operates in three distinctly different but not separate stages: by instinct, by intellect, and by intuition. Wieman's use of the term, "interest," is sufficiently broad to encompass all three of these modes of operation.

> The term interest includes all the activities of a physical organism. Activity is taken to include all 'readiness to act' or 'motor attitude' as well as the gross efforts of limb and trunk. Thinking is activity; it is 'the lambent interplay of motor attitudes.' Every impulse involves a certain readjustment of the organism, however minute and imperceptible may be the changes, and hence is activity. Thus interest may be expressed in various ways and appear in diverse forms. It is 'response of the organism to its environment'; it is 'wish,' want, desire, purpose, instinct, habit, will. It is the tendency of the organism to act in a specific manner; to produce a definite result; to create or sustain a certain situation.[24]

Wieman says he finds it necessary to have some comprehensive term to which "all the phenomena under consideration" can be reduced, so he has adopted the term <u>interest</u> for this purpose, following, as he understands it, the usage of Perry.

It is these Bergsonian categories of interest which Wieman uses as the basis for criticism of Perry's theory of value as liberal harmonization of interests.[25] Again, it is these same categories which Wieman uses to criticize finalistic perfectionism in Hocking's metaphysics of idealism.[26] This clarifies Wieman's saying of his work in Harvard: "In Hocking I found another devoted follower of Royce. But Bergson had already intervened to turn me away from the metaphysics of idealism...."[27]

After recognizing that Wieman's metaphysics has significant aspects in common with Hocking's, as delineated in detail in Chapter III, above, we believe that it is more deeply and widely rooted in the metaphysics of Bergson. Wieman is at home in Bergson's new metaphysics of becoming--rooted in sympathy, the flow of felt quality, real duration which is creative--that transports us beyond the merely causal relations described in the physical sciences, and also beyond the conceptual assumptions of finality. Wieman's metaphysics is a metaphysics of quality.

> Quality, then, is objective fact. It is ultimate reality. It is the substance of which all is made. It can be structured into diverse forms; and, when it is so structured, we have all the different things to be found in this existing world. The world is essentially and substantively quality. It is energy, but energy is quality to human experience, and that means ultimately and absolutely for human living.[28]

The creative flow of felt quality in Wieman is synonymous with real duration in Bergson. However, we are cognizant of the fact that Wieman has sharply distinguished his own interpretation of creativity from creativity as set forth by Bergson:

> ... we must distinguish creativity as here interpreted from creativity as set forth by Bergson. According to him, creativity has no structure and creates no structure. This, plainly, is exactly opposite to what we are saying about creativity, although here, again, in Bergson we recognize a source of insight beyond measure.[29]

We believe there is a significant basis in Bergson for Wieman's interpretation. Bergson distinguishes the flow of duration, as time, from creation. Furthermore, it seems that creation, within the infinite past of duration, appears with but a faint glimmer. This faint glimmer is in the evolving of the _organic_ quality of duration. _Real_ duration involves the presence of creation within it. The continuity of real duration cannot be separated from creation: Bergson says that "'real duration' signifies both undivided continuity and creation."[30] We believe that creativity apart from the continuity of duration could neither have structure nor create structure.

More than a decade after Wieman expressed his criticism of Bergson's conception of creativity, Wieman wrote a significant essay on the flow of felt quality which appears in the longer unpublished manuscript of his "Intellectual Autobiography."[31] We see in this essay a significantly original reinterpretation of Bergson's real duration as the continuity of creativity. Wieman begins by saying that the "ultimate source of security and renewal" in human existence "is the flow of felt quality." He suggests that this flow of felt quality is the ultimate and vital truth diversely articulated in various religions of the world. Furthermore he sees it as "relatively unstructured" but it is

> impossible to experience qualities of sense and feeling without some structure. Therefore the flow of felt quality is only relatively unstructured.... It is unstructured only in the sense that it is the level of experience where new structures are in process of being created but not yet sufficiently definite to do more than awaken vivid awareness of the flow of quality. Thus creativity is immersed in quality, so to speak, thereby carrying all the promise and potency of what human life might become.[32]

Wieman then concludes:

> The claim that flow of quality is creativity itself at the initial stage of its operation is derived from the understanding that felt quality cannot reach consciousness at all unless it is either structured in some way or new structures are burgeoning in it even though these are as yet so unformed that intellect and practice can make no use of them.[33]

So from this context we find Wieman's perspectives on the relatively structured flow of felt quality to be consistent with Bergson's summary statement which relates the enduring universe, the nature of time, duration which means invention, the creation of forms, and the continual elaboration of the absolutely new.[34]

But Wieman has further difficulties with Bergson. These are brought out in the first chapter of his first book where he is setting forth with courage and directness his innovating claim that the methodology of the sciences is to be respected and used in developing knowledge of God in terms of concrete experience. He says:

> We believe nothing is more important at the present stage of human thought than to define God in terms of concrete experience. Failure to do this has led some of the finest scientific thinkers

Bergson's & Whitehead's Philosophy / 81

of our time to regard religion as superstition and nothing else.³⁵

Wieman criticizes the three categories in Bergson's metaphysics of creative evolution: instinct, intellect, and intuition.

We see these categories as basically metaphysical in that they distinguish the domains in organic evolution. Furthermore, they express methods of knowing these domains, and also serve as the basis for critical evaluation of them. In these respects Bergson's metaphysics is operational in connecting creatively metaphysics, theory of knowing, and theory of valuing, all together from the context of the science of biology in its relatedness to the rest of the universe and the entire cosmos. This is creative organismic philosophy.

In Bergson, methods of knowing are evolutionary, and correlative with the domains to which they refer. The three forms of knowing, instinctive, intellectual, and intuitive, are correlative with the metaphysical categories. The source of knowledge is in the felt flow of reality itself: the moving flow of activity. Bergson regards the human intellect

> as relative to the needs of action. Postulate action, and the very form of the intellect can be deduced from it. This form is therefore neither irreducible nor inexplicable. And, precisely because it is not independent, knowledge cannot be said to depend on it: knowledge ceases to be a product of the intellect and becomes, in a certain sense, part and parcel of reality.³⁶

Bergson's concept of knowledge encompasses a wide range of experience which is unacceptable to Wieman. Bergson illustrates what he means by instinctive knowledge by saying:

> When the new-born babe seeks for the first time its mother's breast, so showing that it has knowledge (unconscious, no doubt) of a thing it has never seen, we say, just because the innate knowledge is in this case of a definite object, that it belongs to instinct and not to intelligence.³⁷

Bergson interprets instinctive knowledge in terms of feeling, for he says: "Instinct is sympathy."[38] It is a sympathetic knowing of the unconsciously selected object. However, the consummative evolution of instinct is in insects.[39] The mode of adaptation in the domain of instinctive activity

> is reflected outwardly in exact movements instead of being reflected inwardly in consciousness.... [T]he behavior of the insect involves, or rather evolves, the idea of definite things existing or being produced in definite points of space and time, which the insect knows without having learned them.[40]

Bergson defines intuition, the highest level of evolution, found in man, in terms of instinct by saying:

> ... by intuition I mean instinct that has become disinterested, self-conscious, capable of reflecting upon its object and of enlarging it indefinitely.[41]

The object of reflection is consciousness. By consciousness, Bergson means the vital impetus of life which "consists in a need of creation."[42] Therefore, both instinct, qua instinct, and intuition are directed toward life, but in different ways: the one is an expression of the finality of life in the fixation of it; the other is an expression of real duration in the continuity of creation.

Intellect, in Bergson, refers to the domain of physical causality. This domain is described by the physical sciences in terms of relations between objects of inert matter. Its methodology is mechanistic and its knowledge is an artificial fabrication of real duration, for it is not oriented toward the life process. However, intellect is not separate from instinct and intuition. There are fringe relations with no absolute separations.

We see Bergson's reconstructed way of knowing and valuing as evolutionary, not only in that its source is in the felt flow of real qualitied duration, but in that it is also evolutionary since its source is in the elementary stage of the evolution of intuition. In the course of the evolutionary struggle of the creative vital impetus with the inertia of inorganic matter, the domain of elementary intuition in the flow of reality suffers, in part, from fixation. The result of this fixation is the domain of instinct. Since knowledge of this domain is correlative with instinct itself, it is called instinctive knowledge. This domain is closed to further creation. Intellectual knowledge, traditionally defined as the methodology of the physical sciences, is correlative with the relations between inert material objects rather than between living organisms, and is thereby in opposition to intuitional knowledge, which is correlative with creative organic living relations. Intuitional knowledge, insofar as it is free from the inertia of inorganic causal relations, and also from fixated instinct, is correlative with the intentional creative organic life of expanding and evolving human consciousness. Valuing, like knowing, is intrinsically determined by the biomystical metaphysics of this evolutionary process. Creativity in the flow of real duration is intrinsically evoluationary and is thereby ultimately determinative of increase of value.

In criticizing Bergson's categories of creative evolution, Wieman defines instinctive activity of organisms as

> the first steps which the organism takes in selecting from the mass of stimuli which assails it, those particular elements which are of practical importance. [43]

These steps are operations "of certain automatic mechanisms of behavior." Though these mechanisms "determine the objects of our attention" and "are highly selective," they do not operate to give us the sympathetic feeling awareness of the flow of reality. Wieman says: "They do not render us responsive to, sensitive to, or conscious of, the unanalyzed flow of experience."[44]

In observing Wieman's criticism in context, we see that instinct operates as Wieman says it does. Furthermore, this is the mode of operation which Bergson attributes to instinct as fixated intuition in its elementary evolutionary development. But prior to complete fixation of instinct, instinctive-intuition, or intuitional-instinct does function, with limitations due to the inertia of matter, to give us the sympathic feeling awareness of the flow of reality with consequent responsiveness.

Again, Wieman criticizes Bergson's use of the term knowledge[45] to refer to the wide range of experience which includes, for Bergson, instinctive, intellectual, and intuitional knowledge. Wieman's restricting the term to refer to scientific knowledge alone does not imply that the methodology of the sciences is limited to that set of methods commonly used to describe causal relations in the physical sciences as Bergson's use of scientific methodology requires. We have found that Wieman's second-level commitment to the creative event operates by means of scientific knowledge as expressed by him in the following statement:

> All development of knowledge is by expanding the range of theories which distinguish and relate events in such a way that inference can be extended more widely from what is now observed to other events and possibilities more or less remote in time and space or otherwise inaccessible to immediate observation.[46]

We suggest that Wieman's methodology for knowing as stated here is not so much a rejection as it is a fulfillment of what Bergson was beginning to formulate and use. Our observation of what they have in common, including their organismic metaphysics and their commitment to creativity, is our basis for this suggestion.

Wieman's ultimate first-level commitment to the creative event by means of a denotative definition of God as the source of human good bears similarities to Bergson's intuitional commitment to the vital impetus in real duration which is a union of both continuity and creation, and also a creation of form and of novelty within the natural process of organic evolution, more specifically, within the evolving and expanding of human consciousness. Furthermore, we suggest that the tension experienced by Bergson between his commitment to the domain of intuition and his commitment to the domain of intellect is, in a significant sense, similar to the tension in Wieman between his first and second level commitments. We also see something more than intimations of similarity in their effort to deal creatively with this tension. In each case, the ultimate commitment is to the domain of creativity operative in human experience, more significantly in the expanding of human consciousness. In each case the emerging of novel insights is there. In each case these novel insights are creatively combined in the creation of new perceptions, with consequent expanding of human consciousness. In each case there is a vision of creative human community made possible by symbolic communication and reciprocal interpretation. In each case creative community transcends the classic struggle to solve the problematic relation of individuality to sociality. Bergson's principle of transcendence involves "a balancing between individuation and association"[47] in the context of creative evolution. For Wieman, the transcendence of individuality and sociality for creative community is effected by worship of God.[48]

The following statements, both powerful and poetic, reveal Bergson's and Wieman's creative use of the tension they experience between intellect and intuition. Bergson:

> Thus, to the eyes of a philosophy that attempts to reabsorb intellect in intuition, many difficulties vanish or become light. But such a doctrine does not only facilitate speculation, it gives us also more power to act and to live. For, with it, we feel ourselves no longer isolated in humanity, humanity no longer seems isolated in the nature that it dominates.... All the living hold together, and all yield to the same tremendous push. The animal takes its stand on the plant, man bestrides animality, and the whole of humanity, in space and in time, in one immense army galloping beside and before and behind each of us in an overwhelming charge able to beat down every resistance and clear the most formidable obstacles, perhaps even death.[49]

Wieman:

> No matter what a man treats as the most important thing in the universe, he is worshipping if he puts himself in that attitude toward it in which we can experience the maximum stimulus it can yield. He may be worshipping an idol, but it is worship. If it be the true God, however, or that which approximates the true God, his worship will arouse and organize his impulses for the farthest swing of constructive achievement of which he is capable. Such, we believe, is the rightful work of religion in human living. Its function is creative.[50]

Then, from this closing paragraph in his first book, Religious Experience and Scientific Method, we turn to a statement near the close of his last one, Religious Inquiry, in which the object of true worship is stated in terms of creative evolution.

> Therefore, we have come to the time of final decision in human history, the time when we must consciously and intelligently accept this creativity

as the goal of our existence, or accept the fate of being unfit to undergo the continuing creative transformation of creative evolution, by which and for which we exist.[51]

In our following study of Whitehead as that other organismic philosopher whose influence on Wieman has been both lasting and great, we shall guard Bergson's influence on Wieman for what it is really worth, for Wieman, himself says: "Our indebtedness to Bergson is almost as great as to Whitehead."[52] Furthermore, we shall be mindful of the fact that there is also an indirect influence on Wieman from Bergson through Whitehead, for Whitehead, in naming only a few persons in his Preface to <u>Process and Reality</u>, to whom he is most indebted, says: "I am also greatly indebted to Bergson, William James, and John Dewey."[53]

WIEMAN'S RESPONSE TO WHITEHEAD'S ORGANISMIC PHILOSOPHY OF CREATIVITY

Wieman's general commitment to the process philosophy of creative organicism, which he had found in Bergson's <u>Creative Evolution</u> soon after it appeared in 1911, was a fit context for growing appreciation, beginning about 1920, for Alfred North Whitehead's process philosophy which also became a form of creative organicism.

When Whitehead went to Cambridge University in the early 1880's, he regarded the field of physics as "nearly a closed subject." There was general satisfaction with the Newtonian principles. Then "by the middle of the 1890's" there were beginnings of a new awakening. Einstein was "supposed to have made an epochal discovery." Whitehead says:

By 1900 Newtonian physics were demolished, done for! Speaking personally, it had a profound effect on me; I have been fooled once, and I'll be damned if I'll be fooled again![54]

This event seems to have marked a turning-point in Whitehead's way of thinking. No longer could he think of scientific knowledge or any other kind of knowledge as settled: "There is no more reason to suppose that Einstein's relativity is anything final, than Newton's <u>Principia</u>." So the experience had taught him "to beware of certitude."[55]

He interprets the danger as "dogmatic thought." He sees that "science is not immune from it," and that "it plays the devil with religion."[56]

In Whitehead's reflecting on this experience of more than fifty years earlier, in casual conversation with friends in his home, he relates the evolution of thought and knowledge to organic evolution, as reported by Lucien Price:

> I am, as you see, a thoroughgoing evolutionist. Millions of years ago our earth began to cool off and forms of life began in their simplest aspects. Where did they come from? They must have been inherent in the total scheme of things; must have existed in potentiality in the most minute particles, first of this fiery, and later of this watery and earthy planet.[57]

Whitehead, presenting the ultimate basis of the organismic metaphysics of evolution, says:

> 'Creativity' is the universal of universals characterizing ultimate matter of fact. It is that ultimate principle by which the many, which are the universe disjunctively, become the one actual occasion, which is the universe conjunctively.[58]

Formally stated, "The many become one, and are increased by one."[59]

When Wieman read Process and Reality before it was published, he may well have discovered among the Bergsonian influences within it that Whitehead's profound insight into creativity expressed in terms of "The many become one and are increased by one," is surprisingly similar to the following insight expressed by Bergson:

> Thus, intuition may bring the intellect to recognize that life does not quite go into the category of the many nor yet into that of the one; that neither mechanical causality nor finality can give a sufficient interpretation of the vital process.[60]

Further application of this principle, which Whitehead calls creativity, is related, by Bergson, to the individual person and society in his saying:

> Hence, throughout the whole realm of life, a balancing between individuation and association. Individuals join together into a society; but the society, as soon as formed, tends to melt the associated individuals into a new organism, so as to become itself an individual, able in its turn to be part and parcel of a new association.[61]

The process which organically and creatively relates individuation and association, including the individual person and society, is described by Whitehead as "the production of novel togetherness." This, he says, "is the ultimate notion embodied in the term 'concrescence'."[62]

We see the production of novel togetherness to be the central issue in Wieman's philosophy of creativity. However problematic in the history of philosophy is the issue of the one and the many, or, by extrapolation, the preservation of individual autonomy of persons in relation to order in community, this issue is treated differently by organismic process philosophers. Bergson, Wieman, Whitehead, and others are especially critical of those philosophers who cannot think clearly in terms of process. Bergson criticizes them by saying:

> Just as we separate in space, we fix in time. The intellect is not made to think evolution, in the proper sense of the word--that is to say, the continuity of a change that is pure mobility.... Suffice it to say that the intellect represents becoming as a series of states, each of which is homogeneous with itself and consequently does not change.[63]

The outcome of Whitehead's classic analysis of this set of issues in terms of being and becoming is his Process and Reality. Wieman places these issues not only in the context of process philosophy, organismic metaphysics, and creative evolution, but also directly in the context of philosophy of religion and theology. Wieman's fundamental contribution is in clarification of the imperative need for religious commitment to creativity as an empirical process within human experience.

The production of novel togetherness is evident in Wieman's analysis of the creative event. There is the occurrence of novelty in the emerging of new insights in the first subevent. Togetherness is present in the integrating of these new insights with those already attained. This is the second subevent. The combined operation of the first and second subevents, which yields an expanding appreciative consciousness of one's world, is the third subevent. This is again an experience of novelty. These three subevents, functioning together, produce growth of community among men when the necessary conditions are provided for the release of creativity in human existence. This fourth subevent, which is growth of community, is an experience of togetherness.

The providing of right conditions for release of creativity, as opposed to conditions which obstruct it, makes a significant difference in what human individuals and groups can do about it in terms of their ultimate concern for and ultimate commitment to it. It is this kind of concern and this kind of commitment to creativity which is religious. When this concern and this commitment operate with increasing intelligence, yielding a rich release of creativity in human life, the production of novelty as related to the production of togetherness becomes, we believe, aesthetically rhythmic, so that it is possible to speak, as Whitehead does, of the creative process as the production of novel togetherness.

Careful analysis of Wieman's major writings reveals a multiplicity of varied forms of expressing religious commitment to creativity as production of novel togetherness, even though we find no reference in Wieman's writings where he makes use of Whitehead's phrase. However, its meaning is not only evident in Wieman's four-fold creative event, but like the theme of a symphony, it beats through his works. It is, for example, clearly struck in his Introduction to Man's Ultimate Commitment,[64] then reappearing in a variety of forms through the volume, it is expressed at the close by saying:

> I have explained what I mean by creative and transforming power. I mean two things: [1] interchange which creates appreciative understanding of unique individuality; [2] integration within each individual of what he gets from others in this way, thus progressively creating his own personality in power, knowledge, and capacity to appreciate more profoundly diverse individuals, peoples and things.[65]

Having observed that creativity embodied in concrescence is a fundamental affirmation in the philosophies of creativity of both Whitehead and Wieman, we shall analyze six of Whitehead's basic perspectives which clarify and support this affirmation: (1) relativity and societism, (2) process philosophy and becoming, (3) atomism and actual entities, (4) empiricism and thought, (5) subjectivism and experience, (6) feeling and prehension, and follow the analysis of each perspective with Wieman's response. We shall conclude our study of Wieman's response to creativity in Whitehead by comparing their views on creativity and God.

Relativity and Societism

The principle of relativity which has transformed the field of physics, beginning in the latter part of the nineteenth century, was accepted seriously by Whitehead. From it he derived basic aspects of his philosophy including especially his principle of societism. The import of societism for philosophy of creativity is that nothing exists alone. "Things" traditionally viewed as self-enclosed and independent objects are reinterpreted as events which come into being as structured actual entities within the process of nature, and which have a survival period and pass into other forms of the process. Isolation is a myth invented by the finite intellect.[66] "An actual entity is present in other actual entities,"[67] since everything prehends everything else through feeling.[68] Prehension is the affective interpenetration of events. No entity or event, including God, is absolutely independent.[69]

Societism, for Whitehead, eliminates the vicious dualisms which appear frequently in traditional philosophy "by reason of mistaking an abstraction for a final concrete fact."[70] There is an appearance of dualism between the one and the many,[71] but this "dualism" is a qualified rather than absolute dualism, since "The many become one and are increased by one."

Even though individuality in Whitehead is conditioned by societism, societism does not destroy individuality. Individuals have internal integrity; thus while in the very nature of creativity they are constituted by relations effected by others, and in that sense dependent on others, they are not completely determined by others. Individuals are internally determined and externally free.[72]

Wieman's acceptance of the principle of relativity was certainly an outcome of much previous work on the philosophy of the sciences and their methodology, especially work on Bergson, and with Perry. In acknowledging Perry's contribution to "the way science portrays the world," he says:

> Professor Perry says that science describes in the simplest terms possible.... But the matter of prime consideration ... is the fact that that same mass of experience could be described with equal accuracy in wholly different terms and the object which that description would disclose in the event experienced might be wholly different from what the ordinary simplified scientific description portrays.[73]

By 1917, when Wieman was completing his Harvard dissertation with Perry, he was relating his perspectives on relativity and creative evolution in developing his own empirical philosophy of theistic religion. He had read many other works which were contributing to a metaphysics based on dynamic relations as opposed to fixed substance, including William James, John Dewey, and L. T. Hobhouse. By around 1920, he had read Principles of Natural Knowledge, and The Concept of Nature, by Whitehead. When completing his writing of Religious Experience and Scientific Method in 1925, he had read E. Mach, S. Alexander, J. B. S. Haldane, A. D. Ritchie, and Lloyd Morgan, who had made significant contributions to these trends in his thinking. However, these trends were not fixed. He did not treat them dogmatically. He says:

> We do not wish to set up this metaphysical view as the last word of truth. We are only pointing to it as typical of a movement now going on which renders obsolete the old, exclusive materialistic assumptions of scientific thought, and shows the influence of Biology and the new theory of relativity in recasting the prevailing views of the universe.[74]

Among the resources of the sciences, in addition to biology and the social sciences, which Wieman found most significant at this time for further development of his empirical philosophy of creativity, was this new theory of relativity from the field of physics. He says:

> But perhaps the most radical and important recasting of these basic concepts of science is to be traced to the theory of relativity itself. While this theory is not a metaphysical doctrine, it quite completely breaks down certain assumptions of an earlier Physics.[75]

Wieman then evaluates Whitehead's early contribution as follows:

> The best exponent of the wider applications of relativity is A. N. Whitehead. While he has not himself taken up the positive work of metaphysical reconstruction, he has done the negative work of showing that the metaphysics of materialism is impossible.[76]

Wieman supports his evaluation by quoting from Whitehead's The Concept of Nature in which Whitehead combines basic Bergsonian perspectives including duration or time, creativity, and the limitations of human intelligence, by saying:

> The past and the future meet and mingle in the ill-defined present. The passage of nature which is only another name for the creative force of existence has no narrow ledge of definite instantaneous present within which to operate. Its operative presence which is now urging nature forward must be sought for throughout the whole, in the remotest past as well as in the narrowest breadth of any present duration. Perhaps also in the unrealised future. Perhaps also in the future which might be as well as the actual future which will be. It is impossible to meditate on time and the mystery of the creative passage of nature without an overwhelming emotion at the limitations of human intelligence.[77]

Wieman reports in a footnote to this quotation that Whitehead develops in Science and the Modern World, "the metaphysical implications which we have here detected."[78]

From these perspectives Wieman interprets Whitehead as "coming very close to saying that mind and purpose are at work in all nature." Wieman sees this as a mere suggestion in Whitehead, and in his own further development of his philosophy he regards mind and purpose at work in all nature as merely what "may be,"[79] a mere speculation. However, it is mere speculation untested by empirical methods that is especially objectionable to Wieman as the basis for the development of philosophy and religion.

> We ... are very fearful of speculations which presume a knowledge which they do not possess. The rank growth of mistaken speculation destroys the substance of religion.[80]

But Wieman is not opposing conceptual knowledge as such, since it may be tested experimentally in imagination. He says: "... conceptual knowledge of God, when correct, is the most precious knowledge we shall ever attain."[81] He then refers to Whitehead's latest publications, Religion in the Making, and Science and the Modern World as "exceedingly important" studies "of the nature of God" done "from the standpoint of the mathematician and the physicist." He describes these recent works as a "new attempt at developing an adequate metaphysics on the basis of the new physics" of relativity.

Wieman reinterprets the "Principle of Concretion" as Whitehead's term[82] to designate God. He says "the concrete is precisely the unification of the many into one."[83] The principle of relativity operates in such a way that "Everything which is has some share in the existence" of each event, for example, a flower. In this sense, "the universe is 'concreted' in the flower," and since "all being in some measure enters into the flower," the flower, as Whitehead says, "'prehends' all being."[84] The universe is "organized according to the principle of concretion" and this order which "makes it concrete is God."[85] This order in its rich and full concreteness is aesthetic and all other orders, such as the moral and conceptual orders, are included in the aesthetic order. So at this level of the development of Whitehead's philosophy, Wieman sees his metaphysics as an outgrowth of the principle of relativity expressed in terms of the aesthetic order of the universe whose principle is concretion.

We see that societism in Whitehead significantly exemplifies and clarifies the production of novel togetherness. In its context of relativity, societism operates not in an absolute space and time, but in space-time systems subject to the order of concretion and interpenetration of prehension. Societism relates organically and creatively the novelty of individuals into and out of their world of togetherness.

Process Philosophy and Becoming

Process philosophy is a description and an interpretation of nature from perspectives based on the principle of relativity. Nature is dynamically related activity in which everything is a part of everything else. The basic units in process are the actual entities. These are composed of prehensions interpreted as feeling. The rhythmic alternation between the many diverse novel actual entities and the novel unity of the one is process. Creativity, the many, and the one constitute the ultimate category in process. There are microscopic and macroscopic species of process[86] with evolutionary tendencies in creative advance or transition of the many simpler actual entities to the unification of the more complex actual entity called a nexus or society. This process which is productive of societies, in turn, generates a further diversity of novel actual entities. Both actual entities and societies are organic in nature, so the process is basically organismic.

Societism operates in the production of novel togetherness not statically but as a dynamic process which is becoming. Societistic becoming does not operate like the traditional type of philosophizing frequently observed in philosophical discussions where perspectives are expressed but fail to interpenetrate with sufficient depth to become anything significantly different from what they were. In contrast to this more or less static pseudo-sharing of perspectives, societistic becoming requires real sharing due to the fact that the "inter" is interpenetrating and the change is real. The result is a process of genuine becoming which removes traditional bifurcations from the actual process. The elimination of these bifurcations between subjects and their predicates, subjects and their goals, and conditions and consequences, to mention only a few examples, undercuts the mechanization of natural processes and opens the way for freedom in becoming. Process philosophy as societistic becoming affirms real duration as the continuity of time. Fixations do not belong in a process philosophy of becoming. They are sources of evil whether they be fixed ideas, laws of nature, philosophies, civilizations, or cultures.

Wieman's response to process philosophy and becoming is basic in developing his whole philosophy of creativity. We have found that it was process metaphysics in Bergson's philosophy of evolution which appealed to him and won his commitment to it about a decade before he began to read

Whitehead. Furthermore, the fact that Bergson took seriously the creative advance into novelty, and on this basis rejected the generalizations of mechanistic interpretations of human behavior in traditional materialistic forms of metaphysics, was especially impressive for Wieman. So, when Wieman discovered process philosophy in Whitehead and its import for developing further a creative organismic metaphysics, it was natural that he should become a dedicated reader of Whitehead's books as soon as they appeared. Then, when Wieman was finishing his Religious Experience and Scientific Method with its innovating use of creative process metaphysics for the development of philosophy of religion, he discovered Whitehead's Science and the Modern World, and soon after that, his Religion in the Making. Wieman found both of these volumes to be exciting contributions to the objective he was already pursuing. The fact that Whitehead had received much from Bergson and was making further critical use of his contributions stimulated in Wieman further interest in Whitehead.

In Wieman's original appreciative response to Whitehead, we believe Whitehead's rejection of mechanistic materialism in favor of process philosophy, and his affirmation of the creative advance into novelty are regarded as especially significant.

> In fact, Whitehead is most emphatic in his rejection of materialism; and we believe that his work, together with that of others akin to him, has rendered materialism altogether obsolete among the well informed. Furthermore, his insistence that the event, rather than the object, is the basic fact of nature and that nature is marked by a 'creative advance' lends itself most readily to the religious interpretation. For 'event' and 'creative advance' mean precisely that in nature the past does not drop out of existence with each successive instant, as materialism would declare, but that the past continues operative with the present to shape the future. [87]

During those years from 1925 to c. 1940 when Whitehead the metaphysician and philosopher of religion was analyzing in detail the issues of the new process philosophy of relativity and creative organicism and developing from these analyses a total philosophic system, Wieman found his works to be worthy of careful study both personally and also in his seminars at the University of Chicago. But at the same time he was repulsed by what he regarded as non-empirically related speculation in Whitehead. Whitehead seemed to be aware of this strand of criticism of his works. So he offered a powerful defense of speculative philosophy in <u>Process and Reality</u>, but this did not satisfy Wieman. However, Whitehead's grounding of his philosophy in the actual entities of existence, revealing the influence of his neo-realistic epistemology, was, for Wieman, worthy of support.

For Whitehead, process and becoming, as the alternative to fixation, does not deny the individuality, or "atomism" of actual entities. The actual entity is the locus of becoming. "An 'entity' means 'an element contributory to the process of becoming.'"[88] Becoming, in Whitehead, is not "a uniquely serial advance" in which there is a "continuity of becoming," but there is a "becoming of continuity,"[89] since "'becoming' is a creative advance into novelty."[90]

<u>Atomism and Actual Entities</u>

In the early works of Whitehead, he called an actual entity an event, but in his later works he reserved the term event for a nexus or society of actual entities. The actual entity, as an atomic unit, appears and perishes in its subjective immediacy while the event has a longer survival period. However, the actual entity does not perish objectively, for it passes into some other entity. It is objectively immortal, but subjectively, it perishes in that its intrinsic character is transformed in the process of perishing. The actual entity performs two main functions. One is its own subjective becoming for self-maintenance and self-fulfillment. The other is socially extensive and objective by its passage into other entities. These functions, however distinct, are united in the actual entity which is characterized as a unity. An actual entity is "the unity to be ascribed to a particular instance of concrescence."[91]

Creativity, in Whitehead, is not an abstract freefloating advance outside actual entities. There is nothing, absolutely nothing, apart from individual actual entities and <u>their</u> relations. The actual entity either as one or as many is ultimate, for "there is no going behind actual entities to find anything more real."[92] But actual entities are composed of prehensions which are "Concrete Facts of Relatedness."[93] Whitehead says:

... the first analysis of an actual entity, into its most concrete elements, discloses it to be a concrescence of prehensions, which have originated in its process of becoming.[94]

By means of prehensions operative within the process of becoming or creative advance, the actual entity is objectified in another.[95] Whitehead's theory of objectification is clearly derived from the principle of relativity, but this theory is not a negation of his ontological principle which asserts that "apart from things that are actual, there is nothing." Furthermore, Whitehead says:

> Thus the actual world is built up of actual occasions; and by the ontological principle whatever things there are in any sense of 'existence,' are derived by abstraction from actual occasions.[96]

However, the diversity, individuality, and autonomy of actual entities do not prevent their undergoing a kind of creative "evolution." There are gradations of actual entities. At the lower levels, consciousness is not attributed to them, but at the higher level in man, the actual entities are complex and conscious. The locus of creative evolution is the creative advance through concrescence.

Therefore, we suggest that the major differences among Whitehead scholars regarding his affirmation of both creativity and the one and the many as ultimate can be resolved not only by recognizing that the locus of creativity is actual entities which have ontological being as distinct in their novel unity and novel diversity, but also by seeing that the individuality of actual entities is not lost in the relativity of their prehensive creative advance.

We have already observed that the ultimate tension in Wieman's philosophy of creativity is an outcome of relating order, unity and community to novelty, diversity, and individuality--the classic problem around which so much great philosophy has been oriented. We believe this to be the distinctive problem in Royce, Hocking, Bergson, Whitehead and others who have been most influential in Wieman's philosophic development. Among these philosophers, perhaps Bergson is unique in taking novelty seriously, for he courageously affirmed the limitations of ordered reason and intellect in order to respect the thrust of novelty in creative evolution. Perhaps Whitehead's deep interest in systematic philosophy is nurtured by Bergson's and consequently, his own serious recognition of the fact of novelty. Is not the fact of individuality and novelty the reason for process system-building? Whitehead says: "Process and individuality require one another."[97] Whitehead's balanced emphasis on novelty and process is exemplified in his ultimate category of creativity as related to the one and the many. His more thoroughgoing technical analysis of the issues involved has stirred Wieman not only to profound study of Whitehead's contributions, but also to further critical analysis of Whitehead's effort to develop and maintain this balance between novelty and unitary process.

In order to get the further import of Wieman's criticism of Whitehead on this crucial issue, we believe that further examination of Whitehead's perspectives, including the last three of the six mentioned above, namely, empiricism, subjectivism, and feeling, is now in order.

Empiricism and Thought

Whitehead's acceptance of the modern empirical mood is evident in his referring to William James in the opening of his first chapter of Science and the Modern World.

> The thesis which these lectures will illustrate is that this quiet growth of science has practically re-coloured our mentality so that modes of thought which in former times were exceptional are now broadly spread through the educated world.... This is exactly illustrated by a sentence from a published letter of that adorable genius, William James. When he was finishing his great treatise on the Principles of Psychology, he wrote to his brother, Henry James, 'I have to forge every sentence in the teeth of irreducible and stubborn facts.'[98]

Whitehead sees this new empirical mood of passionate interest in facts as united, "with equal devotion to abstract generalisation...."[99] However, in clarifying the function of reason, he says:

> The basis of all authority is the supremacy of fact over thought, [which] ... means that even the utmost flight of speculative thought should have its measure of truth. It may be the truth of art. But

thought irrelevant to the wide world of experience, is unproductive. 100

Wieman was well prepared for appreciation of this empiricism which he discovered in Whitehead. We recall James' work and his consequent influence of a deep personal nature on Royce at Harvard; Wieman's early conditioning by studying Royce, even as an undergraduate; Hocking's study of Principles of Psychology, which was influential in his decision to go to Harvard to study with James; Wieman's enduring identification with the strand of empiricism in Hocking; Perry's years of work with James and his general acceptance of James' empirical method of inquiry; Wieman's learning this method through his work with Perry, and Wieman's acknowledgments of his indebtedness to Perry, especially in this respect, together with Wieman's own study of James and Dewey --all these and other contributing influences from Wieman's early study of social scientists and psychologists make a significant contribution to Wieman's becoming an empiricist philosopher-theologian.

Whitehead's empiricism is more radical than some of his modern disciples seem to recognize once they become involved in analyzing the complexity of his categories. Submerged in this analysis, it is easy to overlook the import of the analogy Whitehead used to clarify his empiricism.

> The true method of discovery is like the flight of an aeroplane. It starts from the ground of particular observation; it makes a flight in the thin air of imaginative generalization; and it again lands for renewed observation rendered acute by rational interpretation. 101

Yet this empiricism in Whitehead, however radical it may seem to be, is never separated from rational speculation.

> Thus the supreme verification of the speculative flight is that it issues in the establishment of a practical technique for well-attested ends and that the speculative system maintains itself as the elucidation of that technique.... This interplay of thought and practice is the supreme authority. It is the test by which the charlatanism of speculation is restrained. 102

Whitehead's aim in these respects was to seek for two integrated disciplines, the one of speculative thought and the other of practice. The essence of speculation is that "it transcends immediate fact," but "its business is to make thought creative of the future." This is done by developing a "vision of systems of ideas, including observation but generalized beyond it." Whitehead sees "the true use of history" to be the extraction of general principles from it for "the discipline of practice and the discipline of speculation." He refers to the Greek thinkers "who made speculation effective" by their unbounded curiosity, the ideal of clear definition and logical consistency, comprehensive interests, search for "truths of the highest generality," and who "were men with active practical interests."[103]

We find, in Wieman, no disagreement with Whitehead's *empirical* use of speculative thought. In fact, Wieman has made continuous use of it. His *Wrestle of Religion with Truth* is an expression of praise for it. Here he says of conceptual knowledge:

> It is the most precious knowledge we shall ever attain. We must seek this most precious knowledge constantly and treasure up everything that may add to it.[104]

Even though this statement may be symbolic of Wieman's apical period of appreciation for Whitehead, Wieman's aversion to speculative thought then and now is of the kind which concurs with Whitehead's resentment toward what he describes as "the charlatanism of speculation." We find, in Wieman, no stronger polemical expression against this kind of speculative thought than what he has said recently in *Religious Inquiry* about "the followers of Whitehead," and also about Whitehead's own "intricate and complicated system" of philosophy. His statements seem to indicate a clean-cut break from Whiteheadian philosophy.

Subjectivism and Experience

Whitehead not only allies himself with the modern trend in empiricism, but also with the trend in modern philosophy which accepts the principle of subjectivism: "that the whole universe consists of elements disclosed in the analysis of the experiences of subjects."[105] How an actual entity is qualified or influenced by another "is the 'experience' of the actual world enjoyed by that actual entity, as subject." Whitehead calls this "the reformed subjectivist principle" because it is not based on the subject alone which is prehending the actual entity, nor on the datum alone which is prehended, but rather on the relation between the subject and its datum, which relation is the basis for determining "how that subject prehends that datum." Since his subjectivistic principle is based on the relation between these two poles, he says:

> The reformed subjectivist principle adopted by the philosophy of organism is merely an alternative statement of the principle of relativity. 106

Since his principle of subjectivism illustrates relativity in process philosophy, he says: "Process is the becoming of experience."107

For Whitehead, subjectivity is a creative process: "This principle states that the being of a res vera is constituted by its 'becoming.'"108 Therefore, Whitehead's principle is radically different from common sense notions of subjectivity which regard subjects as substantial and fixed. In Whitehead's view, every actual entity is a subject interacting with other subjects. So, "there is no element in the universe capable of pure privacy."109

Since relations are ordinarily abstractions from contrasts, the contrast in this case is between the novel nature of the subject and its datum. Multiple contrasts among prehending subjects and their data are "the basis for the doctrine of organic evolution," and also for a doctrine which "is a commonplace of art."

> This doctrine that a multiple contrast cannot be conceived as a mere disjunction of dual contrasts is the basis of the doctrine of emergent evolution ... [which] doctrine is a commonplace of art. 110

From this context we see that Whitehead's principle of subjectivism is also organismic. He says: "It follows that the philosophy of organism entirely accepts the subjectivist bias of modern philosophy."111

Analysis of relations between the subject and its datum is clarified further by Whitehead in what he has to say about perception. Fundamental to understanding his concept of perception is to see that it undergoes evolution in three modes: (1) Most basic is "causal efficacy," a nonsensuous "intuitive awareness of our own past mental and bodily states and of the wider world beyond as they compel conformation to themselves in the present."[112] (2) "Presentational immediacy," or "perception of the contemporary world as passively illustrating certain sensa,"[113] and (3) "symbolic reference," a mixed mode of efficacy and immediacy in which the percepta from each mode intersect because of an assumed common ground between them which may be locus or shared sense objects. The percepta of presentational immediacy are "distinct, definite, controllable," while those produced by causal efficacy are "vague, not to be controlled, heavy with emotion ... " but "whether analyzed or no," the latter "remains the given uncontrolled basis upon which our character weaves itself."[114]

Whitehead presents his interpretation of evolutionary perception as a corrective of traditional efforts, such as Hume's, to account for causation. He sees their error as a failure to take account of causal efficacy as the ground of perception.

Whitehead rejects traditional subjectivism which affirms that the essence of experience is universals emptied of sensations, as well as the sensationalist view which empties experience of everything but sensations. The outcome in traditional philosophy is to solve the problem of relating bifurcated universals and particulars. Whitehead's corrective substitutes actual entities for particulars and eternal objects for universals. The result is two mutually exclusive classes, but they are integral in the context of experience as feeling.[115]

Wieman's response to this analysis of subjectivism and experience is positive. Whitehead's neo-realistic epistemology, which projects the objectivity of actual entities both as subjects and as the datum of subjects, is wholly acceptable. Wieman, like Whitehead, does not confuse the relation between a subject and its datum, as a <u>happening</u>, with a theory or proposition about the happening. Wieman says:

> The perceptual event itself is a psycho-physical event. If I affirm that the perception happened when it did not, or that it did not when it did, that affirmed proposition is false. But the event itself simply happened. It could not be true or false. Only propositions about it can be.[116]

Wieman also distinguishes the perceptual event which is never fully cognized by the perceiver, or not even cognized at all, from the perceived object. In case the perceptual event is not cognized at all, it would seem that this mode of perception would be a reconception of Whitehead's causal efficacy. Wieman says that the perceptual event, as he understands it, "is never 'in the mind' only," but that "It is physiological since living tissue, nervous and muscular reactions are involved."[117] This perspective is evidently in accord with Whitehead's claim that activities of the body are involved in causal efficacy and also carried over in the higher evolution of perception. Wieman also accepts the richer and more complex content of perception including psychological, sociological, and linguistic data[118] operative, according to Whitehead, at the higher levels of the evolution of perception.

The perceived object, for Wieman, is the datum of the subject, for Whitehead. Wieman sees the perceived object as "always more than the present perceptual event."

> It is this event plus many others all joined together in such a way as to make up a structure of relations. This structure pervading the interrelated events is the perceived object.[119]

From these perspectives offered by Wieman it seems clear that he too interprets perception in terms of relations between the subject and its datum. He says: "This analysis of perception escapes the difficulties involved in narrowing perception down to sense data such as ... many others have done."[120] So, it seems that Wieman's reconception of perception is in accord with Whitehead's reformed subjectivist principle.

Among the six of Whitehead's basic perspectives we have selected for further analysis and for clarification of his philosophy of creativity based on the category of the ultimate as creativity, one, and many, the last, <u>feeling and prehension</u>, is that one which gives to all of these perspectives a ground for meaningful interpenetrating relations.

Feeling and Prehension

Feeling and prehension are technical terms for Whitehead. They are a direct outcome of his effort to develop a total philosophic system in which every entity enters into the constitution of every other entity with some gradation of relevance.[121] In this context it is possible for every entity to have some kind of meaning, either positive or negative, just because every entity has relevance. A feeling is a positive prehension and prehensions are defined as "Concrete Facts of Relatedness."[122] Every prehension has in it those three elements which identify the principle of subjectivism: subject, its datum, and the subjective form which is *how* the subject prehends its datum. Positive prehensions include while negative prehensions exclude their data. The actual entities which constitute the process-units of the world are concrescences of prehensions which have originated in the creative becoming of the world.[123] There are both physical and conceptual prehensions. The former refers to actual entities, the latter to forms or pure potentials which determine the character of actual entities.[124]

Feeling is the condition for integration of physical and conceptual prehensions and also their respective referents in terms of actual entities, and forms as eternal objects. The primitive mode of feeling is *sympathy*: "feeling the feeling *in* another and feeling conformally [physically] *with* another."[125] Whitehead interprets this primitive feeling in the evolution of feeling as the "vector feeling" of physics, that is, a

> feeling from a beyond which is determinate and pointing to a beyond which is to be determined. But the feeling is subjectively rooted in the immediacy of the present occasion: it is what the occasion feels for itself, as derived from the past and as merging into the future. In this vector transmission of primitive feeling the primitive provision of width for contrast is secured by pulses of emotion, which in the coordinate division of occasions appear as wave-lengths and vibrations.[126]

At this primitive level, "feeling is blind," and "relevance is vague," but sensitivity increases in the evolution of feeling with deepening of contrasts by negative prehension which results in the emergence of a new entity called "consciousness." The negative prehension provides an alternative in the prehending process. The consequent feeling of contrast is the condition for emerging consciousness. With emerging consciousness, propositions or theories are formed to choose among alternatives. "Consciousness is" the feeling of the contrast of theory, as mere theory, with fact, as mere fact.[127] Judgments evaluate the relations between mere theory when referring to eternal objects as ideal formal constructs, and mere facts as referring to actual entities. A judgment is essentially "the critique of a lure for feeling."[128]

"Feelings are the 'real' components of actual entities." Actual entities are unitary processes, each in some degree relevant to the other by interpenetrating prehensive feelings which operate creatively in concrescence: the many actual entities become one and in turn produce a novel one. The transition from unity to novel diversity is the condition for concrescence.

We see this process as the ultimate rhythm of the universe. We suggest that it is the basis for Whitehead's perception of the universe as essentially aesthetic and consequently the basis for his philosophic system as an aesthetic system. Feeling functioning creatively is the ultimate condition for the production of togetherness. Creative prehensive feeling in concrescence is the ultimate counter to abstraction.

Wieman's metaphysics of felt quality is certainly akin to Whitehead's, but closeness of kinship is no guarantee against serious conflict. However, Wieman's philosophy, as we have seen, not only accepts conflict, but also thrives on it in so far as conflict can be treated creatively rather than destructively.

Both Wieman and Whitehead often turn to philosophy of art as illustrative of creative use of conflict. It is the aesthetic character of Whitehead's philosophy of felt creative concrescence which especially appeals to Wieman. It is from this context that differences between Wieman and Whitehead arise concerning the nature of creativity and God. In closing our study of Wieman's response to creativity in Whitehead, we shall try to state and clarify these salient differences.

Creativity and God

Wieman's response to creativity in Whitehead is clarified by observing what happens to his continuing tension between his cognitive quest expressed in intellectual religious inquiry and his immediate awareness of the qualitative richness of reality. Whitehead's analysis of the actual world in relation to the inherited past and to future possibilities reaches heights of complex abstraction, perhaps never before attained. Yet his sense of relativity and concrescence is expressed with such depth of feeling for reality that the outcome is a philosophy of creativity which is basically aesthetic. Wieman's response to these contrasting trends in Whitehead may well be characterized as the intensification of his continuing tension.

We observe that the intensification of tension between aesthetic awareness of concrescent reality and abstract intellectual analysis of it carries with it the possibilities for continuous creation of the beauty of holiness in the world and also the creation of abstractions which can divide us demonically and produce in us a philosophy of nihilism which yields the destruction of our world. When this tension mounts, there is the temptation to destroy the tension itself by turning either to abstractions, intellectual and other forms, or to mere feeling awareness of the aesthetic quality of the holiness of reality. Neither Whitehead nor Wieman has succumbed to this temptation. Both seem deeply aware that commitment to mere analysis yields dissipation of meaning, loss of personal identity, and consequent chaos among men Furthermore, they see commitment to mere feeling awareness of the aesthetic quality of reality as a whole to be in effect both sentimental and anaesthetizing with no aesthetic consequence.

We have found that Wieman discovered Whitehead's philosophy as basically aesthetic from his reading <u>Religion in the Making</u> and that he responded appreciatively to it in his <u>Wrestle of Religion with Truth</u>.[129] More recently Wieman wrote a brief essay of some two hundred words, entitled "Summation of Whitehead's Philosophy," which describes it as basically aesthetic.

> Whitehead's philosophy represents the thought of a man who seeks to demonstrate that no set of abstractions can give us the aim of life. Abstractions divert and corrupt our striving and threaten the continuance of life except as they show us the way to attain the fullest possible experience of actuality; and actuality is identical with the aesthetic.[130]

Wieman sees Whitehead's aesthetic philosophy as intrinsically normative for the wide range of human conduct.

> Science, ethics, religion, metaphysics, education, government, sex, marriage, economics, tradition, custom, language are all to be criticized and corrected by the standard implicit in this question: Do they severally and collectively enable us to experience actuality most fully with the understanding that actuality is aesthetic?[131]

Wieman also states what Whitehead means by the chief evils which corrupt our civilization.

> Whitehead claims that the chief evils corrupting our civilization, and the dangers threatening its continued existence, arise from setting up abstractions as the final aim of our striving.[132]

Furthermore, Wieman sees in Whitehead's philosophy as aesthetic, its therapy for the evils which corrupt.

> The order of means and ends must be reversed, if we are to be saved from the fatal escalation of illusion and frustration. Abstractions must be subordinated to serve as means, whereas the final aim must be the fullest possible experience of actuality in its true character which is aesthetic.[133]

What is the import of Wieman's concise summation of Whitehead's philosophy as aesthetic? First, we see that a philosophy as aesthetic is the natural outcome of a philosophy of creativity. The central locus of creativity through history is its aesthetic expression in the fine arts. Secondly, we see that the survival of the fine arts requires a philosophy of art which subordinates abstraction as a means to the final aim which "must be the fullest possible experience of actuality in its true character which is aesthetic." Thirdly, we see that the generalization of philosophy of art as an aesthetic philosophy of creativity for normative guidance in all areas of human conduct is a viable option for confronting and transforming the chief evils in escalating nihilism. These three observations are implicit in Wieman's relating man's dual quest for knowledge and beauty. Wieman relates and analyzes this dual quest in three chapters, entitled "Beauty," "Truth," and "Knowledge," in <u>The Source of Human Good</u>. These chapters, in a significant sense, are his response, born of the intensification of creative tension, for which Whitehead is at least partially responsible.

After our further clarification of Wieman's use of the

concepts--beauty, truth, and knowledge, and how they are related in the context of creativity--we shall analyze his critical response to Whitehead on these issues.

For Wieman, aesthetic objects or situations may be beautiful and/or ugly. In any case they are fascinating.

> But in ugliness one shrinks away even while he is fascinated. In beauty the mind is willingly enthralled, while the ugly thing enthralls the mind against its will. 134

Wieman distinguishes a narrower from a broader meaning of beauty. In the narrow sense, "beauty is aesthetic richness achieved within a unitary structure of events by sharply separating it from all others." In the broad sense, he defines beauty in terms of qualitative meaning in which aesthetic richness is not so limited "but produced in an order of meaning leading on indefinitely and creatively."135

Wieman uses the norm of creativity to compare critically the roles of beauty and ugliness in aesthetic situations.

> True beauty ... is aesthetic form releasing the freedom of human action, the range and keenness of human appreciation, the fulness of intercommunication, and the creative transformations that unfold the depth of quality in the world. Ugliness basically evil in character is aesthetic form hindering all this.... [B]eauty creates history while ugliness prevents its creation. Creation of history is the creation of human existence and the only possible source of its enrichment. 136

Among the various conditions, including political control, which may be provided for managing the affairs of men and for regulating their desires and aversions, Wieman says: "The most important of these conditions is the self-giving of men to these creative processes under the guidance of art." Furthermore, it must be art which expresses and fulfills the lives of industrial workers by making them and their world a part of the cultural matrix. The isolation of the cultural matrix and its arts from the many is an obstruction, in the interest of a few, to the release of creativity in the many, and will eventually cause the whole social system to crack and break. 137 When this occurs, tragic art enables man to walk through devastation and the remaking of the order of life and, in the midst of breakdown, be sufficiently free of obsession and compulsion to undergo the transformation producing a world more rich with meaning.... The most common instance of tragic art serving in this manner is the story of the Cross of Christ.[138]

... Theology can learn more from tragic art, perhaps, than from any other source.[139]

In contrast with tragedy, Wieman sees that comedy can also

make plain that creativity is the way of man's fulfillment.... In humor we live at the breaking edge of life, where worlds are torn down and remade. This quick breakdown and new creative synthesis is what makes us laugh.[140]

But how can man relate creatively art and beauty to truth and knowledge? Wieman says: "Truth and beauty do not coincide."[141] For him, truth is

the specifiable structure of events and possibilities, determined by the feeling-reactions of the organism prior to knowledge but waiting to be known.... [T]ruth is ... artificial and abstract ... lifted out of the concrete matrix ... [and] brought forth by creativity.[142]

Truth, which is "specifiable structures," and knowledge, which is specified structures of truth, can have "richness and depth of qualitative meaning only when they keep close" to this matrix. How abstract specified structures of knowledge can keep close to this matrix which is the locus of creativity, and also the massive wealth of aesthetic value, is problematic. In dealing with this problem, radical for both Wieman and Whitehead, we must examine further their mataphysics in order to clarify Wieman's response to creativity and God in Whitehead.

Since knowledge, for Wieman, is specified structure, there is no way to gain knowledge of anything unless it is structured. Wieman observes that structured relations within and among the events of the world have distinguishable levels known through analysis of their creative evolution. For Wieman, there is a given primordial or aboriginal structure which is creative. This dynamic structure is creative of further levels of structure. It is structured creativity which Wieman refers to as the creative event or God.

Basic conflict between Wieman and Whitehead exists regarding the relation of creativity to God. Whitehead distinguishes God from creativity. Wieman says:

> We do not accept Whitehead's primordial order in the sense of an order distinguishable from the creative event, nor do we interpret creativity as Whitehead does.[143]

We believe that Whitehead's distinction is based on the observable fact that actual entities, or creatures, including men, do try to create, and in their effort to do so, try to make connection between themselves, as actual, and further possibilities of value, or eternal objects. Valuation in man is to be distinguished from valuation in the primordial nature of God, in that valuation in God is an "all-inclusive unfettered valuation"[144] which regulates the realm of possibilities relevant to each occasion. In man's effort to create, he can and often does make the wrong selection from the multiplicity of possible values. In this case the possible value, or ideal possibility, is not relevant to the occasion. The outcome obstructs the creative advance. Whitehead describes this kind of error as "Insistence on birth at the wrong season" and characterizes the wrong selection as "the trick of evil."[145] Man as a creature is free to make wrong selections. He is even free to destroy himself and his world. But God in his primordial nature is non-temporal in that in this form of his being the locus of God is in unification of ideal possibilities of value. However, "The purpose of God is the attainment of value in the temporal world."[146] In attaining this purpose, God's way with man is not brute force but divine persuasion.

Wieman says:

> According to Whitehead, the primordial order waits helplessly for creative events to embody in themselves the eternal objects which are presented to them as possibilities by this order.[147]

We believe that Wieman's interpretation has significance in that the ideal structures of unactualized value are not coercive in their relation to man. They do seem to wait helplessly for their incorporation by man into the process of attaining further value in the temporal world. In this context, God in his primordial function is the supreme respecter of the autonomy of his creatures, not confining their expression of novelty, even permitting chaos among his creatures. Yet further examination of the function of the primordial nature of God, according to Whitehead, seems to indicate that God in his primordial function does more than wait helplessly.

> The non-temporal act of all-inclusive unfettered valuation is at once a creature of creativity and a condition for creativity. It shares this double character with all creatures.[148]

God, as primordial, for Whitehead, determines what is creatively relevant for his creatures in their effort at further actualization of value. God's creative determination functions as a gradient principle of "antecedent ground for the entry of the ideal forms into the definite process of the temporal world."[149] Even though God's grading of possible values to make them creatively relevant may be rejected by man, as a creature, from the context of his autonomy, the creature cannot become anything whatsoever. Man is limited by his own concrete past inherited in the present, by his power of conceptual valuation, by other men and their pasts, and by relevant possibilities presented to him. Yet with these limitations, God's relation to the creative effort of his creatures is not to coerce them, for the creative process is obstructed by coercion rather than released. The primordial function of God, according to Whitehead, provides creatively relevant ideals as a lure for feeling for the creatures.[150] God's primordial persuasion replaces force and becomes victorious over it.[151] "The power of God is the worship He inspires."[152]

Wieman's criticism of the primordial nature of God in Whitehead is sharpened by his saying:

> The primordial order as defended by Whitehead is necessary if every structure that might ever become relevant is to have some kind of reality prior to that creation of a world to which it would be relevant.[153]

Wieman's summary response to Whitehead's defense not only clarifies his disagreement on this issue, but also delineates significant areas of agreement in their respective metaphysical positions.

> There is a determinate order of existence at any given level of creation. There is also a determinate order running through all levels. The latter is the minimal structure of creative energy, the former the structure of the world as created at that level. The primordial order, setting limits to all creation, is not matter or mind or organism or any disembodied primordial order (Whitehead) standing in its own right over and above events, but it is that structure which energy must have to be creative at all.154

About ten years after Wieman wrote the above statement, he analyzed further Whitehead's primordial nature of God by saying:

> ... the primordial order can be called God only because the process which creates us and all the good of human life does in truth conform to the primordial order. Therefore the primordial order is God only because it characterizes the process which creates and sustains us and transforms life toward the greater good. Otherwise stated, the process is God so far as it exemplifies the primordial order.155

Wieman refers to the above statement as an "interpretation or criticism of Whitehead, (whichever it may be)...."

For Whitehead, God is more than his primordial function. He not only performs a mental or conceptual role in the ideal domain of eternal objects, but he also plays a physical role in the expression of physical feelings or prehensions. In this, his consequent nature, God enters the temporal world of physical entities. His consequent nature is derived from his primordial nature. In his consequent nature his conceptual and physical feelings are integrated. His primordial valuational function is one with his role of saving or conserving values in his consequent nature. Each role belongs to God as a unitary entity. He cannot be described apart from such unity. If we were to translate the meaning of these two roles into the language of traditional Christian theology, we might say that God is the judge and savior of men. But this, out of context, would do violence to Whitehead's technical analysis of these roles.

Wieman's critical response to Whitehead's consequent nature of God is in deep contrast with his comparatively appreciative response to God's primordial nature. Wieman says the primordial nature is the essential structure; the consequent nature is inspiring and decorative. The latter is a response to the cries of the human heart in its longing for release from the ultimate tragedy of the world.

> So in the face of this ultimate tragedy Whitehead yields and builds a dome of glory and perfection above this world which we know by observation and reason.... [O]ver this world, with all of its destructive forces and perishings, hovers this perfect consciousness which shows a 'tender care that nothing be lost.'[156]

A decade later, Wieman's criticism is more severe.

> If the consequent nature of God means anything more than ... uncertain progression in the increase of value ... it seems to us a fabrication of the imagination to comfort the human heart in its sore distress over the perishing of precious values.[157]

In our previous discussion of Wieman's criticisms of creativity in Whitehead, we referred to Wieman's recent contribution in Religious Inquiry (1968). We said that his contribution seems to indicate a clean-cut break with Whiteheadian philosophy of creativity;[158] and then deferred our analysis of this set of criticisms until we had presented Whitehead's main perspectives as related to creativity in order to use them as a context for further understanding Wieman's recent response to them.

Wieman introduces these recent criticisms by saying

> I spent several years studying Whitehead's intricate and complicated system with the hope of learning from this great thinker the best available interpretation of religious commitment. But after years of study and critical thinking I reached the conclusion that Whitehead's is not the kind of commitment fitted to save man from his self-defeating propensities and to transform him toward the best that human life can attain. I have, therefore, rejected the Whiteheadian answer to the basic religious question, although I have learned much from this great man.[159]

Among several living Whiteheadian philosophers who

have various disagreements in interpreting Whitehead, Wieman selects Charles Hartshorne's basic interpretation as Whiteheadian, and uses it as the springboard for his criticisms. Hartshorne's interpretation is stated by Wieman in a <u>single brief sentence</u>: "According to Hartshorne, the cosmos is God's body and this body has a 'cosmic consciousness' which is the mind of God."160

Wieman makes four main statements in his preface to his criticisms. First, since there is no evidence that the galactic systems are "organized like a biological organism fit to embody a conscious mind," this view is indefensible and is therefore rejected. But even though disbelieving in "cosmic consciousness," the idea is accepted for examination of its religious significance. Secondly, those who defend belief in "cosmic consciousness" claim that "it exercises supreme control over the total cosmos" but that this control does not deprive "innovating events of all power and initiative of their own." Since this belief does not "contravene the religious idea of God," it is not criticized. Thirdly, the criticism offered is meant to show that "the highest values of human existence, by which and for which we live," are not consistent with the values "cosmic consciousness" must have. This is "the central point of dispute." Fourthly, this inconsistency demonstrates that "cosmic consciousness" cannot be God "in the religious meaning of this word because 'God' is defined as one who sustains the highest values of human life."161

Following this preface, Wieman states concisely what the argument is:

> There is no cosmic consciousness, but if there were one, it must necessarily be of such a nature that it cannot command the religious commitment of our lives, and therefore has not the value attributed to it by giving it the name of 'God.'162

In his further procedure he offers seven criticisms to support this argument. We shall present their essential meanings in summary form:

Wieman's first criticism is based on his claim that the material universe is not opposed but is merely indifferent to human values. However, the material universe may be so organized at least in part, to sustain human values. "But when the cosmos is said to have a conscious purpose of its own, this indifference becomes opposition." He offers an example of the opposition: "... if I fall from a height and am killed, I cannot say that gravitation is opposed to me, since it has no conscious purpose."

Second, prophetic striving for love and justice runs counter to the values of the "cosmic consciousness," for "cosmic consciousness"

> recognizes no values other than satisfactions experienced in its own body, because nothing exists outside of its own body. Love and justice are not values experienced in one's own body, like the taste of food and drink and other sensuous pleasures. Love and justice are experienced in the relations between persons. Since the 'cosmic consciousness' has no interest in anything outside its own body, it can have no experience of love and justice. [163]

Third, if "cosmic consciousness" is and has been in supreme control of the cosmos in all of its vast expanse of space-time and "does not permit evolution issuing in human values to arise" except in some minute spot, it would seem from the perspective of "cosmic consciousness" that human values are "like aberrations or evils." From this perspective "cosmic consciousness" is "unfit to be revered as God."

Fourth, since in Whiteheadian philosophy, "atomic events," or actual entities, seek no values other than those experienced in their own individual bodies until they perish, except human entities, and perhaps to some degree higher animals, it would seem that the atomic events operate, apart from human entities, more like "cosmic consciousness," which is incapable of prehension outside its own body. If there is a likeness between the controlling function of "cosmic consciousness" as "cosmic mind" and the subjective aim of atomic entities, human worship of "cosmic mind" would not be fitting.

Fifth, since atoms and molecules, constituting almost the whole of the cosmos, have no qualitative meaning and value operative within and among them such as we observe in human existence through the use of "language fit to carry symbolized meanings creatively toward infinity," we see no reason for turning to the cosmos as a whole in worshipful commitment to "cosmic consciousness."

Sixth, from the perspective of "cosmic consciousness" as an extreme sensualist incapable of responding to anything outside of its own body because there is nothing outside its own body, "cosmic consciousness" "could not be tolerated in human society," much less worshiped.

In Wieman's seventh and final criticism, he concludes that

> 'cosmic consciousness' cannot be worshiped as God because it can be neither the lure of our aspirations, the guide and support of human striving, nor our savior from the ways of evil.[164]

Whatever justification or lack of justification may be observed in these seven criticisms for rejecting the Whiteheadian answer to the basic religious question, it is clear from the seventh criticism that Wieman is rejecting "cosmic consciousness" as determinately operative of three main functions of the Whiteheadian concept of God. For Wieman, "cosmic consciousness" cannot be the lure of human aspirations. If the conceptual feelings of eternal objects in their total primordial unification is the "cosmic consciousness" which provides the lure for the creatures of the temporal world including man, this, for Wieman, is not the object of religious worship. If this same primordial "cosmic consciousness" grades its eternal objects so as to make them relevant ideals for the creative guidance of man, this "cosmic consciousness" cannot be the ultimate critic for human valuation and striving. Again, to accept "cosmic consciousness" as the ultimate source for saving man from the tragic evils of the world is an illusion.

Why then does Wieman reject "cosmic consciousness" as God? The answer is simple. He sees no empirical evidence to support the claim that there is a "cosmic consciousness" whose nature is characterized by these functions. But there is something different from "cosmic consciousness" which is the ultimate lure for human aspiration, the ultimate guide and support of human striving, and the ultimate savior from the tragic evils of the world. This is structured creative energy undergoing indefinite emergence from level to level of creative advance, operative as creative interchange through symbolized meaning, at the highest known level which is human existence. But human existence cannot carry this high level of creativity beyond a certain point because of the limitations of the biological organism. It is "the humility of life to recognize that we cannot carry it to that infinity toward which it is open.... Awareness of this unattainable reach of creativity is experience of the holy."165

We do not interpret Wieman's rejection of "cosmic consciousness" as a complete rejection of Whiteheadian philosophy of creativity. However deeply rooted within it, "cosmic consciousness" is only one strand in the organismic system. There are other strands including feeling with unlimited range and depth from which both conceptual and physical prehensions are derived. Feeling is the ground of creativity, uniting physical and mental prehensions of concrescence. There is a new romanticism in Whitehead with strands of the physical, phenomenal, voluntaristic, and rational functions of the world-in-the-making woven into it. It is a blend of many colors. It is aesthetic. Wieman recognizes this fact and whenever he criticizes any feature in the system, he seems ever aware that the system unites beauty and truth and that he is at the same time a part of it. His statement in the following note illustrates what we mean to say:

> This criticism is made specifically of Whitehead because we are so profoundly indebted to him that we fear our thought will be confused with his in every particular. This would be a misunderstanding. 166

We suggest that both Bergson and Whitehead have done much for Wieman, including especially two things: (1) they provided conditions which intensified his creative tension between intuitive awareness of the felt qualities of massive reality and further intellectual analysis of the abstractions from reality experienced in its wholeness; (2) they stimulated further creative synthesis of this bi-polar tension without effecting destruction of it.

There is another main philosophic strand of influence in Wieman which needs to be examined. It socializes his philosophy of creativity. It appears early in his career and continues to the present in its impact. It focuses in the works of William James and John Dewey.

Chapter V

CREATIVITY IN WIEMAN AS A RESPONSE TO JAMES' AND DEWEY'S REALISTIC AND EMPIRICAL PHILOSOPHIES

Since the philosophies of William James and John Dewey have so much in common in the area in which we are examining them, we shall interweave their distinct contributions in the course of this study, ever mindful of the individuality of each as related to creativity in Wieman and his response to their philosophies. What all three have in common are, especially, (1) a neo-realistic epistemology, permitting objects to be explored with reasonable scientific objectivity in terms of their relations as events, not as "things"; (2) the empirical method of scientific inquiry, applicable to the study of these relations to obtain evidence, but not fixed certainties; and (3) experience as a basic concept, referring to the interaction of organisms within their environment.

In relating Wieman and Dewey, we find the following statement from Wieman's "Intellectual Autobiography," to be a good introduction, so we shall quote it in full:

> While at Harvard I became acquainted with the work of John Dewey and found him highly stimulating. His influence is also an abiding part of my thought. Dewey caused me to see something I have never forgotten: Inquiry concerning what makes for the good and evil of human life must be directed to what actually and observably operates in human life. Otherwise, the inquiry will produce misleading illusions. The following statements indicate the impact of John Dewey upon my thinking.
> The transcendent, the supernatural, the ineffable, the infinite, the absolute being itself, and other such ideas inevitably lead inquiry astray unless they can be identified with something which observably operates in human life. What is observed is not

necessarily identical with what enters immediately into sense experience. Rather, what we observe is what we infer from sense experience by predicting specific consequences and observing or failing to observe under required conditions what was predicted. Perception, including sense experience, can engage the total personality with all its resources of inquiry--intuition, inference, wonder, meditation, speculation, faith, love, aspiration. Perception always involves sense experience. But profound perception brings into action every means and every power by which knowledge is attained. It is a gross misunderstanding to say that sense experience can give us only knowledge of sense experience. [1]

From this statement it is clear that it is Dewey's empiricism which is most deeply appreciated by Wieman. Since there are different kinds of empiricism, we shall examine its early formation in Dewey as related to contributions from James.

ON THE EARLY FORMATION OF EMPIRICISM IN THE PHILOSOPHIES OF JAMES AND DEWEY

In Dewey's <u>Introduction to Philosophy: Syllabus of Course 5</u>, University of Michigan, February, 1892, he begins section one by <u>identifying</u> philosophy as an all-comprehensive discipline with science for the purpose of realizing "the meaning of experience."

> Philosophy (science) is the conscious inquiry into experience. It is the attempt of experience to attain to its own validity and fullness; the realization of the meaning of experience. [2]

Dewey then proceeds to distinguish philosophy as science, an all-comprehensive discipline, from science as an abstract discipline by saying:

> Science and philosophy can only report the actual condition of life, or experience. Their business is to reveal experience in its truth, its reality. They state what <u>is</u>.
> The only distinction between science and

philosophy is that the latter reports the more generic (the wider) features of life; the former the more detailed and specific.[3]

In section two, Dewey comments on (1) the incompleteness of knowledge when philosophy is separated from science; and (2) the consequent difficulty encountered in bringing philosophy to consciousness:

> The separation of science and philosophy has reference to the incompleteness of knowledge. Although our experience goes on within the whole, the whole is the last thing of which we become conscious <u>as</u> a whole of included factors. Thus the trouble with philosophy is the difficulty of getting the whole, the generic, before consciousness in such a way that it may be naturally reported. The partial thing may be broken off from the whole and then described with comparative ease. But this process of multiplying pieces seems to leave the generic, the whole beyond and out of sight.[4]

The consequence of the separation of philosophy and science is tragic.

> It makes the whole remote, and capable of description only in unnatural ('metaphysical,' 'transcendental') terms. Thus science, as relating to the part, and philosophy as relating to the whole, fall apart. Philosophy suffers by being made vague and unreal; science in becoming partial and thus rigid.[5]

Dewey interprets philosophy and science as moving in two directions, beneficial to both, for "the whole is now more definitely realized than ever before, so that we get a language for reporting it. These two directions are the two phases of action."[6]

The scientific phase of action reveals "in outline, at least, the type action of the individual organism, the process involved in every complete act." This he characterizes as "psycho-physical." The philosophic phase of action is a freer type of action in which social action reveals the principle involved in it. It is the action of the political body. The psycho-physical individual phase of action together with the political or social phase "give us such perception of the whole that we may report the latter, thus translating philosophical truth into common terms."⁷

After completing these introductory clarifications of the nature of philosophy and science, Dewey moves from philosophy in its all-comprehensive sense to psychology, as an abstracted discipline or piece broken off from this all comprehensive whole, to enter into a psycho-physical analysis of action. He begins with "the unit of nervous action" which he calls "the reflex-arc." He informs his students that Spencer, James and Von Hartmann are good background sources for study of reflex action. He suggests James' Psychology, volume 1, pages 12 and 20-21.

The context in James' first chapter for these references in the second is his critical analysis of theories of psychology which he regards as inadequate. These include the "faculty," the "association," and the "mechanistic" theories used to describe and explain the nature of mental acts. James' criticisms of the mechanistic theory are devastating. He contrasts the mechanical action observed in the magnetic field with the attention and attraction observed between Romeo and Juliet. He asks: "Is the Kosmos an expression of intelligence rational in its inward nature, or a brute external fact pure and simple?" He replies:

> If we find ourselves in contemplating it, unable to banish the impression that it is a realm of final purposes, that it exists for the sake of something, we place intelligence at the heart of it and have a religion. If, on the contrary, in surveying its irremediable flux, we can think of the present only as so much mere mechanical sprouting from the past, occurring with no reference to the future, we are atheists and materialists. ⁸

James presents his own functional theory of mentality.

> The pursuance of future ends and the choice of means for their attainment are thus the mark and criterion of the presence of mentality in a phenomenon. [He adds:] We all use this test to discriminate between an intelligent and a mechanical performance. ⁹

The excellence of James' scholarship in zoology, physiology, and neurology and as an M.D. from the Harvard

Medical School prepared him well for analysis of reflex action to which Dewey referred his students. From this and other contributions made by Spencer and Von Hartmann, Dewey, in presenting his theory of the reflex arc, says:

> This term covers not simply the narrower 'reflex' of physiology (the winking of an eye, for example) but every unified action, or completed portion of conduct.[10]

He illustrates what he means by "unified action" with the following examples:

> ... the movement of an amoeba, the impulse of a child for food, the perception of color, a word like 'civilization,' with its whole meaning, a virtuous act, a philosophic theory.[11]

Dewey sees in this "unity of action" that "various conditions are brought to a head or focused ... [and constitute] an expression ... of the Universe attaining a unity in action."[12]

The reflex arc has two sides: (1) "diversity of conditions," and (2) "unity of action." The former is "the sensory side of knowledge"; the latter is "the reflex arc in its unity, ... a moving equilibrium of actions." The former is instrumental to the latter. Dewey extrapolates further, including the structural relations of "causes and effect," and "conditions and end." He accepts James' functional theory of mentality.[13]

DEWEY'S PHILOSOPHY OF INSTRUMENTALISM: A SELF-FACILITATING CREATIVE PROCESS

From this context Dewey develops his philosophy of instrumentalism as a process philosophy which takes the principle of relativity seriously. His pluralistic world of dynamic processes is ever in-the-making. Conditions and end attained are interrelated in that the end attained is constituted by its conditions, giving rise to some further end or consequence. It is the office of human intelligence to provide, in so far as possible, those conditions which are correlative with ends: in effect self-facilitating. This is what Dewey means by creativity.

Activity is creative in so far as it moves to

its own enrichment as activity, that is, bringing along with itself a release of further activities. [14]

It is evident that creative activity, for Dewey, is a social process. He introduces his definition of it from the context of illustrations and analyses of some aspects of economic theory. He says:

> Speaking roughly we may say that native activity is both creative and acquisitive, creative as a process, acquisitive in that it terminates as a rule in some tangible product which brings the process to consciousness of itself. [15]

This statement is an extrapolated reconception of Dewey's analysis of the reflex arc, even at the level of neurology in which sensations as diversified activity are unified in the expression of the wholeness of the reflex arc as a unit of nervous action. The unit is the end product of the act, but this unit is a condition for further action. Unless the further action in the form of conditions is correlative with the end or product to be attained, the activity is not self-facilitating and is therefore not creative. In creative activity the end product of the acquisitive phase of the act is instrumental to the activity in its creative advance.

We see the end product as novel in nature. Dewey says it is this product which "brings the process to consciousness of itself." We say it is because the end product is novel that it performs this vital function. The intrusion of novelty in the orderly flow of a unified process is a shock and therefore problematic until the novel product becomes correlative in a new way with the process as innovative. Dewey's insight which reveals the end product as bringing the process to consciousness of itself is fundamental to understanding his philosophy as a problem-solving process.

We note especially that Dewey characterizes this process as a <u>native</u> activity. [16] We see the import of this insight as meaning that creative activity has roots in nature which are deeper than human nature. However, man with increasing intelligence, can describe conditions for what they are and can also evaluate, select, and provide some conditions for creative advance, but the total responsibility for these latter activities does not belong to man alone. Realization of this fact is man's sense of humility. Humility, for Dewey,

> is not a caddish self-depreciation. It is the sense of our slight inability even with our best intelligence and effort to command events; a sense of our dependence upon forces that go their way without our wish and plan.[17]

However, the "purport" of our sense of humility and dependence "upon forces that go their way without our wish and plan," according to Dewey, "is not to relax effort but to make us prize every opportunity for present growth."[18] This is a definite rejection of perfectionism.

> In morals, the infinitive and the imperative develop from the participle, present tense. Perfection means perfecting, fulfillment, fulfilling, and the good is now or never.[19]

What Dewey means by "the good is now or never" is suggested by the following statements:

> Instruction in what to do next can never come from an infinite goal, which for us is bound to be empty. It can be derived only from study of the deficiencies, irregularities and possibilities of the actual situation.[20]

Though "possibilities of the actual situation" have roots in "the forces that go their way without our wish and plan," the specific locus of these possibilities is <u>within</u> man himself.

> Man continues to live because he is a living creature not because reason convinces him of the certainty or probability of future satisfactions and achievements. He is instinct with activities that carry him on. Individuals here and there cave in, and most individuals sag, withdraw and seek refuge at this and that point. But man as man still has the dumb pluck of the animal. He has endurance, hope, curiosity, eagerness, love of action. These traits belong to him by structure, not by taking thought.[21]

Dewey's classic faith in man is based not only on his native or aboriginal heritage, "the dumb pluck of the animal," his intrinsic structure, but also on the rational, imaginative, hypothetical-experimental connection of "memory of past and foresight of future" which "convert dumbness to some degree of articulateness. " We interpret this to be a distinctly different level of Dewey's faith in man. This second level is faith in the intelligence of man to learn how to evaluate, select, and provide conditions for possible correlation of these conditions with ends pursued so that the result would be self-facilitating, or creative activity. We believe that Dewey's first level aboriginal faith is based on correlativity which functions within nature without man's wish and plan. The second level is not only an outcome of the first, but also is based on trust in the first. Dewey's first and second level faith together reveals the profundity of his naturalism. It is a creatively religious faith.

Creative activity is observed in the neurological functioning of lower animals such as frogs and dogs. Many sensations as acts in the context of hunger, for example, become one in the unit of nervous energy called the reflex arc as a whole, which is an act of expression of the whole individual. The reflex arc is the locus of learning and of habit formation in both the lower animals and man. It is a conditioned act. The response in the reflex arc as a whole is a creative response in that the many acts as sensations become one in a novel conditioned act.

With increasing understanding among men, not merely for any kind of learning whatsoever, but for creative learning which releases self-facilitating rational action, the way is open for indefinite expansion of creative behavior. The rational capacity of man above lower animals for providing experimentally the necessary conditions for creative behavior, and for responding with increasing sensitivity to these conditions and consequences, is the basis for Dewey's radical faith in learning, in education, and in man himself.

CREATIVE EXPERIENCE IN DEWEY AND WIEMAN'S RESPONSE

Creativity, for Dewey, is well rooted in the organic evolution of lower organisms which have the capacity to interact creatively as a functioning part of their environment. In man this capacity for creative activity can become consciously selective and increasingly rational through learning. This distinguishes him from the lower animals.

Ability to respond to meanings and to employ them,

> instead of reacting merely to physical contacts, makes the difference between man and other animals; it is the agency for elevating man into the realm of what is usually called the ideal and spiritual. [22]

Furthermore, Dewey points to "social participation by communication, through language and other tools" as determinative in the development of this human capacity to respond meaningfully. Yet the lower animals, even with their language limitation, are capable of creative aesthetic experience.

> To grasp the sources of aesthetic experience it is ... necessary to have recourse to animal life below the human scale. The activities of the fox, the dog, and the thrush may at least stand as reminders and symbols of that unity of experience which we so fractionize when work is labor, and thought withdraws us from the world. The live animal is fully present, all there, in all of its actions: in its wary glances, its sharp sniffings, its abrupt cocking of ears. All senses are equally on the qui vive. As you watch, you see motion merging into sense and sense into motion--constituting that animal grace so hard for man to rival. What the live creature retains from the past and what it expects from the future operate as directions in the present. The dog is never pedantic nor academic; for these things arise only when the past is severed in consciousness from the present and is set up as a model to copy or a storehouse upon which to draw. The past absorbed into the present carries on; it presses forward. [23]

For Dewey, there are "degrees" of experience. Experience is what the ecologist studies as a science. Dewey's philosophy is a philosophy of ecology. Ecology is the scientific study of the interaction of organisms within their environment. The degrees of experience are measured by the aesthetic quality of this interaction: the more self-facilitating, creative, aesthetic, the higher the degree of experience.

> Experience in the degree in which it is experienced is heightened vitality.... [A]t its height it signifies complete interpenetration of self and the world of objects and events. Instead of signifying surrender

to caprice and disorder, it affords our sole demonstration of a stability that is not stagnation but is rhythmic and developing. Because experience is the fulfillment of an organism in its struggles and achievements in a world of things, it is art in germ. Even in its rudimentary forms, it contains the promise of that delightful perception which is esthetic experience. [24]

The functional quality of an act in its context gives that act its meaning. If the act in context is aesthetic, its meaning is enriched or more qualitative. "The sense of an extensive and underlying whole is the context of every experience and it is the essence of sanity." The mad or insane act is torn from context and stands alone as isolated. It is abstract. It loses its meaning.

A work of art elicits and accentuates this quality of being a whole and of belonging to the larger, all-inclusive, whole which is the universe in which we live. This fact, I think, is the explanation of that feeling of exquisite intelligibility and clarity we have in the presence of an object that is experienced with esthetic intensity. It explains also the religious feeling that accompanies intense esthetic perception. We are, as it were, introduced into a world beyond this world which is nevertheless the deeper reality of the world in which we live in our ordinary experiences. ... [This world beyond is] an enveloping undefined whole that accompanies every normal experience. [25]

In contrast with this kind of creative aesthetic consummatory experience to which Dewey points, is intellectual experience. The distinction which he made in 1892 between these two phases of action, as having two directions, still holds. Intellectual experience is not primary; it is not the ground of experience.

When intellectual experience and its material are taken to be primary, the cord that binds experience and nature is cut. That the physiological organism with its structures, whether in man or in lower animals, is concerned with making adaptations and uses of material in the interest of maintenance of the life-process, cannot be denied. The brain and nervous system are primarily organs of action-undergoing; biologically, it can be asserted without contravention that primary experience is of a corresponding type. Hence, unless there is breach of historic and natural continuity, cognitive experience must originate within that of a non-cognitive sort.[26]

It is these two directions observed by Dewey which are the source of tension in Wieman's philosophy of creativity. Wieman's awareness of these two directions is expressed in his article entitled "Philosophers' Dean: The Dual Dewey"[27] which presents the contrast between Dewey's scientific naturalism and his highest spiritual outreach.

After the publication of Dewey's Carus lectures, Experience and Nature, Wieman reviewed it for The Journal of Religion[28] under the title, "Religion in Dewey's Experience and Nature," and soon afterward, he included it as Chapter XII, "Religion and Reflective Thinking," in his first book, Religious Experience and Scientific Method. Wieman's response to Dewey here, as expressed in the following statement, is typical of many of his later responses to Dewey's writings:

He makes very little explicit reference to religion but his ideas have important bearings on religion. His thought is one of the noteworthy forces shaping modern life and anything so pervasive as religion cannot escape his touch.[29]

Wieman says there are two ideas running through Experience and Nature which he wishes "to develop and use as searchlights to illumine the nature and function of religion."[30] The first is Dewey's "concept of meaningless experience"; the second is his "concept of meaning." We find Wieman's tension exemplified in the depth of this distinction between meaningless and meaningful experience. The former belongs to the mystic at his best; the latter belongs to the thinker at his best. Understanding of the tension between mystical and thinking experience in depth provides the clue to the objectification of originality in a distinctly higher form as presented by Dewey. In order to clarify what Dewey means by this higher form of originality, Wieman proceeds to state, first, what Dewey means by meaningful experience; second, what he means by meaningless experience or "'consciousness' as bare event"; and third, the meaning of radical originality as the outcome in the growth of meaning.

Wieman finds meaningful experience, in Dewey, to be distinctly different from both the subjective psychical and also the objective physical interpretations frequently given in traditional philosophy.

> ... [T]here are many ... things which are neither physical nor psychical existences, and which are demonstrably dependent upon human association and interaction. Such things function moreover in liberating and regulating subsequent human intercourse; their essence is their contribution to making that intercourse more significant and more immediately rewarding.[31]

In further clarification of Dewey's meaning of meaning, Wieman uses Dewey's illustration of the whistle of the policeman in directing traffic. Dewey contrasts the sound of the whistle as a particular, existential space-time event with the "method of social cooperative interaction" which the whistling sound makes effective. Wieman states the import of this contrast by saying: "Meaning is the method by which we control experience."[32] Dewey points to the fact that in the contextual situation of whistle controlling traffic, a multiplicity of activities are involved, but no one of these activities or all of them together form "the meaning of the sound of the whistle."

> ... [T]hey are qualifications of a more secure concert of human activity which, as a consequence of a legal order incarnate in the whistling, forms its significance.[33]

Wieman accepts this contextual interpretation of meaning and emphasizes the import of judgment within this context.

> ... [T]here is something more than this in our meanings which are our system of judgments. In order to control experience we must be able to discriminate the different qualities that enter into it as well as trace the space-time relations in which they occur.[34]

Wieman's further clarification of meaning indicates "that judgment or meaning must consist of a very elaborate and delicate system of pointers" in order that meaning may be freed from ambiguity. The pointers require rules for pointing clearly and these rules constitute a system called logic. Wieman then reminds us that some philosophers become so

deeply involved in developing logical systems that the systems
become formalized and abstract so that they no longer point
to the control of experience and thereby lose their meaning
in relation to experience. He of course recognizes that
some of these formal systems may become relevant to experience
at some later date. But meaning in its fullness
refers to certain events in experience and also to other
meanings. The whistle illustration taken in context shows
how meaning refers to other meanings in that the control of
traffic means law and order on the streets, not only locally,
but also nationally and in the human situation of government.
Wieman says:

> It is plain that a great transformation occurs
> in life, and in the universe with which life deals,
> as soon as meaning begins to engage attention and
> determine conduct, providing that meaning maintains
> its dual reference to events and to other
> meanings. When meaning of this sort flings its
> rainbow over the earth, spiritual life begins. [35]

Knowing what Dewey means by meaningful experience,
Wieman clarifies what Dewey means by "'consciousness' as
bare event." Wieman says it means meaningless experience.
He sees the loss of meaning as the supreme tragedy in human
life.

> The one supreme and indispensable means to ...
> increase of life is meaning. But meaning may
> fail and so life may fail, in either of two ways,
> apart from the failure due to false meaning.
> Meaning may fail to promote life through the loss
> of all meaning whatsoever, or it may fail by the
> development of meanings that no longer apply to
> the events of space-time. In the one case, meaning
> dies, leaving event a widow; in the other case
> meaning becomes divorced, leaving event a divorcee.
> The one is the evil of hyper-sensuality; the other
> the evil of hyper-rationality. [36]

In contrast to the various forms of what Wieman
called misguided mysticism, there is a kind of mystical experience
in Dewey's "'consciousness' as bare event" which
is meaningless, yet significant in growth of meaning if not
cultivated for its own sake. Its significance is made evident
by distinguishing <u>two kinds of originality</u> which appear in the
growth of meaning. Wieman quotes Dewey who makes this
distinction:

> There is a difference in kind between the thought which manipulates received objects and essences to derive new ones from their relations and implications, and the thought which generates a new method of observing and classifying them. It is like the difference between readjusting parts of a wagon to make it more efficient, and the invention of the steam locomotive. One is formal and additive; the other is qualitative and transformative.37

On the basis of Dewey's distinction between these two forms of originality, Wieman describes the higher form as radical originality, illustrated by invention of the steam locomotive, and quotes Dewey's description of the mental state in which it occurs:

> When an old essence or meaning is in process of dissolution and a new one has not taken shape even as a hypothetical scheme, the intervening existence is too fluid and formless for publication, even to one's self. Its very existence is ceaseless transformation. Limits from which and to which are objective, generic, stateable; not so that which occurs between these limits. This process of flux and ineffability is intrinsic to any thought which is subjective and private. It marks 'consciousness' as bare event. 38

Wieman interprets Dewey's "'consciousness' as bare event."

> ... [E]xperience caught in that intervening period when old meanings have faded out and new meanings have not been born.... It is experience which we feel but do not think, although ... [we are] struggling to think ... in some new way, not in the old way.... [T]his is the mystical experience par excellence. 39

Wieman sees the fostering of this mystic consciousness which is "a condition of radical originality" to be "the saving function of religion" in human life.

> Worship at its best is precisely this. It is the great regenerator, renewer, and reconstructor of human life because it fosters that experience which provides for the extreme reconstruction of meanings. It revitalizes old meanings with new insight, brings on 'conversion, ' and once in a while it lifts

human history bodily into new channels, as shown in those periods when great religions have been born.[40]

Wieman suggests that the attitude of humility, beautifully expressed in the lives and works of both Dewey and James, is a precondition for radical originality.

> ... [T]he kind of original thinking which leads to the 'mystic' experience is one in which the thinker struggles to divest himself of every bias and limitation imposed upon him by his mental habits and established meanings.[41]

This attitude of humility in Dewey is religious.

> But a mind that has opened itself to experience and that has ripened through its discipline knows its own littleness and impotencies; it knows that its wishes and acknowledgments are not final measures of the universe whether in knowledge or in conduct, and hence are, in the end, transient.[42]

We observe that humility in Dewey is not self-abasement, for "a mind that has opened itself to experience and that has ripened through its discipline" also "knows that its juvenile assumption of power and achievement is not a dream to be wholly forgotten."[43] But the power and achievement of man is derived from his unity with the universe. This unity is to be preserved. It is a shared responsibility for carrying the universe forward. Meaning is derived from this shared responsibility.

Dewey is aware that shared responsibility of man with nature, of which man is a part, is based not only on faith in man but also on faith in nature. He quotes, with appreciation, from essays of Justice Holmes:

> If we believe that we came out of the universe, not it out of us, we must admit that we do not know what we are talking about when we speak of brute matter.... Why should we employ the energy that is furnished us by the cosmos to defy it and to shake our fist at the sky? It seems to be silly.[44]

But Dewey's faith in man and what common sense

calls human desires and ideals is based on what "nature makes possible."

> Fidelity to the nature to which we belong, as parts however weak, demands that we cherish our desires and ideals till we have converted them into intelligence, revised them in terms of the ways and means which nature makes possible.[45]

Yet Dewey's faith in nature including man is not superficially optimistic.

> When we have used our thought to its utmost and have thrown into the moving unbalanced balance of things our puny strength, we know that though the universe slay us still we may trust, for our lot is one with whatever is good in existence.[46]

In closing his review of Experience and Nature, Wieman makes evident that its chief attraction for him is the way Dewey relates the individual to nature in his outreach for creating a better world. The intimacy of this relationship is expressed in this final quotation:

> The striving of man for objects of imagination is a continuation of natural processes; it is something man has learned from the world in which he occurs, not something which he arbitrarily injects into that world. When he adds perception and ideas to these endeavors, it is not after all he who adds; the addition is again the doing of nature and a further complication of its own domain.[47]

Wieman picks up Dewey's notion of the complication of nature's domain by saying:

> This mergence of the individual with the total movement of all things, this sense of dependence upon the whole and participation in the working of this total movement is surely a religious attitude.[48]

But it is "not pantheistic since the unique contribution of the individual is recognized," and also since

> We become distinct individuals, efficacious in controlling events and contributory to the total outcome of things, only as we develop an operative system of meanings.[49]

Wieman's appreciative response to the religious import of Dewey's philosophy reaches both backward and forward from the time he wrote his review of <u>Experience and Nature</u> in 1925. Wieman reworked Dewey's <u>Human Nature and Conduct</u>, (1922) again and again through the years, always with the conviction that he gained new insights from it with each reworking.[50] When Wieman wrote the statements we have quoted above from <u>Religious Experience and Scientific Method</u>, he may have been recalling Dewey's classic and frequently quoted contribution to understanding the relation between the individual and the "infinite whole" as expressed in the closing pages of <u>Human Nature and Conduct</u>. Here Dewey is expressing his sense of the tragic loss of religion in exclusive cults, dogmas, and myths.

> Religion has lost itself in cults, dogmas and myths. Consequently the office of religion as sense of community and one's place in it has been lost. In effect religion has been distorted into a possession--or burden--of a limited part of human nature, of a limited portion of humanity which finds no way to universalize religion except by imposing its own dogmas and ceremonies upon others; of a limited class within a partial group; priests, saints, a church. Thus other gods have been set up before the one God.[51]

Dewey sees the active relation of the individual to the infinite whole as the true function of religion.

> Religion as a sense of the whole is the most individualized of all things, the most spontaneous, undefinable and varied. For individuality signifies unique connections in the whole.[52]

These insights clarify the function of religion at best as a process which makes for growth of meaning. His understanding of this growth is based on his analysis of the reflex arc, his analysis of the act, and of unified action.

> ... [E]very act may carry within itself a consoling and supporting consciousness of the whole to which it belongs and which in some sense belongs to it.[53]

Shared responsibility, for Dewey, is not only among men in human community, but also between man and nature to which he belongs. The rites and ceremonies of human community symbolize this deeper sharing which is basic religious therapy for human conceit.

> With responsibility for the intelligent determination of particular acts may go a joyful emancipation from the burden for responsibility for the whole which sustains them, giving them their final outcome and quality. There is a conceit fostered by perversion of religion which assimilates the universe to our personal desires; but there is also a conceit of carrying the load of the universe from which religion liberates us. Within the flickering inconsequential acts of separate selves dwells a sense of the whole which claims and dignifies them. In its presence we put off mortality and live in the universal. The life of the community in which we live and have our being is the fit symbol of this relationship. The acts in which we express our perception of the ties which bind us to others are its only rites and ceremonies. [54]

Wieman seems to feel that Dewey has made a significant contribution to further understanding of mystical "consciousness as bare event," and how this kind of consciousness can serve instrumentally the growth of meaning in its finest form of radical originality, so that outworn habits of human conduct can be replaced by new patterns of relevant behavior in a world-in-the-making. Yet at this time in Wieman's career, the tension experienced between mystical consciousness of the whole as worship and the scientific quest for further understanding as work, must alternate. [55]

DEWEY'S REACTION TO THE THEISTIC IMPORT OF HIS OWN RELIGIOUS PHILOSOPHY AS EXPRESSED BY WIEMAN:
Consequent Communications and Wieman's Responses

Wieman's appreciative responses to the religious import of Dewey's philosophy had been expressed in his articles and books for nearly a decade before Dewey, in the spring of 1933, identified himself, not with naturalistic theism, but with non-theistic humanism by signing the "Humanist Manifesto" which included the following statement: "We are convinced that the time has passed for theism...." However, Wieman was well aware that the root referent for theism, for the humanists who projected this Manifesto, was a supernaturalistic interpretation of the nature of God.

The "Humanist Manifesto" appeared soon after the publication of the classic conversations on God between three outstanding scholars from great universities: Douglas Clyde Macintosh of Yale, a Kantian theist; Max Carl Otto of the University of Wisconsin, a non-theistic humanist; and Henry Nelson Wieman of the University of Chicago, an empirical theist. These conversations were first published serially in The Christian Century, and later in 1932 in a volume entitled, Is There a God?[56]

Dewey Reviews "Is There a God?" and Wieman Responds

Dewey reviewed Is There a God? for The Christian Century,[57] saying that he finds much of the discussion in the Conversations to be elusive because of "the indefinite article in the title: Is There a God?" He says this elusiveness applies specifically to Wieman's contribution, and therefore he proceeds by redefining the issue in terms of two questions:

> What is the nature of God; what is or what must be God, in case he or it exists? And the other question, supposing an answer to the first question has been reached by way of fixation of the theme of discourse, is: Is there any being or object in existence which answers the description?[58]

Dewey interprets Wieman as starting from man's subjectively wanting something for human love and devotion, and then shifting to "something objective which generates, supports and constitutes good" which is precisely what Wieman says he means by God. Dewey says he is implying that Wieman's shifting between "something which we may be said intelligibly to find in experience, namely, forces making for the production and extension of goods" and an object of subjective devotion, is due to his effort to adjust to the knowledgeable world of the sciences, but at the same time

> is held back from realizing its full implications because in the end he is overmastered by emotional overtones derived from the earlier conception of an exclusive and jealous God.[59]

It would seem that, in this statement, Dewey senses in Wieman what we have identified as tension between non-analytic awareness and devotion to God as an organic unity in the world and commitment to abstract intellectual analysis of the plurality of conditions necessary for knowing and understanding the world. For Dewey, it seems to be not merely the presence of tension, but a paradoxical predicament from which Wieman fails to emerge by not taking a humanistic stance. It is a shift from traditional worship of God to scientific inquiry, and back again to traditional worship.

Dewey has a second main criticism of Wieman in this review. He accuses Wieman of hypostatization of the following undeniable fact:

> ... there are in existence conditions and forces which, apart from human desire and intent, bring about enjoyed and enjoyable goods, and that the security and extension of goods are promoted by attention to and service of these conditions. 60

Then Dewey asks: "Does this admitted fact throw any light whatever upon the unity and singleness of the forces and factors which make for good?" Replying negatively to his own question, he says that what makes for good "is the expansion and distribution of valid meanings and goods through large ranges of experiences."61

In responding to Dewey's first criticism, Wieman says: "I explicitly denied that man's need was valid ground for man's belief." Wieman proceeds by analyzing Dewey's claim that he [Wieman] shifts from subjective devotion to "something objective which generates, supports and constitutes good." First, Wieman affirms that he and Dewey have a common ground in observing, as Dewey says,

> that there are in existence conditions and forces which, apart from human desire and intent, [italics mine] bring about enjoyed and enjoyable goods, and that the security and extension of goods are promoted by attention to and service of these conditions. 62

But, according to Wieman, there remains the one great criticism that Dewey makes of his position.

> It is that these 'conditions and forces' do not have enough unity to constitute a unitary object of devotion and so cannot be considered God. 63

Wieman tells Dewey that "all that can ever command our highest devotion is what has greatest value, whether it be actual or possible or partly both." Furthermore, for Dewey,

> value lies exactly in this unity between enjoyed or enjoyable goods, and their conditions and consequences.... [T]his connectedness constitutes the value.... The enjoyable goods must be functionally connected with still other goods in such a way as to constitute a meaningful system.[64]

Therefore, according to Dewey's own principles,

> greatest value lies in whatsoever unity there is now, or ever can be, among all the conditions, forces and enjoyable goods that are ever to be had in the present and future of this world's existence.[65]

For Wieman, this is an "organic unity." It "does not diminish variety and diversity, but requires these." Since this organic unity "can alone constitute highest value, it alone should receive our highest devotion ..." and "our utmost reverence and service." If this organic unity "which makes us and our activities and interests functioning members one of another" cannot be called God, then Wieman suggests we give it another name, but "it alone can save us." His closing passionate plea addressed to Dewey is:

> If a sufficient number of us would yield to this functioning unity our ideals and programs and policies, our institutions and needs and hopes, to be reconstructed by its requirements, we should be lifted, molded and renewed, and our civilization would pass triumphantly beyond the disasters that now threaten it.[66]

Three weeks later Dewey's reply reinforces the shift he observes in Wieman's position. He confesses that the purpose of his review was either to drop the concept of God or to frame it "wholly in terms of natural and human relationship involved in our straightaway human experience."[67] He explains that the difficulty he finds with Wieman's chapters is that Wieman is so nearly committed to Mr. Otto's position and yet "he kept introducing another external factor to which he gave the name God."[68]

We shall see how Dewey's further analysis of Wieman's position leads him to the conclusion that Wieman's religion is basically ethical, a fine religious morality touched with emotion, having no quarrel with humanism if he would only follow the logic which his position seems to commit him.

First, Wieman must correct his "strange idea that a humanist is one who separates man both from nature and from himself--or the social environment." Second, the reality of "certain objective forces" which "promote human well-being" is plural and not singular. Third, "that which makes for good, whether it be singular or collective," ... there is nothing about it or them particularly to demand love and adoration." Fourth, if the vital organic unity makes for good, it is because "human thought and action intervene." Fifth, granting this intervention,

> there is an absolutely indispensable connection between 'God,' so defined, and human desire and devotion.... [T]he transformation of objective forces which make for good into the Good itself is unqualifiedly dependent on human desire, loyalty, devotion. [69]

In Wieman's reply, published two weeks later, he tells Dewey he is not interested in "cranking up religious experience" with "a little gadget" called "the concept of God," but that the real problem is "how to make right adjustment" to that "objective reality which is supremely important in the universe and for the life of man." However, our making the right adjustments finds useful these little gadgets called concepts, including the concept of God which certainly must be framed "wholly in terms of natural and human relationship involved in our straightaway human experience" if human relationship is recognized to be a functioning part of nature and its possibilities "because we can in no wise experience, know or deal with anything else."[70]

With regard to Dewey's claim that Wieman first needs to correct his "strange idea that a humanist is one who separates man both from nature and from himself--or the social environment," Wieman says: "I have never claimed that they held such a position," but this is not the real issue. The real issue is twofold:

> (1) Can man dominate and control the process which

> makes for the good of life or must he rather serve and follow it? (2) Can he exploit and use it or must he give his loyalty and affection to it?[71]

Wieman gives Dewey and the humanists a negative answer to the first part of each of the two questions.

In reply to Dewey's persisting claim that the "certain objective forces" are plural and not singular, Wieman says that the growing good

> is the progressive accumulation of a shared body of experience and the development of a cooperative system ... [which are] two different sides of the same thing.... This shared body of experience grows by way of language, art, tested knowledge, education, etc., even when men do not intend it and often when they work against it.... [D]espite ... human plan and intentional effort the cooperative system develops by way of industry, economic exchange, political order, scientific research, etc. ...
> ... When, and in so far as, these institutions and practices function as organs of this single, central growth, they are divine. When and in so far as they do not, they are not divine. They become positively evil when they become independent, separate and plural.[72]

Dewey's third criticism, among the five listed above,[73] claiming that there is nothing about "that which makes for good, whether it be singular or collective," that justifies love and adoration, is, for Wieman, "the supreme issue" between him and Dewey and also "between non-theism and theism." Nearly a third of Wieman's "Reply" of April 5th is given to clarification of this issue. His significant insight is that love and adoration given to separate and exclusive objects as goods is a source of some of the greatest evils, but when these goods are regarded as functional members of that larger organic unity which binds them together, this supreme good commands our highest loyalty and devotion. Wieman is saying that love and adoration given to an abstract good apart from the growth of good exploits goods and wrecks the organic system of growing good which is most worthy of human loyalty. This principle is applicable to human loyalty to all kinds of goods, including a child, a friendship, a home, a culture or any other good as abstract from the organic bonds of growth which makes it good.

Dewey's rejoinder is that if the vital organic unity makes for good, it is because "human thought and action intervene." Wieman replies that if this organic unity did not pervade human activities, humans could have nothing to do with it. But that is a long way from saying that men invent it or that it depends for its existence on the care and attention of men. [74]

Finally, Wieman responds to Dewey's claim that "the transformation of objective forces which make for good into the Good itself is unqualifiedly dependent on human desire, loyalty, devotion."

> In one sense that is true but in such a sense that it applies to everything. A mountain is a mountain only relative to human experience.... But that does not mean that what makes for good is Good only when and if we are conscious of its goodness, any more than a mountain is a mountain only when we are conscious of it. [75]

Wieman concludes:

> God as here presented is by no means identified with man or humanity. A great part of humanity is antagonistic to this organic unity in our midst which is God. A considerable portion of every individual man is antagonistic to it. Also this organic unity extends far beyond present day humanity into the depths of physical and biological existence on the one hand, and into the realm of possibility on the other. [76]

This reply marked the close of four published communications which occurred during a period of approximately two months during the late winter and early spring of 1933. Though initiated by Dewey's review of Is There a God?, and carried forward mainly by the communications between Dewey and Wieman, there were other participants, including especially D. C. Macintosh, one of the three contributors to the volume. During this period the review of the volume by William Ernest Hocking[77] was considered by some scholars to be a major contribution toward further understanding of unresolved conflicts among participants.

Meland's letter to Dewey and Dewey's response

Following all these communications, Bernard E.

Meland wrote an article on the exchange between Dewey and Wieman and sent them copies of it. Dewey's favorable reply included the suggestion that the article be published. Wieman responded with an article for publication. The outcome of these communications between Meland, Dewey and Wieman was an article combining relevant comments from Dewey's letter to Meland, Meland's article, and Wieman's response.

From Dewey's letter to Meland:

> I am extremely glad that you called my attention to your interesting and valuable exposition. I find that it states a point that had been in my own mind in a somewhat inchoate way. I am sure its publication will be helpful in clarifying the minds of others. More specifically, I think you have hit upon the solving word in the discussion between Dr. Wieman and myself.[78]

What Dewey calls Meland's "solving word in the discussion" between him and Wieman is Meland's direct confrontation with the classic problem concerning the nature of God as many or as one. This problem is dealt with again and again in the communications between Dewey and Wieman but Meland brings it into bold relief and subjects it to further critical analysis. He first places the problem in the context of what the "philosophic mystic" does with it when he "urges us to cultivate awareness of the wealth of reality that environs us," and then Meland questions: Does the philosophic mystic "mean to have us focus attention upon the wealth of reality or upon the reality?" Restating the question, he asks:

> Is this objective reality which evokes our sense of wonder and upon which we are dependent to be thought of as a single Object of experience, or as many sustaining activities?[79]

Meland cites references in Wieman's books which indicate that he has dealt with this problem ambiguously.

> On the one hand he speaks of 'those most important conditions ... which must have supreme value for human living,' implying a pluralistic reality, while on the other hand he uses the terms that Something of supreme value, implying a single object of devotion. This discrepancy would seem to clear up in his statement that, 'He [God] would be those

most important conditions which taken collectively
constitute the Something which must have supreme
value for all human living,' if Mr. Wieman carried
this position through consistently. But he goes on
to use the term God, in scientific as well as in
the religious approach to environing reality, as a
single Object, apparently ignoring the pluralistic
elements originally implied in 'those most important
conditions.' In his chapter on 'God and Value' in
the book, Religious Realism, he definitely describes
God as the One in fact as well as in term. That is
to say, he implies that the reality designated by the
term God is a singular element empirically as well
as religiously. Thus the crux of the problem seems
to lie in the use of the term God. [80]

This issue which Meland brings to the fore is clearly
the source of the tension in Wieman's philosophy of creativity.
Furthermore, we recognize it once again as the central problem in this dissertation. We see it as "the crux of the
problem" as Meland states it, between Dewey and Wieman.
The purpose of our previous analysis of their encounter is
to set forth the consummatory meaning of the problem which
threatens separation of their philosophic ways, however much
they have in common, for this issue, as we see it, is the
classic issue in the history of religious philosophy. We believe it is futile to try to dodge it, for it will inevitably surface again and again in almost any context in a variety of
ways when lesser problems are plumbed to their depth. It
is the problem of creativity in Wieman.

Meland's critical analysis of it is the subject matter
for Wieman's further response. If Meland has contributed
"the solving word in the discussion," as Dewey said, we had
better understand it and also Wieman's response.

Meland says, from his analysis of the problem, "it
appears that there is nothing gained in insisting upon conceiving the ultimate character of objective reality either as
the One or the Many."[81] In this case, it would seem that
we may well dub the question, "Is God Many or One?" the
ultimate either/or fallacy. Furthermore, Meland says:

> The fact is, we get nearer to the truth of the
> matter when we recognize that the reality that environs us is both pluralistic and unified.[82]

However, it is evident from Meland's next statement, that this both/and observation does not provide a complete solution to the problem, for the question arises from the context of religious commitment as to whether the One or the Many is superior. He replies:

> ... there is no particular point in contending for the superiority of either the oneness or the many; for oneness is reality synthesized; the many is reality analyzed. 83

But this leads to a further problem, namely, the applicability of the term God in worship, in conceptual theory, and in practical tasks. He says the applicability "depends entirely upon whether the task at hand requires the method of analysis or synthesis." Meland then clarifies applicability in the context of each of these three functions in human life.

> Worship--that experience which relates man to the whole of things, is obviously a synthesizing mood. For worship, then, the term God, understood as a collective representation of this wealth of sustaining activities, seems thoroughly legitimate. But in reflective tasks, where the objective is avowedly that of discerning the empirical nature of sustaining reality; and in practical tasks, where the objective is that of adjusting to those empirical conditions of supreme importance, the preliminary method at least would seem to be analytic, and would therefore call for terms expressive of the empirical phenomena thus encountered. 84

Meland concludes that "coming to terms with the universe ... implies two approaches to reality":

> ... the one, the worship experience in the contemplative sense, which is a synthetic approach, involving deep emotional enjoyment of our relation to the total cosmic environment as well as loyal commitment to its demands and opportunities; the other, the theoretical and experimental investigation of sustaining reality as well as practical adjustment to its activities, which are analytic in approach, affording insight into the nature of those elements in environment which support man, and helping him to achieve triumphant living. 85

James' & Dewey's Philosophies / 145

Therefore, Meland's response to the philosophic mystic who urges us to cultivate awareness of the wealth of reality is a dualistic alternating response between analytic theoretical and analytic experimental investigation of the Many conditions constituting the wealth of reality, and loyal worshipful emotional commitment and enjoyment of the totality of cosmic reality as One.

Meland offers further observations to support his conclusion: (1) Since "the term God is essentially a religious or contemplative concept," it is the nature of the religious mood and method of the worshiper to synthesize the Many conditions of reality into One. (2) If one is to avoid confusion in an effort to understand and make practical adjustments to the many conditions of reality, an empirical, analytic, scientific procedure is needed, in which case the role of the worshiper, including his language and method, is abandoned. (3) Even though thinking of God as structure or process, or system of progressive integration, is helpful and "gets at the basic character of that which sustains and creates value, this kind of thinking does not reduce objective reality to an empirical Oneness, except in religious worship." (4) The system, like any system, including the system of progressive integration, is a multiplicity of functions, pluralistic in character. "There is a working together, a coordination of functions" in the system, "but that coordination is the abstract pattern."[86]

Wieman's response

In Wieman's response he recognizes Meland's contribution to this question between him and Dewey as "most valuable and clarifying." He sanctions much of what Meland says, but in closing offers four criticisms.

Wieman affirms Meland's both/and approach to the wealth of reality including the principle of alternation between scientific analysis of the many conditions of reality and worshipful commitment to reality as one. He interprets the alternation as a change of perspective on reality which is consistent with the application of the principle of relativity to all experience.

It means that you cannot talk intelligently about any reality until you specify the viewpoint and other conditions under which it is experienced.[87]

In summary form, Wieman restates the question and answers it:

> Now then, is that wealth of reality which we call God one or many? It is both. From the standpoint of practical efficiency and scientific analysis, it is many. From this standpoint of loving devotion it is one. [88]

The criticisms which Wieman offers of Meland's position seem to be subissues which do not qualify his affirmation of Meland's main contribution. His first criticism is based on Meland's claim that "there is no particular point in contending for the superiority of either the oneness or the many." Wieman responds by saying:

> I think the oneness of the universe is not functionally important.... But there is something in the universe that has a oneness which is functionally of the utmost importance. It is that totality of conditions which constitutes the growing good.... This oneness is the oneness of God.
> So we say it is the oneness, not the manyness, of God that is most important. This is so because it is the unity, the organic connectedness, of the conditions which constitutes the good.... The oneness of them is reality just as much as the manyness. [89]

This last statement seems to say that even within the context of changing human perspectives and attitudes toward reality by means of which it can be treated as many or as one, there is within reality a growing unitary good which is actual, whose activities sustain one another and mean one another, and carry further possibilities for good. This again reveals the neo-realism of Wieman's value system. Even the unity of it is empirically actual and is not determined by the worshiping synthesizing mind of man.

In Wieman's second criticism of Meland, he says Meland "seems at times to speak of this oneness of God as though it were the same as the oneness of the cosmos." Without documentation, Wieman says: "This, I think, is a mistake." Wieman's interest here seems to be the preservation of his pluralistic metaphysics and of God as the one system of growing good in a context of many other activities which obstruct rather than support the growing good.

Third, Wieman suggests that Meland "seems to imply that in emotional worship God is one, but to intellectual understanding God must be many." In response, Wieman says: "An intellectual *as* *well* *as* appreciative understanding of the oneness of God is just as important as a grasp of the manyness."[90]

Fourth, Wieman's neo-realistic empiricism as related to the unity of God becomes explicit.

> Mr. Meland further writes as though the manyness were empirical, while the oneness was not. I hold that the oneness is just as empirical as the manyness. We truly experience the oneness of God whenever we experience that great goodness that consists in the unity of many conditions, each of which is indispensable to the goodness experienced. Our experience of the goodness is experience of the oneness of the operative conditions which sustain and constitute it.[91]

Fifth, Wieman disclaims Meland's saying that the functional aspect of any system is pluralistic, not unitary.

> I cannot see that this is true at all. The important functioning of heart, lungs, glands, etc., in an organism is unitary, not pluralistic. When they function pluralistically the man becomes sick, and if they become very pluralistic he dies. So also the factors that go to make up the good of a social culture or a home or an economic system or any other great good, must function as a unity if there is to be any good.
> In summary, the important functioning of God is unitary, not pluralistic, because God is the organic connectedness (unity) of all the different conditions which are necessary to the growing good. The good is precisely this organic connectedness. God is this organic connectedness.[92]

We believe the import of this series of communications between Wieman and Dewey and Meland is especially significant for a further understanding of creativity in Wieman as a response to both James and Dewey. Creativity in Wieman is expressed not in the explicit language of creativity but in the language of organic connectedness or unity. In his closing statement quoted above, in which he is disclaiming that the functional aspect of any system is pluralistic by referring to "the important functioning of heart, lungs, glands, etc., in an organism," as unitary, we do not interpret his meaning as analogical. It is, instead, a literal indication of his metaphysics of creative organicism. We believe that a thorough and explicit development of Wieman's metaphysics in these communications, despite Dewey's aversion to the use of the term because of its traditional speculative connotation, would have clarified and strengthened his position. The ground for doing this had already been well cultivated, especially in his work on Bergson, Hocking, and Whitehead. In the closing lines of his Harvard dissertation, Wieman describes the functional nature of God as "the progressive creation of cosmic history through the mutual determination of wills."93 However, this series of communications does not prove to be Wieman's last opportunity to bring out the theistic religious import of Dewey's philosophy.

Wieman Reviews "A Common Faith": Consequent Communications and Wieman's Responses

About a year and a half later, Wieman reviews Dewey's A Common Faith. 94 Wieman begins his review with the following paragraph:

> John Dewey has served the world richly in many walks of life. Now at last in the ripeness of his years he turns to religion, and his service here is equal to any he has given. Some of us have known for a long time that he was a deeply religious man. Furthermore, many of us have seen in all his writings the implicit outline of a noble religion. But he never made it explicit. You had to get it between the lines. It was like invisible ink, waiting to be made plain for all to see. Now at last he has stated it. We are not disappointed. 95

Even though Wieman says that Dewey, in this volume, has moved in the statement of his religious faith from an implicit to an explicit expression of it, he continues his characteristic style of reviewing Dewey's works not only by clarifying their content, but also by developing their further import. Wieman's method of reviewing, commenting on, and criticizing the works of other philosophers is not merely to serve as a reporter but also to show how the work fits or does not fit into the growth of meaning. He uses the work for this purpose simply because his entire philosophy is organized around growth of meaning. However, this method is easily misunderstood, for it is sometimes difficult to distinguish the report from its import as Wieman sees it.

Wieman continues his review by listing concisely Dewey's main contributions to further understanding of what concerns the religious person: He makes "important and clarifying distinctions" regarding the nature of religious experience (see pages 12 and 13). He "describes that transformation of the will ... which most of us recognize to be conversion, and declares that it is necessary to enter the religious way of living" (see pages 17 and 33). He distinguishes "faith that is essential to religious living from faith that is mere intellectual assent" (see pages 22, 23, and 33). He shows "the value of mystical experience and distinguishes its misuses from its true importance" (see pages 35 and 36).

> He pronounces non-theistic humanism as futile and mistaken and thus clearly separates himself from that movement with which many have identified him [see pages 53 and 54]. Above all, he declares his knowledge of God and devotion to God.
>
> This knowledge of God for Dewey is not merely a belief which may or may not be true, on which one 'bets his life.' Dewey is convinced, and we share the conviction, that religion has been degraded and weakened by clinging to beliefs for which we have no assured evidence. [96]

Wieman is profoundly impressed with Dewey's distinction between religion as an isolated special interest forced to compete with other special interests in contrast with what religion once was when it gave

> character, meaning, direction, dignity to the total social process, the collective life of the group.... [It was] the utmost outreach and glory of the life of man so far as the individual could imaginatively compass that life. [97]

Wieman quotes Dewey as saying that this change from religion as guidance for the whole of life to religion as more or less isolated within the church as one among other institutions is "the greatest revolution that has taken place in religion during the thousands of years that man has been upon this earth."[98] He appreciates Dewey's distinguishing the religious from the unreligious attitude.

> The essentially unreligious attitude is that which attributes human achievement and purpose to man in isolation from the world of physical nature and his fellows.[99]

Furthermore, he appreciates Dewey's distinguishing the religious attitude from religion in its institutional forms which so frequently suffer from fixed beliefs, rites, and ceremonies, and which are more or less exclusive from their context in the world and are unable to benefit as they should from current critical modes of inquiry. Wieman reaffirms Dewey's longstanding interest in discarding supernaturalism, as well as those subjectivistic expressions of religion which elevate human desire, rather than the desirable as a consequence of further understanding of value and the growth of value. Wieman asks: "What is this religious attitude Dewey talks about?" He replies:

> It is devotion to an ideal reality which exercises control over one's conduct. It is loyalty in service and adoration to what one holds to be supremely worthful, not only for himself alone, but for all human living.[100]

Wieman says further that Dewey "is discussing the reality which is the rightful object of man's supreme devotion." To quote Dewey:

> We are in the presence neither of ideals completely embodied in existence nor yet of ideals that are mere rootless ideals, fantasies, utopias. For there are forces in nature and society that generate and support the ideals. They are further unified by the action that gives them coherence and solidity. It is this active relation between ideal and actual to which I would give the name 'God.'[101]

Wieman goes further, using the terms of his own philosophy to develop the import of the nature of God as Dewey presents it. In doing this, Wieman gives five reasons for God's being superhuman without implying in any way either that God is supernatural, or that God "has a mind, intelligence or personality ... superior to man," but because God "is more than personality, mind or intelligence."[102] First, the activity which connects the actual and the ideal

> sustains and promotes the highest values with scope and power greater than any single personality possibly could, no matter how greatly magnified....
> Second, this activity ... carries possibilities of value far beyond what men can sense or imagine except as the values emerge in existence or human consciousness, and as man's capacity is developed to appreciate them.
> Third, this activity ... generates, develops and brings to highest fulfillment human personality. Man does not make it. It makes men. Human personality is dependent on this mesh of interaction for the very breath of its existence and all its highest development....
> Fourth, this activity ... exercises the might of gentleness as no human could do. Its might is the might of growth, and growth is always gentle beyond any of the works of man.
> Fifth, it is superhuman because man must be mastered by it in order to receive the sustenance, development and high fulfillment that it can bring. In so far as man tries to master it, he loses the values which it pours into human life.[103]

Furthermore, the import of the nature of God as Dewey presents it in terms of "the active relation between ideal and actual" is not exhausted by observing that it is superhuman. Wieman sees it as exercising "rightful sovereign authority over every impulse and habit, institution and practice, dream and desire of man." However, it is "neither omnipotent nor omniscient." It is not brute force. It commands "our highest loyalty by reason of supreme worthfulness."[104]

Still further import of this activity to which Dewey refers as God, is that it answers prayer "when prayer is understood to be adjustment of human personality to it." Also God

> comforts and sustains in time of trouble and disaster, if warm fellowship of sympathetic hearts is solace, for it is this activity which unites us in bonds of brotherhood. Even when human companionship is not available, it is comforting to

> know there is an activity that forever works to draw the world and men into closer bonds of mutual support, and does fold the world about us with sustaining arms even when many forces work to destroy us.[105]

We note especially in this review that Wieman's interpretation of the <u>connection</u> between the actual and the ideal, does not emphasize <u>organic unity</u> and <u>organic connectedness</u>, but <u>creative unity</u>.

> Here is an operative reality which brings into dynamic, creative unity many different activities, so that ... the existing things of nature are transformed from brute fact into bearers of meaning and value.[106]

He also quotes Dewey's description of this operative reality, or "<u>active</u> relation between ideal and actual," which makes use of two additional terms: "community of causes and consequences" and "matrix within which our ideal aspirations are born and bred."

> The community of causes and consequences in which we, together with those not born, are enmeshed ... is the matrix within which our ideal aspirations are born and bred.[107]

So Wieman is calling this community type of relation between causes and consequences a creative unity. This, then, is the matrix within which ideals are born and bred. Dewey adds that this matrix "is the source of the values that the moral imagination projects as directive criteria and as shaping purposes."[108] It is evident from Wieman's closing paragraph in this review that he sees no basis for criticism of the role Dewey has given to moral imagination in this additional statement:

> The religious function will not come again to the earth to fill human life with passionate devotion to God until we discover God operating in the practical, everyday concerns of human living in some such way as Dewey indicates.[109]

Aubrey's letter to Dewey and Wieman: responses from Dewey and Wieman

Following the publication of <u>A Common Faith</u>, and

Wieman's review, both non-theistic humanists and supernaturalists were confused by Dewey's adverse criticism of each of these religious philosophies. Dewey's forthright and complete rejection of supernaturalism, as responsible for maintaining the separation of the spiritual nature of man from nature to which man belongs, and of the separation of nature including man from the source of religious values, was disconcerting to all kinds of supernaturalists, but for the nontheistic humanists this rejection of supernaturalism was the focal source of their deep appreciation for Dewey. He was keenly aware of this fact. Moreover, we see the concerted effort of the non-theistic humanists to negate supernaturalism and to domesticate religion within natural human experience to be the real basis for Dewey's affiliations with humanism. However, his adverse criticism of the religious philosophy of the non-theistic humanists was even more confusing to them, for they had regarded him as belonging with them, while the supernaturalists had no basis for such claims. The outcome, on the one hand, was open opposition from the supernaturalists and, on the other hand, requests from nontheistic humanists for further explanation of his position.

Wieman's review of A Common Faith made it more difficult for these non-theistic humanists--if not only Wieman's report of Dewey's faith, but also its import, as interpreted by Wieman, was to be judged correct--for Wieman had said in his review:

> He [Dewey] pronounces non-theistic humanism as futile and mistaken and thus clearly separates himself from that movement with which many have identified him (pp. 53, 54).[110]

During this period of confusion, Edwin Ewart Aubrey wrote a reply[111] to Wieman's review of A Common Faith and sent copies of it to Dewey and Wieman.

Aubrey's formal criticism of Wieman's review begins with the claim that Wieman's emphasis on Dewey's use of the phrase, "forces in nature and society that generate and support the ideals," can be read in two ways:

> ... either (following Whitehead's view) as affirming the existence of some more-than-human principle of progressive integration which is operative in the cosmos and partly in man; or (following Mr. Dewey's previous utterances) as affirming the power of corporate human intelligence to draw the actual

> given of nature and the projected ideals of the imagination together in a plan of directed activity. 112

Here, Aubrey's attributing Wieman's interpretation of this phrase in question, as coming from Whitehead, and of placing it in contrast with Dewey's previous utterances, is a significant method used to persuade Dewey that what Wieman is saying is to be identified with the more speculative metaphysics of Whitehead and far removed from Dewey's <u>previous</u> utterances which affirm, according to Aubrey,

> the power of corporate human intelligence to draw the actual given of nature and the projected ideals of the imagination together in a plan of directed activity. 113

It is evident that Aubrey is implying that Dewey's "previous utterances" remain normative for interpreting Dewey's religious philosophy, and furthermore, that there is no indication in Dewey's recent work, <u>A Common Faith</u>, for believing, as Wieman does, that Dewey's thinking on God has undergone creative development; for, Aubrey says: "A careful reading of <u>A Common Faith</u> fails to reveal that Mr. Dewey has gone beyond the second interpretation."114

Aubrey says Wieman's Whiteheadian interpretation

> might be implied <u>on the basis of Mr. Wieman's own premises</u>; but that is not the same thing as imputing the views to Mr. Dewey. Mr. Wieman's wish is perhaps father to his thought in this respect. There seems to be no warrant in the book for his declaration (presumably in exposition of Mr. Dewey) that 'this activity which unites the actual and the ideal is not merely the conscious, intelligent effort of men'; and it is significant that no quotations are offered in support of this interpretation. 115

Aubrey proceeds in an effort to document his own claim by selecting references from <u>A Common Faith</u> which emphasize four main points: (1) that which connects the actual and the ideal is "<u>not externally imposed</u> ..." (page 16, emphasis added by Aubrey); (2) the unity or connection referred to by Dewey signifies not a single Being, but the unity of loyalty and effort evoked by the fact that many ends are one in the power of their ideal, or imaginative, quality to stir and hold us (page 43). [116]

(3) values take on unity "through imagination"; (4) the values "need no external criterion and guarantee for their goodness" (emphasis added by Aubrey). Aubrey concludes that

> the integrative power binding actual and ideal is still restricted, in Mr. Dewey's thought, to human imaginative intelligence. This interpretation is further reinforced by ... the author ... 'all significant ends and all securities for stability and peace have grown up in the matrix of human relations' (page 70). [117]

Finally, after this effort to document Dewey's past and present philosophic position as essentially a form of non-theistic humanism, and to describe the locus of God, according to Wieman's interpretation of Dewey, as somewhere exterior or trans-human to human imagination and the matrix of human relations, Aubrey says: "Mr. Dewey is not yet talking of a God who is a trans-human power or principle of integration, as the review by Mr. Wieman seems to claim." Aubrey then decides that he cannot escape the fact that Dewey does have a core of divinity in his religious philosophy; hence he says that Dewey is talking "of a divinely creative human intelligence."[118] Then he adds: "And this is substantially the position which Mr. Dewey has expounded for years."

Wieman responded to Aubrey's letter by saying:

> I had not realized ... that my words about Dewey could be so greatly misunderstood. I do not identify Dewey's idea of God with that of Whitehead.... It is very plain that Dewey repudiates such an idea, emphatically and consistently. Ideals and possibilities [for Dewey] have no existence. They are to be brought into existence as fully as possible. [119]

Wieman then points to the import of Dewey's statement on the community of causes and consequences as the matrix for growth of value in which our ideal aspirations are born and bred.

> This matrix ... is not created by our ideal striving except in part. Further, it carried possibilities which men have not yet consciously apprehended.
> It is this matrix, this community, this operative system, of inter-functioning activities with its possibilities, that held the actual and the ideal together ... not in the sense that the ideals are already in existence in God or anywhere else. But without this actuating matrix these possibilities could not be held as ideals by intelligent human beings because they would not be either discoverable or workable. A careful reading of my review of Dewey's book should make plain that I attribute nothing else than this to him.¹²⁰

Wieman says that the use of his phrase, "progressive integration" in interpreting Dewey's thought may be misleading, but that he used it to clarify the fact that "the community or matrix grows."

Wieman concludes his reply by saying that however much the ideas of God have varied, the term when used sincerely means "what, by right of supreme importance, commands the most inclusive and sovereign loyalty of human living." Furthermore, Dewey's "search for the supremely worthful, stripped as it is of all traditional bias and wishful thinking, should be widely shared."[121]

Dewey's published response to Aubrey and Wieman together indicates that after reading Wieman's reply, he would not modify his "complete approval" as given in his letter to Aburey previously. He says: "In fact, Mr. Wieman's reply has only made it clearer to me that he has read his own position into his interpretation of mine."[122]

Dewey thinks there is a fundamental distinction to be made between what he and Wieman mean by that which connects the actual and the ideal. According to Dewey, it is

> the union of ideals with some natural forces that generate and sustain them, accomplished in human imagination and to be realized through human choice and action....
> ...
> The unification of these, [forces] was, I said, the work of human imagination and will.[123]

We note especially Dewey's terse form of expression in this response to Wieman. It is not characteristic of him. He is especially disturbed by Wieman's interpretation of the com<u>m</u>unity of causes and consequences <u>as the matrix</u> for growth of value in which our ideal values are born and bred. Dewey wants to give these expressions an interpretation which is unrelated to anything he might call God. He says that the chapter which is entitled "The <u>Human</u> Abode of the Religious Function" has nothing in its context about God. The community of causes and consequences refers to the human community of intelligence and also to the need for transferring to intelligence "some of the zeal and devotion ... expended upon the supernatural." Community is a symbol of what the human imagination "calls the universe." This imaginary object called "the universe" or matrix is not to be identified with this community. Furthermore, this community is not "something to be worshiped." Dewey thinks Wieman "slips from the human community over to all nature as embracing man."¹²⁴

We believe what Dewey calls slipping over to <u>all</u> nature as embracing man is the clue to one of his main difficulties in understanding Wieman, for Dewey's conception of nature is not monistic but pluralistic. If Wieman slips over to all nature as embracing man, his conception of nature must be monistic. The presence of evil or actual disvalues in nature is the real reason for Dewey's pluralism. Not all of nature including human nature embraces man. For Dewey, the negation of value is just as real as positive value. We see clearly from the following passage how criticism of Wieman's slipping over is linked with the fact that Dewey takes evil seriously.

> It is quite true that in my whole philosophy I regard man as part of nature. But Mr. Wieman when he says that 'this matrix' (referring to my passage as quoted) is 'what holds ideal and actual "together"' slips from the human community over to all nature as embracing man. When we come to nature as this larger, inclusive matrix, I supposed that I had made it clear that I regarded nature in this sense as the matrix in which bad human impulses and habits are also 'born and bred.'¹²⁵

After Dewey has accepted both a naturalistic and a pluralistic interpretation of nature as the whole of existence and its possibilities, he faces the problem of determining

the basis for the growth of value in human life, which is
really the classic problem of determining the basis for the
wise guidance of human conduct. Since the general nature
of human conduct is its <u>actual</u> causes and consequences, wise
guidance is determined by learning how to deal intelligently
with causes and consequences which are the actual data for
selection by thought and action from the totality of nature.

> The 'causes and consequences' mentioned in the
> passage refer to the work of intelligence.
> ...
> I supposed I had made it clear that the 'actual'
> to which I referred was something <u>selected</u> by
> human thought and action out of the totality [uni-
> verse or matrix].[126]

Wieman's reply, to which Dewey did not respond, was
the last communication between them. Wieman sensed that
Dewey was reacting against the very real and significant import of his own philosophic growth of meaning expressed in
A Common Faith. This is not the first time that Wieman
had caught the deeper religious import of another man's philosophy before the other person had been able to develop and
express it clearly and explicitly. As with Whitehead[127] in
the mid-twenties, so with Dewey in the mid-thirties, except
that Whitehead suffered no insurmountable obstruction to his
own further rapid development, while in Dewey's case, as
we shall see, a decade passed before we find evidence of
significant change.

We recognize the difficulty encountered in reviewing
another man's religious philosophy, as Wieman does, by
centering attention on its import for further growth of meaning, for the import is what is implied and this places the
burden upon the reviewer to determine what a statement does
or does not imply, certainly one of the most complex issues
in the history of logic. The review does not <u>create</u> further
meaning if it is confined to mere reporting, but if it suggests
what is implied for further meaning, and the reader cannot
apprehend the implication as real, the reviewer may be ac-
cused of wishful thinking or prejudice by reading into the
work in question what is not there. This is the live issue
between Dewey and Wieman. This seems evident from the
opening paragraph in Wieman's reply:

> On a number of points I have always differed
> strongly with Professor Dewey. Generally these

were points where it seemed to me he failed to
follow through to the inevitable implications of his
position. In the passages from A Common Faith
around which this discussion has arisen, it seemed
to me that he had at last carried two of these implications to their logical fulfillment. But the letter above contradicts this. [128]

In this final response, Wieman deals with just these
two implications and how they are related. They are:

... (1) the way the actual world and its possibilities of value are united and (2) the unity of this
organization of the actual which carries these possibilities. [129]

On the first implication Wieman states how he agrees
with Dewey and then in what respect he disagrees.

I agree with Dewey in saying that what has 'actually functioned in human experience in its religious
dimension' has been this union of actual and ideal;
but I disagree with his present momentary claim
that this union is solely the work of human imagination and choice. That is so patently contrary to
fact that I can scarcely believe he means it even
now. [130]

The fact presented by Wieman is that "many ends of
endeavor pictured in human imagination are grossly evil,
some foolish and frivolous, others impossible of any sort of
approximation." Furthermore, "before human imagination
existed, its future emergence was a possibility of the then
existing world." Therefore, "Human imagination is only one
of many activities which work together to make these possibilities genuine possibilities" for growth of value. Wieman
concludes his discussion of this implication by telling Dewey
that if he denies this he will not only be "going contrary to
obvious fact," but also to "his own prior commitments."[131]

If the way that conditions of the actual world are
united with genuine possibilities for growth of value is not
by human imagination alone, the further question which
arises is: What is the nature of the uniting process? Wieman deals with this question under the second implication
mentioned above. For Wieman the process of uniting is the
work of a unitary system which is more deeply and more

reliably rooted in nature including human nature than human imagination alone, as claimed by Dewey.

Wieman analyzes the unity in the value-making process in the following way: Unity "is always relevant to some function," rather than existing "in an absolute sense, which cannot be considered multiple."

> Whatever has unity, has it only by virtue of serving some one function. With respect to that one function it is unitary. With respect to multiple functions it is multiple. [132]

Second, since "the highest value is the greatest possible unification of values" in which the activities "sustain one another and mean one another ... the function of generating and sustaining them must be a unitary function."[133]

Third, what makes an activity bad is that it does "not function together with the others under the dominance of this one supreme function of promoting the highest possibilities of value."[134] The religious function of man is commitment to this one supreme operative functional unity which is God.

Fourth, Wieman points to what happens in the growth of a child to illustrate this kind of unity.

> The infant organism in the beginning strives for some end or other, not because it has a purpose, nor even imagination, but because physiological propulsions and environmental conditions interact to give direction to its striving. But the interaction does not stop there. It carries possibilities of value. It goes on to develop imagination and intelligence in the infant. This first activity of the infant organism, without purpose and without imagination, operates on the environment in such a way as to change it. This changed state of the environment reacts again on the infant to cause some experience of comfort or discomfort that is now associated with his own action. The association of these experiences with these interactions develops in the infant: imagination, purpose, the sense of meaning, and the ability to make choices. [135]

Dewey does not reply.

Relevant correspondence between Jacobson and Dewey

While Dewey did not reply to Wieman at this time, nearly fifteen years later in his correspondence with Nolan P. Jacobson, regarding an article by Jacobson,[136] Dewey makes a reference to Wieman. In Dewey's letter of May 25, 1949,[137] he says in a parenthetical statement: "(You have helped me understand what it is that with my admiration of Wieman's work has always stood between that work and my acceptance of its standpoint.)" The standpoint in question is Dewey's previous assumption that Wieman's interpretation of nature is monistic as opposed to Dewey's pluralism.

In Jacobson's article he is clarifying the creativity of the greatest possible value in terms of the unity of function of three events based on human need, integration of nature and human nature, and "quantitative widening and qualitative enriching of the human community of creative interaction."

> The unity of these three events is the unity of function, the function of being everywhere and under all conditions creative of the greatest possible value within the time and place.... The unity resides in the fact that in all its manifestations the structured process is creative of value.... This unity, discoverable in the midst of events that are subject to constant change, is the only type of permanence or stability that men require, or ever have required in their active transactions with the surrounding world.[138]

Jacobson clarifies the issue further in his letter to Dewey as of June 8, 1949.

> ... if these three crucial events, ... locked in a structure, ... and interrelated be defined ... as God; then I have implied no reservoir of value standing beyond but only a structured process passing history along to no particular consummation at all.[139]

In Dewey's reply of June 13, he says:

> A genuinely naturalistic philosophy of religion will, as I see it have to be the expression of a religious

outlook which has not as yet taken any agreed upon form--to me, naturally, of the kind indicated in an outline way in my <u>Common Faith</u> book.[140]

Jacobson's reply to Dewey as of July 9 analyzes in further detail what he believes Dewey and Wieman have in common in their respective philosophies of religion. He says: "You must know that your own approach to matters of religion is immensely popular with both myself and Wieman...."

Referring to Dewey's theory of inquiry, Jacobson says:

> The whole point of your long and fruitful labor has been as you said in your last letter to get people to employ this method.... Now, Wieman does not have only a theory of inquiry, although he goes along fully with you there; he has a theory of the way value increases, value defined as qualitative meaning, a conception that I assume he took almost bodily from you. Witness that Wieman insists ... that no man can tell precisely <u>what</u> qualitative meaning will emerge. The contingency is Wieman's way of celebrating the power of 'God.' Wieman has followed a simple method, once your own work is presupposed. He has sought to discover the pattern followed in man's growth of appreciative awareness; part of the pattern he insists is beyond the control of man and could not possibly be achieved by man--it is, ergo, God.
> Notice that Wieman belabors everyone who says anything about God other than God in the doings that are involved in this growth.... I would say that he is much closer to you than you appreciate. If God be defined as that upon which man's value development depends, and providing there be nothing said of any divine existence other than in the development itself....[141]

Jacobson pursues the issue further, more specifically with regard to Dewey's use of the term "God."

> Finally, let me add that some things you say have always been a source of encouragement to Wieman. Concerning the narrow and shallow (and perhaps nonexistent) gulf separating you, consider your remark in <u>Experience and Nature</u>: 'All

criticism worthy of the title is but another name for that revealing discovery of conditions and consequences which enables liking, bias, interest to express themselves in responsible and informed ways instead of ignorantly and fatalistically.' (431). If inquiry reveals a pattern or structure in the growth of anything whatever men might agree is supremely worth pursuing ... might we not in addition to encouraging in ourselves a 'religious' quality of living in such pursuit also use the term 'God' to refer to whatever part of that pattern or structure lies beyond the control of man and does not result from his own conscious effort?[142]

In Dewey's letter of July 16, closing the correspondence, he says:

> ... to my own discredit in some measure ... I acquired a prejudice against his [Wieman's] way of thinking when we had a little exchange via the Christian Century. After I had done my best to state my point of view, he said in the course of a published comment that doubtless I later was sorry for something I said which, as I recall, was the nub of my position. Though his article invited reply I dropped the discussion, as his interpretation of what I wrote seemed to me so gratuitous as to make anything further on my part wholly useless. I may add that I wouldn't have felt so strongly if I hadn't a high opinion of Wieman.[143]

We believe that Dewey's response to this situation, fifteen years later, is significant; but we would add that Wieman's later responses to Dewey are equally significant, and for our purposes are worth noting.

Wieman's 1961 and 1970 responses to Dewey

Wieman's 1961 response is recorded in the opening chapter in his Intellectual Foundation of Faith,[144] under the title "Faith Asks a Question," which sets the stage for the following chapter on "John Dewey Answers." The question is not about our many interests or the many goods in existence, but "about the direction in which all of life should move." The question which faith asks can be stated in many ways:

> What can save man from his self-destructive propensities? What can bring into action the depth and wholeness of man's being? ... What can actualize most completely the constructive potentialities of human existence? What can bring this partially created being to the full maturity of his powers and values? What can carry human history and human society and the individual to these attainments?[145]

Wieman follows a three-fold procedure for answering the question of faith. First, he describes the current condition of man.

> In our time civilization has built up the suppressed potentialities of man to a greater intensity than in the past. Consequently they demand release more insistently than ever.... Also we are training men and establishing institutions devoted to the study of these suppressed potentialities and the problem of how to release them constructively. This is what every educational institution is supposed to be doing, whether or not it does it effectively.[146]

Second, he formulates the basic problem.

> The basic problem is two-fold. It is: (1) to search out and set up the conditions most favorable for creativity and (2) seek appreciative understanding of the opposing way of life in order to acquire from the 'enemy' whatever virtues are there. Only in this way can creativity operate effectively in human life.[147]

Third, in closing this first chapter, he suggests that we seek the finest contributions yet offered for solving the basic problem.

> With this understanding of the moral and religious problem of human life, it will be profitable to examine the work of some of the most influential men of our time who are working upon it. We shall look at John Dewey first, not because we think that his explicit teaching has done more than any other to show the way, but he is more intimately a part of our American life than many of the others and we

may find, underneath his explicit teaching, something of profound importance.¹⁴⁸

Chapter two, "John Dewey Answers," includes Wieman's greater tribute to Dewey, and also his adverse criticism of Dewey's analysis of the referent for the term "God." Wieman's tribute is to be distinguished from his earlier treatments of Dewey, in that now it is expressed in the terminology of creativity. It also suggests what Dewey's faith has in common with the best in the Christian tradition.

Wieman's approach to Dewey's answer to the religious problem is centered in Dewey's living faith, which, Wieman says, "runs deeper than words." It is what Dewey says and does when he is not thinking about faith or talking about religion that his living faith is most clearly revealed. Wieman feels that Dewey's real personal faith tends to recede into the background or be concealed rather than exhibited whenever Dewey begins to theorize about it. However, Wieman states what he conceives it to be: a certain "kind of communication which Dewey believed to be more important than anything else in the world."¹⁴⁹ Wieman's conviction that communication is central in Dewey's faith is the outcome of more than forty years of careful study of Dewey's thought and action and a personal conference¹⁵⁰ with Dewey which, for Wieman, exemplified this kind of communication.

> I never met a man more simple, kind and gentle. Nothing striking about his appearance, ... so much so, that some philosophers who were opposed to his views went around saying that John Dewey was ... no philosopher at all ... not only because of his appearance and manner but also because he worked on problems of everyday life.... ¹⁵¹

Wieman cites various passages in Dewey's Experience and Nature to indicate what Dewey means by this kind of communication:

> Of all affairs, communication is the most wonderful.... [T]hat the fruit of communication should be participation, sharing, is a wonder by the side of which transubstantiation pales.... [C]ommunication and its congenial objects are objects ultimately worthy of awe, admiration, and loyal appreciation.

> They are worthy as means because they are the
> only means that make life rich and varied in meanings. They are worthy as ends, because in such
> ends man is lifted from his immediate isolation
> and shares in a communion of meanings.... When
> the instrumental and final functions of communication live together in experience, there exists an
> intelligence which is the method and reward of the
> common life, and a society worthy to command affection, admiration and loyalty.... Thus communication is not only a means to common ends but is
> the sense of community, communion actualized.[152]

Wieman summarizes Dewey's religious commitment as

> the kind of communication which continuously
> creates[153] and sustains in being the human mind
> and personality, human society and culture and
> human history when history means the resources
> for human living accumulated by past generations
> and communicated to the present.[154]

It is this deep, wide-ranging, and continuously operative role of creativity in communication which Wieman finds in Dewey's living faith, but Dewey, he says, "did not discuss it under the head of religion."

> We observe this faith to be more implicit than explicit, yet it is explicitly pervasive in Dewey's way of living.
> It is not isolated in some one field of activity, division of
> study, or some one institution. In a sense, the religious
> life is lost in the whole of living and thereby saved. It is
> this lost and living faith found in Dewey which has been
> Wieman's continued concern when dealing with Dewey in an
> effort to express the import of his religious philosophy.
> Dewey seems ever fearful lest his faith should become an object of exhibition rather than a common faith shared by all
> men.

We believe it is this context in which this kind of communication operates with the attitude or spirit of communion in creative community that causes Wieman to relate the living faith of Dewey to the faith of the founder of Christianity.

> ... [T]he disciples ... experienced a transformation of their lives and character ... by the kind

of communication they had with Jesus.... The
revelation was the transforming power of this kind
of communication.... God as revealed in Jesus
Christ is the transforming, saving power of this
kind of communication which creates appreciative
understanding of one another and transmits the
values of one to the other.[155]

Furthermore, Wieman suggests that Dewey and Jesus had something in common in their adverse criticisms of the fixations of institutionalized religion.

Wieman's criticism of Dewey's analysis of the meaning of God as that "active relation which connects the ideal and the actual" is based on Dewey's further interpretations[156] which for Wieman, are ambiguous.[157] But on further examination of this criticism nearly a decade later,[158] Wieman's paper entitled "My Misinterpretation of Dewey's Religious Faith,"[159] clarifies the context of his 1961 criticism of Dewey, states in summary form the content of his criticism, presents his correction, and expresses deep regret for his misinterpretation.

Wieman, in clarifying the context of his 1961 criticism says:

> In his book A Common Faith John Dewey gives
> to the word 'God' the religious meaning it has for
> him in the faith by which he lives. In my book
> Intellectual Foundation of Faith I criticize this
> meaning he gives to the divine. I now see in retrospect that my criticism was mistaken. Controversy arose between us in The Christian Century
> 12/5/34 under conditions that developed misunderstanding between us. I wish here to correct the
> misinterpretation of him which I set forth in my
> Intellectual Foundation of Faith, pp. 40-44.[160]

Wieman summarizes this criticism:

> On these pages I criticize Dewey on the ground
> that he identified God with three separate realities:
> (1) God is the ideal provided that the ideal unifies
> many values and commands the full allegiance of
> the individual, thereby unifying his personality under
> its control.
> (2) God is the exercise of imagination which unites

the ideal with the actual processes of the existing world so that the ideal is not merely a construction of the imagination but shapes and guides the process of living.
(3) God 'is also connected with all the natural forces and conditions--including man and human association--that promote the growth of the ideal and that further its realization.... For there are forces in nature and society that generate and support the ideals.' (Quotation from Dewey.)[161]

Wieman presents his correction of his earlier criticism:

> I am wrong when I say that Dewey represents these three as separate and independent matters. For Dewey they are three different aspects of the same reality. The ideal taken by itself is not to be identified with God. Rather for Dewey God is what operates in human existence to create the ideal and is served by the ideal when the ideal directs men to seek out and provide the conditions under which this creativity can operate most effectively to transform human existence toward the greatest good.
>
> For Dewey the ideal is an essential part of religious living only when 'the ideal itself has its roots in natural conditions; it emerges when the imagination idealizes existence by laying hold of possibilities offered in thought and action.... The idealizing imagination seizes upon the most precious things found in the climacteric moments of experience and projects them.... They are had, they exist as good, and out of them we frame our ideal ends.' (Quotation from Dewey.)
>
> Dewey is saying that ideals are religious only when they arise to direct conduct in service of what we experience in 'climacteric moments.' What we then experience is not merely an ideal; it is actual. Ideals are religious only when they unify the personality and direct our ruling loyalty to the service of this actuality.
>
> What then is this actuality which is the basic concern in religious living for John Dewey? He makes plain what it is in many of his writings. It is a kind of communication. As I study what Dewey says about this kind of communication I find it to

> be very much what I mean by creative interchange. I have been led to misinterpret Dewey because of his emphasis on the ideal. But for Dewey, unlike many humanists, the ideal by itself is not the matter of religious concern. Rather the ideals of religious significance rise out of this creative communication to direct conduct in its service by searching out and providing conditions most favorable for its operation and further realization.
>
> As Dewey says, this kind of communication (or creative interchange) commands religious commitment only when we give to it our most inclusive and commanding ideals. This is the same as saying, to use my own words, that it becomes religious for us only when we give to it our ruling commitment. These are different ways of saying the same thing.[162]

Wieman closes his paper by expressing deep regret for his misinterpretation of Dewey:

> I hereby express my deep regret that I misinterpreted John Dewey in my book <u>Intellectual Foundation of Faith</u> and failed to see the deep accord between us. This shows how confusing and misleading the word 'God' can be when used in the midst of the issues of modern life. I myself am coming more and more to avoid its use because of these confusions. Dewey himself began to regret this use of the word in his book <u>A Common Faith.</u> Here again I find myself in accord with Dewey.[163]

In retrospect, we find that we have discovered two significant misinterpretations: one by Dewey of Wieman and one by Wieman of Dewey. Each of these misinterpretations has its source, according to both Dewey and Wieman, in <u>The Christian Century</u> controversy of December 4, 1934.[164]

Furthermore, we have before us two signficant confessions: one from Dewey and one from Wieman. Dewey confesses in his correspondence[165] with Nolan P. Jacobson that he had "acquired a prejudice against his [Wieman's] way of thinking." This prejudice was based on Dewey's assuming mistakenly that Wieman's concept of nature is monistic rather than pluralistic, with the implication that God, for Wieman, is <u>external</u> to human existence.[166] Wieman confesses misinterpretation of Dewey's analysis of what the word "God" should refer to.[167] Wieman had assumed mistakenly that, for Dewey, ideal ends, natural forces and conditions, as well as human imagination are "three separate realities," each of which is identified in some way with God. Dewey's interpretation of the word is therefore judged to be ambiguous and mistaken. But when Wieman discovers that, for Dewey, ideal ends, natural forces and conditions, and imagination are all one process and that when this process functions creatively, or in Wieman's terms is subject to creative interchange, he realizes that he and Dewey are saying the same thing.

However signficant these reconceptions on the part of both Dewey and Wieman may seem to be, we feel that there is a need for further clarification of the basic concepts involved and of their relations within the context of creativity as divine. These basic concepts are: ideal, natural forces and conditions, and imagination.

CLARIFICATION OF DEWEY'S CONCEPTS: IDEAL, NATURAL FORCES AND CONDITIONS, AND IMAGINATION IN THE CONTEXT OF CREATIVE INTERCHANGE

Certainly the relations of these concepts in the context of creativity as divine are not of any type or pattern whatsoever. To fit the context of creativity the relations are necessarily creative. Since creativity is a process, these relations should be structured as process and not separated, fragmented, and fixated. Since creativity is characterized by continuity, these relations should be self-facilitating rather than mutually frustrating and self-destructive. Since the interchange within creative relations is consistent, these relations should operate consistently rather than inconsistently. Since divine creativity is to be distinguished from merely human creativity which often creates more or less fragmented, fixated, frustrated, inconsistent, and self-destructive situations, we are confronted with the question as to whether ideals, natural forces and conditions, and imagination may be so related as to function as a genuinely creative process which may serve as the source for transforming human life from less creative to more creative living.

As early as 1891, Dewey characterized an ideal as a method of thought. But not all ideals as methods of thought are intelligent.

> Processes of intelligence which have their nature fixed in themselves, apart from fact and having to be externally applied to fact, are pure myths .... [168]

In contrast with these mythical "processes of intelligence" are the intelligent modes which

> are simply the various forms which reality progressively takes as it is progressively mastered as to its meaning, --that is, understood. Methods of thought are simply the various active attitudes into which intelligence puts itself in order to detect and grasp the fact. Instead of rigid moulds, they are flexible adaptations.... They are only the ideal evolution of the fact--and by 'ideal' is here meant simply the evolution of fact into meaning. [169]

We use this illustration from Dewey's early analysis of the logic of methods of intelligent thought in order to present the context for understanding Dewey's use of concepts. An ideal, a condition, or imagination are not used intelligently, in order to be understood, when they are treated substantively as nouns apart and fixed in themselves. Instead, to understand them, they must be analyzed functionally in terms of the principle of relativity. Note that the illustration cited serves a double function. It not only indicates the nature of intelligent modes of thought for understanding concepts, but it also includes the adjective "ideal," and illustrates its functioning. Application of Dewey's principle would require that if one were to project an intelligent mode of thought as one's ideal to be actualized, one would begin to think <u>ideally</u>, which in this case would mean that one should think in terms of "the evolution of fact into meaning."

This method of thinking is based on William James' description of the way mentality operates[170] as stated in his <u>Principles of Psychology</u> which Dewey used as a text in some of his courses in his early teaching career. According to James, if one is to think intelligently, in contrast to a mechanical performance, the pursuance of ideals is "the pursuance of future ends" and their attainment depends on "choice of means." This, he says, is "the mark and criterion of the presence of mentality." This is a process description of mentality and of the functional nature of ideal ends operationally conceived.

Conditions, for Dewey, also operate in this process context and are a necessary function in the operation of an ideal. Therefore, ideal ends and their conditions cannot be separated meaningfully. They can only be distinguished for analytic purposes. This Jamesian insight is fundamental to the development of Dewey's instrumentalist theory, not of value but of valuation, which is the result of an empirical, teleological, and critical study of active relations which constitute valuing. Therefore, ideal ends and their conditions are relational activities. Yet some conditions which we employ for the actualization of ideal ends-in-view produce in the ends attained different consequences from those desired, in which case we experience a problematic situation or failure, except that the failure may be used as a negative correlation which may be eliminated from future effort, and as a stimulus for further thoughtful analysis of the problem situation.[171] However, if there is insufficient skill in the practice of thoughtful analysis and experimental effort to w toward a hoped-for solution of the problem, then interest, imagination and desire may become so confused and frustrated that intelligent effort is displaced by unorganized impulsive activity, which may run the course between violence and despair.[172] The only recourse from these forms of desperation is to learn the disciplines which the way of intelligence offers and to develop its skills at the more mature level of sensibility.

The physical forces of nature, such as movement, sound, color and their novel relations in the growth of organisms, especially in the growth of a child, provide the elemental conditions as means for transformation of unorganized impulse into aesthetically intelligent ways of thinking and acting. These forces and conditions, as means are not inferior in the constituent roles they play in the process of creative growth of meaning and value. Dewey's acceptance of this fact exemplifies his radical naturalism.

> For the closer man is brought to the physical world, the clearer it becomes that his impulsions and ideas are enacted by nature within him. Humanity in its vital operations has always acted upon this principle. Science gives this action intellectual support. The sense of relation between nature and man in some form has always been the actuating spirit of art.[173]

This does not mean that Dewey's perspectives on the relations between natural physical forces and conditions on the one hand and the arts of intelligence on the other hand are of an either-or nature. Without creative interplay, "the tang of overt conflict and the impact of harsh conditions"[174] threaten the very destruction of man and the arts of intelligence grow pallid and thin. This bifurcation creates alternation between harsh or even horror tactics and individual and mass expression of sentimental sensuality. The outcome is dissipation of the capacity of persons, especially of children, for natural emergence of creative imagination and the maturing of aesthetic sensibilities.

Loss of sense of the necessities involved in the physical forces and conditions of nature as related to the actualization of whatever ideals man may project is not only obstructive, but disastrous for creative growth of meaning and value. Dewey's sense of experience is the sense of ecological necessities. Failure to recognize them is the way to nihilism. Correlation, which is the essential object of scientific effort, does not respond positively to any whim or fancy embodied in ideal ends. But novelty gives rise to the necessity for correlation. These insights provide for man the opportunity to understand what art in life really is.

> For art is the fusion in one experience of the pressure upon the self of necessary conditions and the spontaneity and novelty of individuality. [175]

But this fusion of the natural necessities of the forces and conditions with novel ideal ends-in-view requires in man something other than fancy and fantasy. It requires imagination.

For Dewey, the arts of life are not given to man by the conveyance of mere information, however computerized. The locus of imagination is communication:

> Instruction in the arts of life is something other than conveying information about them. It is a matter of communication and participation in values of life by means of the imagination, and works of art are the most intimate and energetic means of aiding individuals to share in the arts of living. Civilization is uncivil because human beings are divided into non-communicating sects, races, nations, classes and cliques. [176]

Communication in its fullness is communion among friends who have intimate affection one for the other. It is this kind of communication to which Wieman points as the center of Dewey's living faith.[177] It is the source of acceptance and appreciative understanding of one for the other even in situations of intense conflict. It is the context for fulfillment of man's quest for identity.

> Friendship and intimate affection are not the result of information about another person even though knowledge may further their formation. But it does so only as it becomes an integral part of sympathy through the imagination.[178]

Imagination is an essential aspect of those relations which are growth of meaning as appreciative understanding among men. When there is a creative interchange of imagination between men, growth of understanding is made possible by the outreach of imagination into the life of the other. This kind of imagination expands the appreciative consciousness of each communicant in the process of communication. It makes communication viable. It makes qualitative meaning possible. It is embodied in the interests, desires and aims of the communicants.

> It is when the desires and aims, the interests and modes of response of another become an expansion of our own being that we understand him.[179]

It is significant to know that Dewey's <u>Art as Experience</u> has its origin in the William James lectures delivered at Harvard University in the winter and spring of 1931, and that further work on these lectures was continued for several years until they were published in the spring of 1934. Not until Dewey had completed more than three-fourths of the volume did he say anything about imagination while writing this philosophy of art.

> IN [sic] what precedes, I have said nothing about imagination. 'Imagination' shares with 'beauty' the doubtful honor of being the chief theme in esthetic writings of enthusiastic ignorance. More perhaps than any other phase of the human contribution, it has been treated as a special and self-contained faculty, differing from others in possession of mysterious potencies. Yet if we judge its nature from the creation of works of art, it desig-

nates a quality that animates and pervades all processes of making and observation. It is a *way* of seeing and feeling things as they compose an integral whole. It is the large and generous blending of interests at the point where the mind comes in contact with the world. When old and familiar things are made new in experience, there is imagination. When the new is created, the far and strange become the most natural inevitable things in the world. There is always some measure of adventure in the meeting of mind and universe, and the adventure is, in its measure, imagination.[180]

Dewey's further clarification of the role of imagination, when properly distinguished from fantasy, reverie, dream, supernatural apparition, or some special faculty, indicates that imagination is that kind of fluid "solution" which holds all other elements together in the aesthetic situation. These elements include sense, emotion, and reason within the context of physical forces and conditions which are connected in the growth of meaning and value with ideal ends projected. This fluid solution is not, for Dewey, a "hung-up" type of imaginary activity confined to mere speculation or "inner vision." In essential art, there is creative interchange between what is sometimes called inner and outer vision.

There is a stage in which the inner vision seems much richer and finer than any outer manifestation. It has a vast and enticing aura of implications that are lacking in the object of external vision. It seems to grasp much more than the latter conveys. Then there comes a reaction; the matter of the inner vision seems wraith-like compared with the solidity and energy of the presented scene. The object is felt to say something succinctly and forcibly that the inner vision reports vaguely, in diffuse feeling rather than organically. The artist is driven to submit himself in humility to the discipline of the objective vision. But the inner vision is not cast out. It remains as the organ by which outer vision is controlled, and it takes on structure as the latter is absorbed within it. The interaction of the two modes of vision is imagination; as imagination takes form the work of art is born.[181]

This creative interaction between the physical forces and conditions which provide the raw materials for objects of art-in-the-making and the projected possibility as an art object or ideal end-in-view is precisely what Wieman refers to as creative interchange. But Dewey calls it "imagination." It is evident from the passage quoted above that this kind of imagination is creative. It is creative of further possibilities to be brought out of or educed from the raw materials or natural forces and conditions of nature. For Dewey, the <u>embodiment</u> of these possibilities "is the best evidence that can be found of the true nature of imagination."

Dewey also turns to philosophy to illustrate what he means by creative interaction which he calls "imagination."

> There are moments when he [the philosopher] feels that his ideas and ideals are finer than anything in existence. But he finds himself obliged to go back to objects if his speculations are to have body, weight, and perspective. Yet in surrendering himself to objective material he does not surrender his vision; the object just as an object is not his concern. It is placed in the context of ideas and, as it is thus placed, the latter acquire solidity and partake of the nature of the object.[182]

Dewey was uniquely sensitive to the fixations of habit, including the mechanical use of words. He was careful to distinguish his use of "imagination" and the "imaginative" from "imaginary" activity which "passes because it is arbitrary." The imaginative has an enduring quality "because, while at first strange with respect to us, it is enduringly familiar with respect to the nature of things." The "close observation of nature" by the creative artist "discovers qualities existing in her which have never been portrayed before, and thus forms a style which is original."[183] The aesthetic situation or object of art which embodies this quality of originality is a "revelation." It is a "quickened expansion of experience." The human contribution is not the only one: "art is also the quickened work of nature in man." Aesthetic expression "strikes below the barriers that separate human beings from one another." It is "the most universal form of language," expressing "the common qualities of the public world." It is "the freest form of communication.... The sense of communion generated by a work of art may take on a definitely religious quality."[184]

We find Dewey's sensing of the religious quality in art to be not only profoundly informative for his philosophy of art, but also for his total philosophic way of living. Understanding of experience is a root condition for all philosophic endeavor. This means understanding of the degrees or levels of experience in its evolution. Consummatory experience is aesthetic.

> For aesthetic experience is experience in its integrity.
> ... [A]ll the elements of our being that are displayed in special emphases and partial realizations in other experiences are merged in esthetic experience.[185]

Imagination is the creative interaction among the elements of our being. It is "that which holds all other elements in solution." It is what makes experience fluid rather than fixated. It is the freedom-giving process quality of experience. It is that <u>active</u> relation which connects the actual forces and conditions of nature with ideal ends projected. This kind of creative connection within experience gives it integrity. Wieman's term, "creative interchange," is a good way to refer to it. But it should be given the name "God," as Dewey affirmed in <u>A Common Faith</u>, and which he defended fifteen years later after receiving much adverse criticism from non-theistic philosophers.

Following Dewey's counsel, we would say that if philosophers wish to understand experience <u>as</u> experience in its most advanced evolutionary form, then they must go to aesthetic experience as creative ecological interchange between organisms and their environment.

> ... [S]ince art is the most direct and complete manifestation there is of experience <u>as</u> experience, it provides a unique control for the <u>imaginative</u> ventures of philosophy.
> In art as an experience, actuality and possibility or ideality, the new and the old, objective material and personal response, the individual and the universal, surface and depth, sense and meaning, are integrated in an experience in which they are all transfigured from the significance that belongs to them when isolated in reflection.[186]

For Dewey, it is creative aesthetic experience--with

its aesthetic perceptions, its aesthetic attitudes or predispositions for the guidance of action, its actual embodiment in the lives of common men effecting a common living faith in nature's creative process--that is the critic and the corrective for the fragmentation of experience. This kind of living faith is a faith in the growth of meaning and value which is transformative of the demonic divisiveness of traditional non-process and non-creative philosophies.

> Of art as experience it is also true that nature has neither subjective nor objective being; is neither individual nor universal, sensuous nor rational. The significance of art as experience is, therefore, incomparable for the adventure of philosophic thought. [187]

We find Dewey's neither/nor denials of the either/or polarizations of philosophic thought to be founded on his living faith that within the pluralistic processes of nature's ways there is an incomparable way. It is the way of creative, imaginative, moral, viable, aesthetic experience.

IMPORT OF JAMES FOR CREATIVITY IN DEWEY AND WIEMAN

Wieman's deep appreciation for William James is expressed early in Wieman's philosophic career in a ten-page essay[188] in which he analyzes the main contributions and limitations of James as he sees them.

For Wieman, it is William James as a person who "makes his work of such incomparable value." Wieman's summary analysis of James' main characteristics recognizes the

> intellectual honesty that enabled him to observe accurately and record fairly all the facts that came to his attention, without allowing his own theories to distort or obscure them.... [It also recognizes an] ... intellectual humility ... which revealed the inadequacy of all his own thinking and then would calmly admit that there were mysteries he had not begun to fathom. And he would throw out suggestions that would have brought ridicule upon a smaller man from the representatives of scientific thought.... Above all, he had that childlike spirit that continued to grow and develop new ideas to the

very end--new ideas that rendered his earlier theories untenable.[189]

We sense in James the radical tension which is reflected and reconceived in Wieman. One pole of this tension is James' well-known radical empiricism. It is also strongly reflected and reconceived in the philosophies of both Perry and Dewey. It is this radical empiricism in James which commands Wieman's deepest appreciation, not merely for its actualization in James, but for its further import.

> And the wonderful thing is that he himself has given us the key to open the door which he could not enter. It is no honor to us that we can go where he could not. It is only because of him that we can enter in. That key of radical empiricism which he found so late in life, too late to use himself for the opening of many doors, he had given to us.[190]

The other pole of the radical tension which appears in James' philosophy is, we believe, no less radical than his radical empiricism. Therefore, we shall refer to it as his radical MORE. We see this tension in James as the focal source of his creativity which is exemplified in his philosophy. But in the explicit language of creativity, he says little about it. This creative tension between his radical empiricism and his radical MORE, the one scientific in expression, the other mystical, is the context from which his profound interest in the scientific study of religion is combined and balanced by his interest in religious mysticism. These religious interests and studies are not narrow or provincial, but display range and depth which penetrate the whole of philosophy and life.

Wieman's response to James' mystical interests and expressions as reconceived in Hocking is appreciative;[191] but Wieman reacts against some of James' suggestions on mysticism.

> James suggests that 'if there be higher spiritual agencies' they cannot be found in the world of sense. Things material must exclude things spiritual; we must turn away from the material world, close all the senses that yield us knowledge of it, and find some hidden other sense which will give us knowledge of the spiritual world. Here is that pitiful blunder that always leads to confusion.[192]

As we have observed under many circumstances, Wieman is a stern watchman in guarding the way to knowledge. For him, the way of mystical awareness alone as a way of knowing should be marked "Closed." However, he is understanding of James who would not close that way.

> ... [W]ith that broad sympathy and marvelous acquaintance with all the ways of the human heart, he recognized this to be the way so dear to many, and, in passing, acknowledged it to be a way which some might wish to follow; and he would not close the path to them. [193]

Knowing James' mind, disciplined by radical empiricism, Wieman says: "James did not himself go that way."

Though Wieman reacts strongly against some of James' suggestions on mysticism, he is appreciative of the principles which operate in James' sense of the MORE and which direct our sensibilities regarding both the limitation and the expansion of knowledge. For Wieman, there are qualities in events and their relations which are always more than man, at best, can sense, think, analyze or know; yet with increasing skill in developing better disciplines for knowing based on sensitivity and receptivity to the revelations of creativity which expand human consciousness, indefinite growth in knowledge appears possible. From these perspectives we may say that divine creativity does operate as the MORE in Wieman's way of knowing and valuing. Wieman's life-long search is based on his effort to understand "what operates in human life with such character and power that it will transform man as he cannot transform himself...."[194] According to Meland, Wieman's emphasis on the grace of divine creativity or the redemptive power of God as limiting man's role "to providing the conditions through which creativity can occur" collapses "the distinction between the creative and the redemptive themes." The outcome for human creativity is that

> the freedom of man, or the authenticity of his creative efforts, appears more muted than in either Whitehead or James. Man's works when they are creative, tend to become created goods which can be seen as being demonic or as being destructive of good such as creative event provides. [195]

According to this interpretation of Wieman's limitation of the autonomy of human creativity, there is a significant distinction to be made between James and Wieman as to contrasts and relations (by analogy, dissonance and counterpoint) between human and divine creativity. "Eachness" in James is muted in Wieman.

Meland interprets James' "eachness" from James' perspectives on radical empiricism:

> The point is that the only creativity that could be overtly known or acknowledged by him was that creativity of the human spirit in its attentive and volitional acts, projected as an adventure in thought and moral action within the exigencies of existence as being purposeful and exploratory, or crucial and necessary, given the option of choice and decision.[196]

In contrast with "eachness" in James, Meland interprets James' "all" or MORE by saying:

> The best way I know of stating this more inclusive view of James, whereby his 'eachness' and the 'all' can be simultaneously taken into account is to say that James conceived of each individual stream of experience as participating in a depth of relations which exceeds its conscious experience, except in marginal ways as a horizon of the More.[197]

From our analysis of creativity in Dewey, it seems evident that he follows faithfully the radical empirical "eachness" in James, yet with overtones of the mystical MORE included. Wieman is determined to actualize empirically more of the mystical MORE, in the interest of further knowledge of the nature of God. This effort, we believe, is an outcome of what Wieman means when he says of James, "... the wonderful thing is that he himself has given us the key [of radical empiricism] to open the door which he [late in life] could not enter."[198] This reference to James increases our understanding of Wieman's early and continuous effort to develop an empirical theology. "Eachness" is exemplified in Wieman's early statement of his philosophy of creativity.

> We can be satisfied only in achievement which reaches beyond our own subjective disposition. We must be able to change the world beyond ourselves

> in some significant and eternal manner. The good which we desire is the power to so achieve; it is the actual process of so achieving, not the results of such achievement.[199]

Then in this closing paragraph of his dissertation, he quotes Hocking: "In whatever sense God is to triumph in history, in that same sense must I triumph also."[200] With the following comments, Wieman closes his dissertation:

> God's triumph, as we have described it, is not a future event. It is a continuous present process. It is the progressive creation of cosmic history through the mutual determination of wills. When I participate in His community I create and I triumph, in my small way, even as God.[201]

While these references seem to exemplify a balance of contrast in what we are calling creative tension in Wieman, and what Meland refers to as creative dissonance or counterpoint, Wieman's emphasis on the absolute sovereignty of God as the source of every created good, together with man's role as providing further conditions, supplies evidence to support Meland's claim. This claim would be strengthened insofar as these conditions are truncated from the continuity of creative interchange between conditions and ideal ends. But in this case, either the conditions or ends, whichever perspective one may choose, become an obstruction to and a drop-out from the creative process, which is definitive of the nature of an evil activity in the context of creativity as normative. These evil activities are what Wieman would lend effort to prevent and transform. But this process of transformation is again ultimately dependent on the redeeming grace of God.

> The ordeal of this transformation might almost reach the limits of endurance for the most transformable and might destroy all others. This ordeal of transformation seems to be the theme of the Christian myth about the 'last things,' or 'the end of the world.' This 'end of history' is always imminent, although we never know when it will come. History may periodically move up toward such a transformation, then swing back, then up again and back, in the great social crises. It swings back because man lacks the faith to undergo the transformations demanded of him.

It may be that in the great crises of historic transition man has come more than once very near to the gates that open into the Kingdom of God but could not pass through because he was unable to yield up what he desired in opposition to creative transformation, or was unable to endure what was demanded in the way of hardship. And so, refusing to go on, he had to fall back disastrously, in suffering and loss, to some lower level. Perhaps even now, in the present historic situation, we are moving up to such a time of trial and choice. Possibly the magnitude of power and momentum of movement in the social process today may carry us beyond our power to hold back, until we are driven, through a thousand or ten thousand years of transformation, across the great divide separating us from 'the end of history' and that great good which will be produced when man is able to receive it and do his part. [202]

We interpret the sovereignty of God in Wieman not as a mere hang-over from his early Calvinistic conditioning, but as a criticized belief based on empirical analysis of the more simple structure of creativity operative in the lower levels of creative evolution, in comparison with its more complex structure operating within the expanding consciousness of man in the communicative process of learning. Central in learning is the creative emerging of imaginative insights, their creatively critical integration in the human self, their creatively appreciative expansion within the growing worlds of persons, and the creative transformation of these worlds through growing creative community. We see the import of Wieman's reconception of God as: God the creator, the functioning catalytic agent of creativity in the creative evolution of life; incarnate as creative event in the sons of God; and present as the holy spirit of creative interchange in creative community.

We observe Dewey's philosophy of creativity as a unique effort to make use of radical empiricism in the development of a morally and aesthetically religious philosophy of living, ever cognizant of the "eachness" in James, but finally efficient in developing the basis for a creative ethics as exemplified in his Theory of Valuation, and consequently an aesthetically religious living faith as exemplified in both Art As Experience, and A Common Faith. Though the story of creative interchange between Dewey and Wieman has already been told, there is a further exemplification of creative tension in the principle of creativity in Dewey, or what we may well call, from its aesthetic context, the principle of creative counterpoint.

> From the philosophic point of view, I see no way to resolve the continual strife in art theories and in criticism between the classic and the romantic save to see that they represent <u>tendencies</u> that mark every authentic work of art. What is called 'classic' stands for objective order and relations embodied in a work; what is called 'romantic' stands for the freshness and spontaneity that come from individuality. At different periods and by different artists, one or the other tendency is carried to an extreme. If there is a definite overbalance on one side or the other the work fails; the classic becomes dead, monotonous, and artificial; the romantic, fantastic and eccentric. 203

It is easy to miss the presence of creative counterpoint in Wieman's four-fold analysis of the nature of God by a more casual reading of its 1-2-3-4 point structure. Upon further examination, we find it to be a highly accelerated rhythmic unitary system of deep and intense contrasts:

rhythmic contrasts

    between emerging imaginative insights

            and those already had

in critical creative interaction

occurring within expanding appreciative consciousness

creating novel unity

            in one's expanding world

creating deeper contrasts

            with other expanding worlds

    undergoing creative critical interchange

conflict creating community

Chapter VI

SUMMARY AND CONCLUSION

In our effort to contribute to further understanding of the nature of creativity in the religious philosophy of Henry Nelson Wieman, we have found in it a form of creative tension which appears in its early development and which continues with variations in its structural pattern. We found a clear expression of this tension in his first book, Religious Experience and Scientific Method.[1] The tension is between "two sides of discovery." One side is "wide open mystic awareness" of "the rich, novel fullness of concrete experience." The other side is "theorizing ... with its analysis, discrimination, definition and experimentation." When these two sides of discovery are separated, "mystic awareness flounders helplessly and blindly," while scientific theorizing "becomes a barren definition of concepts without yielding anything to enrich life..."; but "when these two are united and rightly balanced ... life becomes abundant" as exemplified by "the artist, the prophet, the moral and social reformer, the scientific genius, the religious seer...."[2]

We believe that Wieman's central problem in the development of his philosophy of creativity has been that of understanding the conditions for uniting these two sides of discovery. Our study indicates that this problem was motivational for his life commitment to religious inquiry, made first as a college senior, continuing through more than six decades, and expressed in the title of his last book, Religious Inquiry: Some Explorations (1968).

Conditions in Wieman's early life that were favorable for the creation of tension calling for religious inquiry include his home as the manse of the Presbyterian church, and his conditioning within the church as related to his study during high school years of Darwin's theory of evolution; and in college, his experiencing the contrast between the philosophy underlying Calvinistic supernaturalism, with its belief in miraculous events, and his serious study of the philosophy of idealism, with its strong commitment to logical reasoning.

Further contrast was afforded by three years of study in a Calvinistic theological seminary and consequently its award for a year of graduate work. During this time he studied the philosophy of idealism in its greater centers in Germany. Returning to the States, he served for several years in a Presbyterian pastorate for both laymen and university students. During these first three decades of Wieman's life, he was strongly conditioned in a context of contrasting philosophic tendencies by what he has called "the doing of creation" emphasized by the Judeo-Christian tradition. We see this conditioning as a fitting context for impregnation, birth, and maturing of a philosophy of creativity, if further necessary conditions can be provided for its actualization.

Wieman's reading Henri Bergson's classic philosophy of <u>Creative Evolution</u> during those years in the pastorate proved to be the necessary condition for impregnation. Bergson's contribution to the understanding of creativity, especially from the context of biology and other scientific disciplines, with his basic orientation in the whole field of philosophy, opened the way for both novel emerging insights in Wieman and also their unification, aided by Bergson's more mystical consummatory emphasis on intuition which surmounts the role of mere intellect as defined then by the physical sciences.

This experience with Bergson was indeed a kind of creative conversion for Wieman. It was significant in the formation of his decision to enter Harvard University to study for a doctorate in philosophy and to continue religious inquiry as a teacher within a college or university setting. Harvard was for him a source for further experience of tension between open mystical awareness of the massive fullness of reality and disciplined analysis of the issues of life. These two sides of inquiry were not separated in Wieman's select professors, Ralph Barton Perry and William Ernest Hocking; but Perry's philosophy was in significant respects a reconception of the radical empiricism of William James and the disciplined scientific inquiry of John Dewey; while Hocking was a critical disciple of Josiah Royce and a convert to the mysticism of the MORE in William James. Wieman's writing of his dissertation under Perry while being engaged at the same time in an intensive study of Hocking's religious philosophy of creativity as expressed in The Meaning of God in Human Experience, especially its four closing chapters on the four creative acts of God, provided the necessary conditions for further intensification of the kind of tension in him which we have described. Wieman's dissertation presented a creative organization of interests in direct opposition to Perry's theory of their ideal harmonization. He saw the latter as impractical and invalid: impractical because he could see no reason to believe that all human interests could ever be harmonized, and invalid because a world devoid of human conflict would neutralize the conditions essential for thought and action.

Instead of harmonization, Wieman proposed the clarification and organization of interests based on a reconception of Bergson's three basic categories: instinct, intellect, and intuition. Instinct he reconceived as adaptation. "Adaptive interest applies to all activities having unconscious teleology, such as automatic habit and primitive instinct." Intellect functions as scientific or instrumental interest which "includes everything done with deliberate recognition of its utility." Intuition is reconceived as functionally creative. Creative interest functions with "zest and enjoyment" in the growth of a "clarified and quickened consciousness." All of these interests, he argued, are needed in the efficiencies of living; but adaptive and instrumental interests should be so organized as to serve creative interest.

Interest, for Wieman, is a broad concept, synonymous with experience in Dewey. Creativity, in Wieman, at its highest evolutionary level yet known, is intrinsically operative within human interest or experience as creative interaction or interchange between human organisms and their environment. For Wieman, God as creativity is intrinsically creative; intelligent human commitment to divine creativity includes its total space-time span, whatever that may be; but intelligent commitment does not permit one to commit the genetic fallacy of directing his commitment to anything less than its highest, evolutionary exemplification including future possibilities for further creative advance.

Bergson's basic categories, analytically and critically reconceived by Wieman, continue to be operative in the further development of his philosophy of creativity. For example, Bergson's sense of the limitations of scientific instrumentalism remains within Wieman's sensibilities. This greater sense of limitation has served as a conditioning factor in his full acceptance of Dewey and has stimulated his search for whatever mysticism there is in Dewey. Again, Bergson's tension between intellect and intuition continues to be appreciated by Wieman because it helps Wieman to define it more fully as it operates within his own sensibilities. Wieman, as with many others, has had difficulty in discovering the possibility of a creative connection between intellect and intuition in Bergson. However, we have found that Bergson's own struggle with this problem led him to believe in the further creative evolution of intellect as the hoped-for solution. Wieman seems to have accepted this suggestion, for in his Harvard dissertation he says:

> While intelligence has been developed as a means in the course of biological evolution, our proposition is that in human life it becomes the supreme end both of individual and of social existence.³

Therefore, Wieman seems to have identified creative interest with intelligence, which gives further indication of his affinity with Dewey's position.

But Wieman's further religious inquiry into the nature of creativity was highly stimulated also by William Ernest Hocking. We discover tension operative in Hocking's principle of alternation between work and worship, intelligent analytic work and mystical awareness in devotion to God. Wieman accepted this principle but neither he nor Hocking was wholly satisfied with it. Hocking gives intimations of a mystical unity which surmounts the paradoxical nature of the principle. The tension in Wieman, however, is intensified. Meland sees it as a "stumbling-block" in Wieman's philosophy of creativity. Three decades after Wieman closed his work with Hocking at Harvard, Wieman presented an innovative reconception of Hocking's four fundamental acts of God expressed in his closing chapters of The Meaning of God in Human Experience. Wieman criticizes and expands Hocking's term "creative event" and uses it to designate what he, himself, means by the four-fold nature of God. This he presents as the basis of his philosophy of creativity in his work, The Source of Human Good. But Wieman sees the creative event, and also any other event, as more than man may be able to analyze, think or know in its fullness. Therefore mystical awareness of the rich massive fullness of the reality of God is essential to further analytic understanding of God's nature. But mystical awareness alone does not yield knowledge of God or any other event. The

Summary and Conclusion / 189

term "knowledge" is used by Wieman to refer to the highly analyzed raw data of experience which have been subjected to sensitive feeling awareness combined with disciplined observations in a context of consistent reasoning, yielding testable hypotheses used experimentally, and either negated or verified by positive or negative correlativity. We believe that this is the context for understanding the further import of creativity in Wieman. We shall state what the nature of it really is after further consideration of creativity in Wieman as related especially to Whitehead, James, and Dewey.

Wieman, on reading Whitehead during the twenties, found him to be profoundly impressive. He saw in Whitehead possibilities for the emergence of a neo-religious metaphysics before Whitehead had begun to express his thought in those terms. Wieman's Religious Experience and Scientific Method is an innovative expression of what he was referring to as a possibility in Whitehead; and before Wieman's volume was ready for the press, he discovered that Whitehead had moved in this direction in his Science and the Modern World, published in May 1925. Wieman's volume was not published until February 1926. Then, when Whitehead's Religion in the Making appeared in September 1926, Wieman found in it a great contribution to the philosophy of creativity. After the publication of his article[4] on Whitehead's concept of God, he was recognized for his ability as an interpreter of Whitehead's neo-religious metaphysics.

Wieman found in Whitehead, especially in Process and Reality, a highly technical analysis of the classic tension-producing problem of relating one's immediate mystical awareness of God as Being to God as actual Becoming. However significant Whitehead's formal statement of the relationship--in terms of both "The many become one, and are increased by one"[5] and his less formal statement, "Thus the 'production of novel togetherness' is the ultimate notion embodied in the term 'concrescence'"[6]--these forms of expression did not satisfy Wieman's empirical bent. Furthermore, Whitehead's distinction between God and creativity was not acceptable to him. For Wieman, God as known is the empirical structure of creative becoming. The being of creativity as creativity is becoming.

In recent years, Wieman has become increasingly critical of Whitehead's more abstract speculative tendencies, not only in Whitehead, but also in Whiteheadian scholars.

In Wieman's last book, Religious Inquiry, his adverse criticism of these tendencies indicates a breaking away in favor of a more empirical philosophy of creativity which would be more directly involved in the existential situation of human conflict and its transformation by empirical means. However, one of the finest tributes given Whitehead in recent years, is, we believe, Wieman's summary interpretation of Whitehead's philosophy as aesthetic. From this aesthetic perspective, we see how meaningful Whitehead's philosophy can be for further creative transformation of the tension in Wieman.

Wieman's epistemological neo-realism, which seems to hover above and behind him like a guardian angel, is ever present to aid him in seeing events and their relations as they really are. Perry and Whitehead seem to belong to this company, but this guardianship seems to create something of a problem for Wieman, especially in his understanding of Dewey and of Dewey's understanding of Wieman. From this context Wieman has interpreted Dewey's "ideal, natural forces and conditions, and imagination" as events in sheer objectivity, related though not to be confused each with the other, or with the referent for the term "God"; while Dewey, who is less sensitive to epistemological neo-realism, sees "ideal, natural forces and conditions, and imagination" as not only intrinsically interwoven in their relations, but also contextually interwoven with what he should call "God." Therefore, Dewey and others less sensitive to this "angel" think that the locus for God, according to Wieman, is somewhere exterior to human experience, which is really shocking for Wieman since for him this is not at all the case.

With the aid of Nolan P. Jacobson, who had done his doctoral work with Wieman, Dewey, in correspondence with Jacobson, confessed that he had acquired a prejudice against Wieman's view. [7] The present author, on the other hand, after further examination of Wieman's Intellectual Foundation of Faith, "John Dewey Answers," Chapter Two, asked Wieman to read it again and to comment on it, and as a result, received from Wieman a paper confessing his misinterpretation of Dewey. [8] The reconciliation seems especially significant for both the affirmation of Dewey's naturalistic theism and the clarification of Wieman's creative tension between the human effort to provide conditions for the actualization of ideal ends and the locus of God in this context of what Dewey has called "imagination," and what Wieman calls "creative interchange." However, we see this reconciliation between Dewey and Wieman as being worthy of further critical study, more at least than we can give it at this time.

We have observed that there is a core of common meaning in what we have called the two levels of Dewey's living faith and Wieman's two-level commitment. The common meaning is in the kind of creative tension in each case. In Wieman, it is the creative tension which we have described above in various contexts in a variety of ways. The first level or ultimate commitment is "to whatever does in truth operate in human life to make life better" before one knows either <u>what</u> it is or "what the greater good might be." The second-level commitment is to that religious inquiry which yields evidence of the nature of that which operates in human life to make life better. In Wieman, these two levels are interdependent and at best operate through creative interchange. [9]

The two levels in Dewey's living faith are: (1) faith in man's native or aboriginal heritage which functions correlatively in nature without man's wish or plan; (2) faith in the capacity of man to learn how to participate intelligently in the process of providing conditions which may prove to be correlative with genuinely ideal ends, effecting a self-facilitating creative process. [10]

Wieman likens Dewey's living faith as operative in his daily living to that which Jesus Christ had in the normal course of his every-day life. Yet, whatever excellence exists in Dewey's faith, further understanding of it may well depend on his rich heritage from William James who defined for Dewey the nature of mentality as operative intelligence at work in the correlation of means-ends. Furthermore, James' <u>Psychology</u> gave to Dewey an analysis of reflex action which was used by Dewey for constructing his theory of the reflex arc and consequently the creative unifying processes of nature which occur in the process of learning through communication and communion. [11] We believe that this continuing creative process is at least suggestive of what James meant by the "MORE." This suggested dimension of the MORE in James is certainly functional in Wieman's mystical awareness of God in his first or ultimate level commitment. Furthermore, we have found that Wieman's empirical theology is related in depth to the radical empiricism in James and Dewey, even as he seeks to go beyond it in expressing definitively and empirically what operates in human life with such character and power that it will transform man as he cannot transform himself, saving him from evil and leading him to the best that human life can ever reach, provided that he meet the required conditions.[12]

CHAPTER NOTES

PREFACE

1. Henry Nelson Wieman, "Intellectual Autobiography" (unpub., Carbondale: Southern Illinois University, Archives, 1957), p. 1. [See abstract of "Intellectual Autobiography," in The Empirical Theology of Henry Nelson Wieman, ed. by Robert W. Bretall, Vol. IV of The Library of Living Theology, ed. by Charles W. Kegley and Robert W. Bretall (New York: Macmillan 1963), pp. 3-18. Also an Arcturus Book (Carbondale: Southern Illinois University Press, 1969).]

2. Henry Nelson Wieman, Religious Experience and Scientific Method (New York: Macmillan, 1926), p. 197. Republished, Carbondale: Southern Illinois University Press, 1971.

CHAPTER I

1. Wieman, "Intellectual Autobiography," unpub., p. 57.

2. Ibid., p. 1.

3. Henry Nelson Wieman, Intellectual Foundation of Faith (New York: Philosophical Library, 1961), p. 55.

4. Ibid.

5. Henry Nelson Wieman, The Source of Human Good, (Chicago: University of Chicago Press, 1946), p. 299. [Republished as an Arcturus Book (Carbondale: Southern Illinois University Press, 1964.]

6. Wieman, Intellectual Foundation of Faith, p. 55.

7. Henry Nelson Wieman, "The Organization of Interests" (unpub. Ph.D. dissert., Dept. of Philosophy, Harvard University, 1917), p. 33. [Also Southern Illinois University Archives.] Chapters I, "Introductory," and II, "Adaptive, Instrumental, and Creative Interests," Henry Nelson Wieman, Seeking a Faith for a New Age (Metuchen, N.J.: Scarecrow Press, 1975), Cedric L. Hepler, editor.

8. Wieman, "Intellectual Autobiography," unpub., pp. 8, 9.

9. Ibid., p. 8.

10. Ibid.

11. Wieman, "Intellectual Autobiography," unpub., p. 11.
12. Ibid.
13. Ibid.
14. Ibid.
15. Ibid.
16. Ibid.
17. Henry Nelson Wieman, "Empiricism in Religious Philosophy," in Philosophy, Religion, and the Coming World Civilization; Essays in Honor of William Ernest Hocking, ed. by Leroy S. Rouner (The Hague: Martinus Nijhoff, 1966), p. 185. Republished in Wieman, Seeking a Faith for a New Age (Metuchen, N.J.: Scarecrow Press, 1975), Cedric L. Hepler, editor.
18. Wieman, "Intellectual Autobiography," unpub., pp. 11-12.
19. Ibid., p. 12.
20. Ibid., p. 11.
21. Ibid.
22. Ibid.

CHAPTER II

1. Wieman, "The Organization of Interests," p. 1.
2. Ralph Barton Perry, "The Definition of Value," The Journal of Philosophy, Psychology, and Scientific Methods, XI (March 12, 1914), 149.
3. Ibid., p. 153.
4. Ibid., p. 152.
5. Ibid., p. 153.
6. Ibid., p. 152.
7. Ibid., pp. 152-153.
8. Wieman, "The Organization of Interests," p. 2.
9. Ibid.
10. Ibid.
11. Ibid., p. 3.
12. Ibid.
13. Ibid.
14. Ibid., p. 4.
15. Ibid., p. 7.
16. Ibid., p. 1.
17. Perry, "The Definition of Value," p. 157.

Chapter Notes--II / 195

18. Ibid., p. 158.

19. Ralph Barton Perry, "Contemporary Philosophies of Religion," The Harvard Theological Review, VII (July 1, 1914), 378-395.

20. Ibid., p. 395.

21. Ralph Barton Perry, Realms of Value (Cambridge, Mass.: Harvard University Press, 1954), p. 119.

22. Ibid., p. 122.

23. Ibid., p. 123.

24. Ibid.

25. Ibid., p. 132.

26. Ibid., p. 133.

27. Ibid., p. 134.

28. Ibid.

29. Wieman, "The Organization of Interests," pp. 12-33.

30. Ibid., p. 8.

31. Ibid., p. 7.

32. Ibid., p. 8.

33. Ibid., pp. 8-9.

34. Ibid., p. 9.

35. Ibid.

36. Wieman, "Intellectual Autobiography," unpublished, p. 12.

37. Henry Nelson Wieman, "Sources of Moral Confusion," Man's Ultimate Commitment (Carbondale: Southern Illinois University Press, 1958), Chapter VI, pp. 117-134. [Republished as an Arcturus Book, 1965.]

38. Ibid., p. 130.

39. Ibid.

40. Ibid.

41. Ibid., pp. 130-131.

42. Ibid., p. 118.

43. Ibid., pp. 118-119.

44. Ibid., pp. 120-121.

45. Ibid., p. 121.

46. Ibid., p. 122.

47. Henry Nelson Wieman, "God and Value," in Religious Realism, ed. D. C. Macintosh (New York: Macmillan, 1931), p. 158. Republished in Wieman, Seeking a Faith for a New Age,

(Metuchen, N.J.: Scarecrow Press, 1975), Cedric L. Hepler, editor.

    48. Ibid.

    49. Wieman, Religious Experience and Scientific Method, p. 6.

    50. Ibid., pp. 160-161.

    51. Ibid., pp. 161-163.

    52. Ibid., p. 161.

    53. Ibid., p. 160.

    54. Ibid., p. 197; vide supra, pp. xviii-xix, at n. 2.

CHAPTER III

    1. William Ernest Hocking, The Meaning of God in Human Experience (New Haven, Conn.: Yale University Press, 1912), pp. xix-xx.

    2. Ibid., p. xx.

    3. Ibid.

    4. Wieman, "Empiricism in Religious Philosophy," p. 184.

    5. Vide supra, Chapter II.

    6. Wieman, "Empiricism in Religious Philosophy," p. 185.

    7. Ibid., p. 184.

    8. Ibid., pp. 181-197.

    9. Hocking, The Meaning of God in Human Experience, p. xxii.

    10. Rouner, Philosophy, Religion, and the Coming World Civilization, pp. 14-15.

    11. Ibid., p. 16.

    12. Ibid.

    13. John E. Smith, Introduction to The World and the Individual, by Josiah Royce, Vol. I (New York: Dover Publications, 1959), p. x.

    14. Ibid.

    15. Leroy S. Rouner, Within Human Experience (Cambridge, Mass.: Harvard University Press, 1969), p. 16.

    16. Ibid., p. 16.

    17. Ibid.

    18. Ibid., p. 19.

19. Hocking, The Meaning of God in Human Experience, p. 246.

20. Rouner, Within Human Experience, p. 22.

21. Ibid., p. 23.

22. Ibid., p. 25. From James' letter to Miss Frances R. Morse, April 12, 1900, quoted in The Thought and Character of William James by Ralph Barton Perry (Boston: Little, Brown, 1935), II, pp. 326-327.

23. Rouner, Within Human Experience, p. 24.

24. Hocking, The Meaning of God in Human Experience, p. xv.

25. Ibid.

26. Ibid., pp. 161-162.

27. Wieman, The Source of Human Good, p. 195.

28. Hocking, The Meaning of God in Human Experience, p. xxii.

29. William Ernest Hocking, "The Elementary Experience of Other Conscious Being in Its Relations to the Elementary Experience of Physical and Reflexive Objects" (unpub. Ph.D. dissert., Harvard University, 1904; in Archives, Harvard's Widener Library).

30. Richard C. Gilman, The Bibliography of William Ernest Hocking from 1898 to 1951 (Waterville, Me.: Colby College, 1951).

31. D. S. Robinson, "Hocking's Contribution to Metaphysical Idealism," in Philosophy, Religion, and the Coming World Civilization, ed. Rouner, p. 62.

32. Ibid.

33. Ibid.

34. Hocking, Preface in Royce's Metaphysics by Gabriel Marcel, as quoted in "Hocking's Contribution to Metaphysical Idealism" by Robinson in Philosophy, Religion, and the Coming World Civilization, ed. Rouner, p. 61.

35. Ibid.

36. Ibid.

37. Ibid.

38. Hocking, The Meaning of God in Human Experience, p. 463.

39. Ibid., p. 445.

40. Ibid., p. 462.

41. See documented reference to Hocking's specific use of the concept, "creative event," and the more limited function of its referent than in Wieman's use of it, pp. 37-42 supra.

198 / Chapter Notes--III

42. Hocking, The Meaning of God in Human Experience, pp. 445-446, 462.

43. Ibid., p. 460.

44. Wieman, "Intellectual Autobiography," in The Empirical Theology of Henry Nelson Wieman, ed. Bretall, p. 6.

45. Ibid.

46. Vide supra, p. 28 at n. 34.

47. Wieman, Religious Experience and Scientific Method, p. 303.

48. Ibid.

49. Vide supra, p. 30 at n. 43.

50. Vide supra, p. 1 at n. 2.

51. Wieman, Religious Experience and Scientific Method, p. 9.

52. Wieman, "Intellectual Autobiography," in The Empirical Theology, p. 6.

53. Hocking, The Meaning of God in Human Experience, pp. 450-451.

54. Ibid., p. 451.

55. Ibid.

56. Ibid., p. 460.

57. Ibid., pp. 447.

58. William Ernest Hocking, The Coming World Civilization (New York: Harper, 1956), Appendix pp. 190-199. First published in The Christian Century, March 8, 1933.

59. Hocking, The Coming World Civilization, p. 193.

60. Ibid., pp. 198-199.

61. Ibid., p. 199.

62. Ralph Barton Perry, Present Philosophical Tendencies (New York: Longmans, Green, 1912), p. 321. In this passage Perry includes quotations from G. E. Moore, as follows: "The Refutation of Idealism," Mind, n.s., vol. XII (1903), pp. 442, 449, 453. Cf. also, "The Nature and Reality of Objects of Perception," Proceedings of the Aristotelian Society, n.s., vol. VI (1905-06).

63. Wieman, "The Organization of Interests," p. 1.

64. Ibid.

65. Wieman, The Source of Human Good, Chapter III, pp. 54-83.

66. Vide supra, p. 36 at n. 20.

67. Wieman, Religious Experience and Scientific Method, Chapter VI, pp. 160-188.

68. Hocking, The Meaning of God in Human Experience, pp. 462-484.
69. Ibid., p. 463.
70. Wieman, The Source of Human Good, pp. 56-83.
71. Hocking, The Meaning of God in Human Experience, p. 462.
72. Ibid., p. 465.
73. Ibid., p. 467.
74. Ibid., p. 466.
75. Ibid., p. 468.
76. Ibid., p. 467.
77. Ibid., pp. 465-466.
78. Ibid., pp. 470-471.
79. Ibid., p. 470.
80. Wieman, The Source of Human Good, Chapter III and the "Technical Postscript," pp. 297-309.
81. Wieman, "The Organization of Interests," Chapter XIII, "God in Creative Religion," pp. [239-254].
82. Henry Nelson Wieman, "Anxiety Mastered by Commitment," Religious Inquiry: Some Explorations (Boston: Beacon Press, 1968), pp. 67-95.
83. Hocking, The Meaning of God in Human Experience, p. 137.
84. Ibid., p. 472.
85. Wieman, Religious Experience and Scientific Method, p. 84.
86. Hocking, The Meaning of God in Human Experience, p. 485.
87. Ibid., pp. 488-502.
88. Ibid., p. 489.
89. Ibid., p. 502.
90. Ibid., p. 503.
91. Ibid.
92. Ibid., p. 504.
93. Ibid.
94. Ibid., p. 505.
95. Ibid., pp. 505-509.
96. Ibid., p. 510.

97. Ibid., pp. 511-513.
98. Hocking, The Meaning of God in Human Experience, p. 502, as quoted by Wieman in "The Organization of Interests," p. [254].
99. Wieman, "The Organization of Interests," p. [254].
100. Ibid.
101. Ibid.
102. Application and Record of Work of Henry Nelson Wieman as a student in Park College, 1904-1907, Carbondale, Southern Illinois University, Archives.
103. Personal observations and interpretations by the author from many courses with Wieman.
104. Wieman, The Source of Human Good, p. 59.
105. Ibid., p. 62.
106. Ibid., p. 59.
107. Ibid.
108. Ibid., pp. 62-63.
109. Hocking, The Meaning of God in Human Experience, p. 516.
110. Ibid., p. 518.
111. Ibid., p. 520.
112. Ibid., p. 521.
113. Ibid., pp. 522-524.
114. Wieman, The Source of Human Good, p. 64.
115. Ibid., p. 58.
116. Ibid., p. 65.
117. Vide supra, n. 1, p. 51, at n. 59.
118. Wieman, The Source of Human Good, p. 66.
119. Ibid.
120. Ibid.
121. Ibid., p. 67.
122. Ibid.
123. Ibid., pp. 68-69.
124. Hocking, The Meaning of God in Human Experience, pp. 14-26.
125. Ibid., p. 205.
126. Wieman, Man's Ultimate Commitment, p. 305.
127. Vide supra, Chapter II.

128. Wieman, The Source of Human Good, p. 64.
129. Ibid., p. 65.
130. Wieman, "Empiricism in Religious Philosophy," p. 185.
131. Ibid.
132. William Ernest Hocking, Experiment in Education (Chicago: Henry Regnery, 1954), p. 226, quoted by Wieman in "Empiricism in Religious Philosophy," p. 184.
133. Wieman, "Empiricism in Religious Philosophy," p. 186.
134. Ibid.
135. Webster's Third New International Dictionary (Springfield, Mass.: G. & C. Merriam Co., 1961) "coherence," p. 440.
136. Wieman, "Empiricism in Religious Philosophy," p. 187.
137. Ibid., p. 186.
138. Ibid., pp. 185-186.
139. Hocking, The Meaning of God in Human Experience, p. 225.
140. Ibid., pp. 206, 223.
141. Wieman, "Empiricism in Religious Philosophy," pp. 192-193.
142. Hocking, The Meaning of God in Human Experience, p. 110.
143. Ibid., p. 175.
144. Ibid., p. 203.
145. Wieman, The Source of Human Good, p. 93.
146. Ibid., p. 90.
147. Ibid., p. 91.
148. Ibid., p. 92.
149. Ibid., p. 88.
150. Ibid., p. 93.
151. Hocking, The Meaning of God in Human Experience, p. 418.
152. Ibid., pp. 424-425.
153. Ibid., p. 427.
154. Ibid.
155. Vide supra, pp. 55-59.
156. Wieman, "Empiricism in Religious Philosophy," pp. 188-189.
157. Ibid., p. 189.

158. Ibid.
159. Wieman, Religious Inquiry: Some Explorations, p. 80.
160. Ibid., p. 81.
161. Ibid., p. 94.
162. Ibid., p. 81.
163. Ibid., pp. 94-95.
164. Ibid., p. 82.
165. Ibid., p. 83.
166. Ibid.
167. Vide supra, p. 62, at n. 154.
168. Vide supra, pp. 63-67.
169. Henri Bergson, Creative Evolution, trans. by Arthur Mitchell (New York: Henry Holt, 1911; New York: Random House, 1944 [Modern Library]).
170. Vide supra, p. 5, at n. 20.

CHAPTER IV

1. Henry Nelson Wieman and Bernard Eugene Meland, American Philosophies of Religion (Chicago: Willett, Clark, 1936), p. 212.
2. Vide supra, p. 4, at n. 12.
3. Wieman, "Intellectual Autobiography," unpub., p. 13.
4. Bergson, Creative Evolution, p. 14.
5. Ibid., p. xxv, n. 1.
6. Ibid., p. 25.
7. Vide supra, p. 72, at n. 4.
8. Ibid., p. 273.
9. Ibid., pp. 373-374.
10. Ibid., p. 372.
11. Ibid., pp. 372-373.
12. Vide supra, p. 72, at n. 5.
13. Ibid., p. 373.
14. Ibid., p. 290.
15. Ibid., p. 195.
16. Ibid.
17. Ibid., pp. 324-325.
18. Vide supra, pp. 65-66, at n. 163.

19. Ibid., p. 195.
20. Ibid., p. 282.
21. Ibid., pp. 291-292.
22. Vide supra, p. 4, at n. 12.
23. Wieman, "The Organization of Interests," p. 11.
24. Ibid., p. 4.
25. Vide supra, pp. 8-19.
26. Vide supra, pp. 55-59.
27. Vide supra, p. 5, at n. 20.
28. Wieman, The Source of Human Good, p. 303.
29. Ibid., p. 194.
30. Vide supra, p. 72, at n. 5.
31. Wieman, "Intellectual Autobiography," unpub., pp. 40-43.
32. Ibid., p. 41.
33. Ibid., p. 43.
34. Vide supra, p. 72.
35. Wieman, Religious Experience and Scientific Method, p. 10.
36. Bergson, Creative Evolution, p. 168.
37. Ibid., pp. 162-163.
38. Ibid., p. 194.
39. Ibid., p. 148.
40. Ibid., p. 162.
41. Ibid., p. 194.
42. Ibid., p. 274.
43. Wieman, Religious Experience and Scientific Method, p. 43.
44. Ibid.
45. Ibid., pp. 43-44.
46. Wieman, "Empiricism in Religious Philosophy," p. 186.
47. Vide supra, p. 76-77, at n. 20.
48. Vide supra, p. 63, at item (1).
49. Bergson, Creative Evolution, p. 295.
50. Wieman, Religious Experience and Scientific Method, p. 383.
51. Wieman, Religious Inquiry, pp. 195-196.
52. Wieman, The Source of Human Good, p. 194.

53. Alfred North Whitehead, Process and Reality (New York: Macmillan, 1929), p. vii.

54. Lucien Price, Dialogues of Alfred North Whitehead (Boston: Little, Brown, 1954), p. 345.

55. Ibid., p. 302.

56. Ibid., p. 346.

57. Ibid.

58. Whitehead, Process and Reality, p. 31.

59. Ibid., p. 32.

60. Bergson, Creative Evolution, p. 195.

61. Ibid., p. 282.

62. Whitehead, Process and Reality, p. 32.

63. Bergson, Creative Evolution, p. 179.

64. Wieman, Man's Ultimate Commitment, p. 4.

65. Ibid., p. 305.

66. Alfred North Whitehead, Modes of Thought (New York: Macmillan, 1938), pp. 12-13.

67. Whitehead, Process and Reality, p. 79.

68. Alfred North Whitehead, Science and the Modern World (New York: Macmillan, 1925; and New York: New American Library of World Literature, 1948 [a Mentor Book]), p. 133.

69. Alfred North Whitehead, Religion in the Making (New York: Macmillan, 1926), p. 108.

70. Alfred North Whitehead, Adventures of Ideas (New York: Macmillan, 1933), p. 245.

71. A. H. Johnson, Whitehead's Theory of Reality (Boston: Beacon Press, 1952), p. 168.

72. Whitehead, Process and Reality, p. 41.

73. Wieman, Religious Experience and Scientific Method, pp. 103-104.

74. Ibid., p. 152.

75. Ibid., pp. 152-153.

76. Ibid., p. 153.

77. Alfred North Whitehead, The Concept of Nature (Cambridge University Press, 1920), p. 73; in Religious Experience and Scientific Method, p. 153.

78. Wieman, Religious Experience and Scientific Method, p. 153.

79. Ibid., p. 181.

Chapter Notes--IV / 205

80. Henry Nelson Wieman, The Wrestle of Religion with Truth (New York: Macmillan, 1927), p. 181.

81. Ibid.

82. "In the place of Aristotle's God as Prime Mover, we require God as the Principle of Concretion." Whitehead, Science and the Modern World, p. 174.

83. Wieman, The Wrestle of Religion with Truth, p. 184.

84. Ibid., p. 183.

85. Ibid., p. 185.

86. Whitehead, Process and Reality, p. 326.

87. Wieman, Religious Experience and Scientific Method, pp. 180-181.

88. Whitehead, Process and Reality, p. 43.

89. Ibid., pp. 52-53.

90. Ibid., p. 42.

91. Ibid., p. 323.

92. Ibid., pp. 27-28.

93. Ibid., p. 32.

94. Ibid., p. 35.

95. Ibid., pp. 320-321.

96. Ibid., pp. 64, 113.

97. Whitehead, Modes of Thought, p. 133.

98. Whitehead, Science and the Modern World, pp. 2-3.

99. Ibid., p. 3.

100. Alfred North Whitehead, The Function of Reason (Princeton, N.J.: Princeton University Press, 1929; and Boston: Beacon Press, 1958), p. 80.

101. Whitehead, Process and Reality, p. 7.

102. Whitehead, The Function of Reason, pp. 80-81.

103. Ibid., pp. 81-83.

104. Wieman, The Wrestle of Religion with Truth, p. 181.

105. Whitehead, Process and Reality, p. 252.

106. Ibid., p. 252.

107. Ibid.

108. Ibid.

109. Ibid., p. 324.

110. Ibid., p. 349.

111. Ibid., p. 253.

112. Schubert M. Ogden, "Present Prospects for Empirical Theology," in The Future of Empirical Theology, ed. Bernard Eugene Meland, Vol. VII of Essays in Divinity, Jerald C. Brauer, gen. ed. (Chicago: University of Chicago Press, 1969), pp. 81-82.

113. Ibid., p. 81.
114. Whitehead, Process and Reality, pp. 270-274.
115. Ibid., p. 239.
116. Henry Nelson Wieman, "Perception and Cognition," The Journal of Philosophy, XL (February 4, 1943), 73.
117. Ibid., p. 74.
118. Ibid.
119. Ibid., p. 75.
120. Ibid.
121. Whitehead, Process and Reality, p. 66.
122. Ibid., p. 32.
123. Ibid., p. 35.
124. Ibid., pp. 32, 70, 163.
125. Ibid., p. 246.
126. Ibid., p. 247.
127. Ibid., p. 286.
128. Ibid., p. 294.
129. Vide supra, p. 93.
130. Henry Nelson Wieman, "Summation of Whitehead's Philosophy" (unpub. essay, Carbondale, Southern Illinois University, Archives, n.d.), p. 1.
131. Ibid.
132. Ibid.
133. Ibid.
134. Wieman, The Source of Human Good, p. 138.
135. Ibid., p. 134.
136. Ibid., pp. 139-140.
137. Ibid., pp. 149-153.
138. Ibid., p. 156.
139. Ibid., p. 158.
140. Ibid., p. 159.
141. Ibid., p. 161.
142. Ibid., p. 168.

143. Ibid., p. 192.
144. Whitehead, Process and Reality, p. 47.
145. Ibid., p. 341.
146. Whitehead, Religion in the Making, p. 100.
147. Wieman, The Source of Human Good, p. 192.
148. Whitehead, Process and Reality, p. 47.
149. Whitehead, Religion in the Making, p. 152.
150. Whitehead, Process and Reality, p. 522.
151. Whitehead, Adventures of Ideas, p. 31.
152. Whitehead, Science and the Modern World, p. 192.
153. Wieman, The Source of Human Good, p. 189.
154. Ibid., p. 195.
155. Wieman, "Intellectual Autobiography," unpub., pp. 14-15.
156. Wieman and Meland, American Philosophies of Religion, p. 240.
157. Wieman, The Source of Human Good, pp. 193-194.
158. Vide supra, p. 100.
159. Wieman, Religious Inquiry, pp. 39-40.
160. Ibid., p. 40. In a personal conversation between the present author and Charles Hartshorne at the 1970 meeting of the American Philosophical Assoc., Western Division, Hartshorne said: "I agree with everything that Wieman affirms. It is what he denies that I disagree with." He commented on his own treatment of Wieman's philosophy without any reference to it on my part, by saying: "In what I have done, I should have given more consideration to what Wieman is saying." Following this conversation, Hartshorne said, in a letter dated May 11, 1970: "The more I think about it the more I regret not making explicit connections with Wieman's splendid analysis of the human forms of 'creative synthesis' when discussing the topic in my new book, especially in the value chapter. Not only would this have been fairer, it would have greatly strengthened the book in its practical-ethical-religious bearings. I think I can defend my views against his sharp attack in that recent article, but I have no defence at all for having failed to recognize and profit by his important work. This was a real blunder. I must look for an opportunity to do better."
161. Ibid., pp. 40-41.
162. Ibid., p. 41.
163. Ibid., pp. 41-42.
164. Ibid., p. 44.
165. Ibid., p. 37.

166. Wieman, The Source of Human Good, p. 193.

CHAPTER V

1. Wieman, "Intellectual Autobiography," in The Empirical Theology of Henry Nelson Wieman, pp. 8-9.
2. Jo Ann Boydston, gen. ed., John Dewey, The Early Works, 1882-1898; vol. 3--1889-1892, Early Essays and Outlines of a Critical Theory of Ethics (Carbondale: Southern Illinois University Press, 1969), p. 211.
3. Ibid.
4. Ibid.
5. Ibid.
6. Ibid., p. 212.
7. Ibid.
8. William James, The Principles of Psychology, Vol. 1 (New York: Dover Publications, 1950), p. 8 [first pub. by Henry Holt, 1890].
9. Ibid.
10. Boydston, Dewey, Early Essays and Outlines..., p. 212.
11. Ibid.
12. Ibid.
13. Vide supra, p. 121, at n. 9.
14. John Dewey, Human Nature and Conduct (New York: Random House, 1930 [Modern Library]), p. 143 [first pub. by Henry Holt, 1922].
15. Ibid., pp. 142-143.
16. Vide supra, p. 123, at n. 15.
17. Dewey, Human Nature and Conduct, p. 289.
18. Ibid.
19. Ibid., pp. 289-290.
20. Ibid., pp. 288-289.
21. Ibid., p. 289.
22. John Dewey, Experience and Nature (Chicago: Open Court Pub. Co., 1925), p. vi.
23. John Dewey, Art As Experience (New York: G. P. Putman's Sons, 1934 [Capricorn Books]), pp. 18-19.
24. Ibid., p. 19.
25. Ibid., p. 195.

26. Dewey, Experience and Nature, p. 23.

27. Henry Nelson Wieman, "Philosophers' Dean: The Dual Dewey," The Christian Register, CXXVIII (November, 1949), 22-24.

28. Henry Nelson Wieman, "Religion in Dewey's Experience and Nature," The Journal of Religion, V (September, 1925), 519-542.

29. Wieman, Religious Experience and Scientific Method, p. 322.

30. Ibid.

31. Dewey, Experience and Nature, p. 196.

32. Wieman, Religious Experience and Scientific Method, p. 334.

33. Dewey, Experience and Nature, p. 196.

34. Wieman, Religious Experience and Scientific Method, p. 335.

35. Ibid., p. 339.

36. Ibid.

37. Ibid., p. 342, quoting Dewey in Experience and Nature, p. 222.

38. Ibid., quoting Dewey, Experience and Nature, p. 221.

39. Wieman, Religious Experience and Scientific Method, p. 343.

40. Ibid., p. 345.

41. Ibid., p. 347.

42. Dewey, Experience and Nature, p. 420, quoted by Wieman in Religious Experience and Scientific Method, p. 349.

43. Ibid., quoting Dewey, Experience and Nature, p. 420.

44. Ibid., p. 418.

45. Wieman, Religious Experience and Scientific Method, pp. 349-350, quoting Dewey, Experience and Nature, p. 420.

46. Ibid., p. 350, in Experience and Nature, p. 420.

47. Ibid., p. 350, quoting Dewey.

48. Ibid.

49. Ibid., p. 351.

50. Information received by the author from personal conversation with Wieman.

51. Dewey, Human Nature and Conduct, pp. 330-331.

52. Ibid., p. 331.

53. Ibid.

210 / Chapter Notes--V

54. Ibid., pp. 331-332.

55. Wieman, Religious Experience and Scientific Method, p. 352.

56. Henry Nelson Wieman, Douglas Clyde Macintosh and Max Carl Otto, Is There a God? A Conversation with an Introduction by Charles Clayton Morrison (Chicago: Willett, Clark, 1932). Morrison was the editor of The Christian Century.

57. John Dewey, "A God or The God," The Christian Century, L (February 8, 1933), 193-196.

58. Ibid., p. 194.

59. Ibid., p. 196.

60. Ibid.

61. Ibid.

62. Henry Nelson Wieman, "Mr. Wieman and Mr. Macintosh 'Converse' with Mr. Dewey," The Christian Century, L (March 1, 1933), 299, quoting Dewey.

63. Ibid.

64. Ibid., pp. 299-300.

65. Ibid., p. 300.

66. Ibid.

67. John Dewey, "Dr. Dewey Replies," The Christian Century, L (March 22, 1933), 394.

68. Ibid.

69. Ibid., p. 395.

70. Henry Nelson Wieman, "Mr. Wieman Replies to Mr. Dewey," The Christian Century, L (April 5, 1933), 467. Here again we observe Wieman's neo-realistic epistemology functioning freely and fully by subordination of the concept of God to the objective reality of God. Whether Dewey gets the full force of it is problematic. Of course "objective reality of God," for Wieman, does not imply that God is an "external factor," either external to nature or to human experience as a part of nature.

71. Ibid.

72. Ibid., pp. 466-467.

73. Vide supra, p. 140.

74. Ibid., p. 467.

75. Ibid.

76. Ibid.

77. Vide supra, p. 34.

78. The Editor's Introduction to Bernard Eugene Meland, "Is God Many or One?" The Christian Century, L (May 31, 1933), 725-726, quoting Dewey.

79. Bernard Eugene Meland, "Is God Many or One?" The Christian Century, L (May 31, 1933), 725.

80. Ibid.

81. Ibid., p. 726.

82. Ibid.

83. Ibid.

84. Ibid.

85. Ibid.

86. Ibid.

87. Henry Nelson Wieman, "Is God Many or One?" The Christian Century, L (May 31, 1933), 726.

88. Ibid., p. 727.

89. Ibid.

90. Ibid.

91. Ibid.

92. Ibid.

93. Wieman, "The Organization of Interests," p. 254.

94. John Dewey, A Common Faith (New Haven, Conn.: Yale University Press, 1934).

95. Henry Nelson Wieman, "John Dewey's Common Faith," The Christian Century, LI (November 14, 1934), 1450.

96. Ibid.

97. Ibid.

98. Ibid., p. 1450, quoting Dewey.

99. Dewey, A Common Faith, p. 25.

100. Wieman, "John Dewey's Common Faith," p. 1451.

101. Dewey, A Common Faith, pp. 51-52.

102. Wieman, "John Dewey's Common Faith," p. 1452.

103. Ibid.

104. Ibid.

105. Ibid.

106. Ibid., pp. 1451-1452.

107. Ibid., p. 1452, quoting Dewey.

108. Ibid., quoting Dewey.

109. Wieman, "John Dewey's Common Faith," p. 1452.

110. Vide supra, p. 149, at n. 96.

111. Edwin Ewart Aubrey, "Is John Dewey a Theist?" The Christian Century, LI (December 5, 1934), 1550.

112. Ibid.

113. Ibid.

114. Ibid.

115. Ibid.

116. Ibid.

117. Ibid.

118. Ibid.

119. Henry Nelson Wieman, "Is John Dewey a Theist?" The Christian Century, LI (December 5, 1934), 1550-1551.

120. Ibid., p. 1551.

121. Ibid.

122. John Dewey, "Is John Dewey a Theist?" The Christian Century, LI (December 5, 1934), p. 1551.

123. Ibid.

124. Ibid.

125. Ibid., p. 1552.

126. Ibid.

127. Vide supra, p. 92, at notes 76 and 78.

128. Wieman, "Is John Dewey a Theist?", p. 1552.

129. Ibid.

130. Ibid.

131. Ibid.

132. Ibid., p. 1553.

133. Ibid.

134. Ibid.

135. Ibid. Punctuation corrected in closing sentence.

136. N. P. Jacobson, "Marxism and Religious Naturalism," The Journal of Religion, XXIX (April, 1949).

137. Letter, John Dewey to N. P. Jacobson, May 25, 1949, Carbondale, Southern Illinois University, Archives.

138. Jacobson, "Marxism and Religious Naturalism," pp. 108-109. Jacobson documents his statement as a contribution from two sources: George Herbert Mead, Movements of Thought in the Nineteenth Century (Chicago: University of Chicago Press, 1946), pp. 42-43; and Wieman, The Source of Human Good, p. 299.

139. Letter, N. P. Jacobson to John Dewey, June 8, 1949, Carbondale, Southern Illinois University, Archives.

140. Letter, John Dewey to N. P. Jacobson, June 13, 1949, Carbondale, Southern Illinois University, Archives.

141. Letter, N. P. Jacobson to John Dewey, July 9, 1949, Carbondale, Southern Illinois University, Archives.

142. Ibid.

143. Letter, John Dewey to N. P. Jacobson, July 16, 1949, Carbondale, Southern Illinois University, Archives.

144. Henry Nelson Wieman, Intellectual Foundation of Faith (New York: Philosophical Library, 1961).

145. Ibid., p. 1.

146. Ibid., p. 28.

147. Ibid., p. 12.

148. Ibid., p. 29.

149. Ibid., p. 31.

150. This conference may have occurred at the time Dewey was at the University of Chicago when he gave one of the addresses in the Memorial Service for George Herbert Mead in 1931.

151. Wieman, Intellectual Foundation of Faith, p. 31.

152. Ibid., pp. 32-33, quoting Dewey, Experience and Nature, pp. 166, 205-206.

153. Vide supra, pp. 165-166.

154. Wieman, Intellectual Foundation of Faith, p. 33.

155. Ibid., p. 35.

156. Vide supra, pp. 156-158.

157. Wieman, Intellectual Foundation of Faith, p. 51.

158. After further analysis of Dewey's idea of God, including Wieman's criticism in Intellectual Foundation of Faith, I called Wieman at his home in Grinnell, Iowa, June 14, 1970, and asked him if he would reread chapter two, "John Dewey Answers," in Wieman's book, Intellectual Foundation of Faith, and send me any comments he might wish to offer. Wieman asked if there was any particular issue to which he should give special attention. I replied negatively. Later in the day, Wieman called, saying his criticism of Dewey was a misinterpretation. His correction and letter of June 15 arrived June 18, 1970.

159. Henry Nelson Wieman, "My Misinterpretation of Dewey's Religious Faith," (unpub. ms., Carbondale, Southern Illinois University, Archives, June 15, 1970), pp. 1-3.

160. Ibid., p. 1.

161. Ibid.

162. Ibid., pp. 2-3.

163. Ibid., p. 3.

164. Vide supra, pp. 153-159.

165. Vide supra, pp. 161-163.

166. Vide supra, pp. 152-160.

167. Vide supra, p. 169.

168. John Dewey, "The Present Position of Logical Theory," in Dewey, Early Essays and Outlines..., ed. Boydston, p. 133 [first published in The Monist, II (October, 1891), 1-17].

169. Ibid.

170. Vide supra, p. 121, at n. 9.

171. John Dewey, Theory of Valuation (Chicago: University of Chicago Press, 1939), Section V, "Ends and Value," and Section VI, "The Continuum of Ends-Means," pp. 35-50. From Vol. II, No. 4 of the International Encyclopedia of Unified Science (1939), ed. Otto Neurath, Rudolf Carnap and Charles W. Morris.

172. John Dewey, Human Nature and Conduct, Part Two: "The Place of Impulse in Conduct," pp. 89-171.

173. Dewey, Art as Experience, p. 339.

174. Ibid., p. 281.

175. Ibid.

176. Ibid., p. 336.

177. Vide supra, pp. 165-167.

178. Dewey, Art as Experience, p. 336.

179. Ibid.

180. Ibid., p. 267.

181. Ibid., p. 268.

182. Ibid.

183. Ibid., p. 269.

184. Ibid., pp. 269-270.

185. Ibid., p. 274.

186. Ibid., p. 297.

187. Ibid.

188. Wieman, "William James," Religious Experience and Scientific Method, pp. 311-321.

189. Ibid., p. 311-312.

190. Ibid., p. 320.

191. Vide supra, pp. 25-27.

192. Wieman, Religious Experience and Scientific Method, p. 317.

193. Ibid.

194. Vide supra, p. 1.

195. Bernard Eugene Meland, "Creativity in William James" (a research paper of 25 pages, prepared for the Society for Philosophy of Creativity and presented in its 1967 meeting with the Western Division of the American Philosophical Assoc.), p. 24.

196. Ibid., p. 16.

197. Ibid.

198. Vide supra, p. 179, at n. 190.

199. Wieman, "The Organization of Interests," p. [254].

200. Ibid., quoting Hocking, The Meaning of God in Human Experience, p. 502.

201. Wieman, "The Organization of Interests," p. [254].

202. Wieman, The Source of Human Good, pp. 288-289.

203. Dewey, Art as Experience, p. 282.

CHAPTER VI

1. Vide supra, pp. xviii-xix, at n. 2, and p. 20, at n. 54.

2. Ibid.

3. Wieman, "The Organization of Interests," p. 258.

4. Henry Nelson Wieman, "Professor Whitehead's Concept of God," The Hibbert Journal, XXV (1926-1927), pp. 623-630; reprinted as Chapter XI, "The Concept of God," The Wrestle of Religion with Truth (1927), pp. 179-190.

5. Whitehead, Process and Reality, p. 32.

6. Ibid.

7. Vide supra, p. 163, at n. 143.

8. Vide supra, pp. 168-169.

9. Vide supra, pp. 64-67.

10. Vide supra, pp. 124-125.

11. Vide supra, pp. 121-123.

12. Vide supra, p. 1, at n. 2.

BIBLIOGRAPHY

BOOKS

Bergson, Henri. Creative Evolution. Translated by Arthur Mitchell. New York: Random House, 1944. (Modern Library.)

──────. The Creative Mind. Translated by Mabelle L. Andison. New York: Philosophical Library, 1946.

──────. An Introduction to Metaphysics. Translated by T. E. Hulme. New York: Bobbs-Merrill, 1949.

──────. The Two Sources of Morality and Religion. Translated by R. Ashley Audra and Cloudesley Brereton. Garden City, N. Y.: Doubleday, 1954.

Bernstein, Richard, ed. Perspectives on Peirce. New Haven, Conn.: Yale University Press, 1965.

Boydston, Jo Ann, gen. ed. John Dewey, The Early Works, 1882-1898. Vol. 3, 1889-1892. Early Essays and Outlines of a Critical Theory of Ethics. Carbondale: Southern Illinois University Press, 1969.

Bradley, Francis Herbert. Appearance and Reality. New York: Macmillan, 1897.

Brandt, Richard B. Value and Obligation. New York: Harcourt, Brace & World, 1961.

Bretall, Robert W., ed. The Empirical Theology of Henry Nelson Wieman. Vol. IV of The Library of Living Theology. Edited by Charles W. Kegley and Robert W. Bretall. Carbondale: Southern Illinois University Press, 1969. (Arcturus Books.)

Castell, Alburey, ed. Essays in Pragmatism by William James, New York: Hafner Pub. Co., 1948.

Cobb, John B., Jr. A Christian Natural Theology Based on the Thought of Alfred North Whitehead. Philadelphia: Westminster Press, 1965.

──────. God and the World. Philadelphia: Westminster Press, 1969.

Cole, Stewart G., ed. This Is My Faith. New York: Harper & Brothers, 1956.

Dewey, John. Art as Experience. Capricorn Books. New York: G. P. Putnam's Sons, 1958.

⸺. A Common Faith. New Haven, Conn.: Yale University Press, 1934.

⸺. Experience and Nature. Chicago: Open Court Pub. Co., 1925.

⸺. Human Nature and Conduct. New York: Random House, 1930. (Modern Library.)

⸺. The Quest for Certainty: A Study of the Relation of Knowledge and Action. New York: Minton, Balch & Co., 1929.

⸺. Theory of Valuation. Chicago: University of Chicago Press, 1939.

⸺, and Tufts, James H. Ethics. New York: Henry Holt, 1936.

Gilman, Richard C. The Bibliography of William Ernest Hocking from 1898 to 1951. Waterville, Me.: Colby College, 1951.

Gunter, P. A. Y., ed. and trans. Bergson and the Evolution of Physics. Knoxville: University of Tennessee Press, 1969.

Hanna, Thomas, ed. The Bergsonian Heritage. New York: Columbia University Press, 1962.

Hartshorne, Charles, and Weiss, Paul, eds. Collected Papers of Charles Sanders Peirce. Cambridge, Mass.: Harvard University Press, 1931-1935. 6 vols.

Hocking, William Ernest. The Coming World Civilization. New York: Harper & Brothers, 1956.

⸺. Human Nature and Its Remaking. New Haven, Conn.: Yale University Press, 1918.

⸺. The Meaning of God in Human Experience. New Haven, Conn.: Yale University Press, 1912.

⸺. The Self: Its Body and Freedom. New Haven, Conn.: Yale University Press, 1928.

⸺. Thoughts on Death and Life. New York: Harper & Brothers, 1937.

_____. Types of Philosophy. New York: Charles Scribner's Sons, 1929.

James, William. Essays on Faith and Morals. Selected by Ralph Barton Perry. New York: World, 1962. (Meridian Books.)

_____. The Principles of Psychology. New York: Henry Holt, 1890 [reprinted, Dover]. 2 vols.

_____. The Varieties of Religious Experience. New York: Longmans, Green, 1902.

Johnson, A. H. Whitehead's Theory of Reality. Boston: Beacon Press, 1952.

Lowe, Victor; Hartshorne, Charles; and Johnson, A. H. Whitehead and the Modern World. Boston: Beacon Press, 1950.

McDermott, John J., ed. The Writings of William James: A Comprehensive Edition. New York: Random House, 1967. (Modern Library.)

Macintosh, Douglas Clyde, ed. Religious Realism. New York: Macmillan, 1931.

Marcel, Gabriel. Royce's Metaphysics. Translated by Virginia and Gordon Ringer. Chicago: Henry Regnery, 1956.

Meland, Bernard Eugene. America's Spiritual Culture. New York: Harper & Brothers, 1948.

_____. Faith and Culture. New York: Oxford University Press, 1953.

_____., ed. and co-author. The Future of Empirical Theology. Vol. VII of Essays in Divinity. Edited by Jerald C. Brauer. Chicago: University of Chicago Press, 1967-69. 7 vols.

_____. Higher Education and the Human Spirit. Chicago: University of Chicago Press, 1953.

_____. The Realities of Faith. New York: Oxford University Press, 1962.

Minor, William S., ed. Charles Hartshorne and Henry Nelson Wieman. Carbondale: Southern Illinois University for Foundation for Creative Philosophy, 1969. (Philosophy of Creativity Monograph Series, vol. 1.)

_____. "Public Interest and Ultimate Commitment." Nomos V: The Public Interest. Edited by Carl J. Friedrich. New York: Atherton Press, 1962.

Murphey, Murray G. The Development of Peirce's Philosophy.
Cambridge, Mass.: Harvard University Press, 1961.

Ogden, Schubert M. "Present Prospects for Empirical Theology."
The Future of Empirical Theology. Edited by Bernard Eugene
Meland. Vol. VII of Essays in Divinity. Edited by Jerald C.
Brauer. Chicago: University of Chicago Press, 1967-69.
7 vols.

_____. The Reality of God and Other Essays. New York:
Harper & Rowe, 1966.

Perry, Ralph Barton. General Theory of Value. Cambridge, Mass.:
Harvard University Press, 1926.

_____. Present Philosophical Tendencies. New York: Longmans, Green, 1912.

_____. Realms of Value. Cambridge, Mass.: Harvard University Press, 1954.

_____. The Thought and Character of William James. Boston:
Little, Brown, 1935. 2 vols.

Price, Lucien. Dialogues of Alfred North Whitehead. Boston:
Little, Brown, 1954.

Rouner, Leroy S., ed. Philosophy, Religion, and the Coming
World Civilization. Essays in Honor of William Ernest Hocking. The Hague: Martinus Nijhoff, 1966.

_____. Within Human Experience. Cambridge, Mass.: Harvard
University Press, 1969.

Royce, Josiah. The Problem of Christianity. New York: Macmillan, 1913. 2 vols.

_____. The World and the Individual. New York: Dover Publications, 1959. 2 vols.

Schilpp, Paul Arthur, ed. The Philosophy of Alfred North Whitehead. Vol. III of The Library of Living Philosophers. New
York: Tudor Pub. Co., 1941.

_____, ed. The Philosophy of John Dewey. Vol. I of The Library of Living Philosophers. New York: Tudor Pub. Co.,
1939.

Sherburne, Donald W., ed. A Key to Whitehead's Process and
Reality. New York: Macmillan, 1966.

Thompson, Manley. The Pragmatic Philosophy of C. S. Peirce.
Chicago: University of Chicago Press, 1953.

Whitehead, Alfred North. Adventures of Ideas. New York: Macmillan, 1933.

_____. The Aims of Education. New York: New American Library of World Literature, 1949. (Mentor Books.)

_____. The Concept of Nature. Ann Arbor: University of Michigan Press, 1957.

_____. The Function of Reason. Boston: Beacon Press, 1958.

_____. Modes of Thought. New York: Macmillan, 1938.

_____. Nature and Life. Chicago: University of Chicago Press, 1934.

_____. Process and Reality. New York: Macmillan, 1929.

_____. Religion in the Making. New York: Macmillan, 1926.

_____. Science and the Modern World. New York: New American Library of World Literature, 1948. (Mentor Books.)

Wieman, Henry Nelson. The Directive in History. Boston: Beacon Press, 1949. (Phoenix Books.)

_____. Intellectual Foundation of Faith. New York: Philosophical Library, 1961.

_____. Man's Ultimate Commitment. Carbondale: Southern Illinois University Press, 1958.

_____. Methods of Private Religious Living. New York: Macmillan, 1929.

_____. "Neo-orthodoxy and Contemporary Religious Reaction," in Religious Liberals Reply. Boston: Beacon Press, 1947.

_____. Now We Must Choose. New York: Macmillan, 1941.

_____. Religious Experience and Scientific Method. New York: Macmillan, 1926.

_____. Religious Inquiry: Some Explorations. Boston: Beacon Press, 1968.

_____. The Source of Human Good. Arcturus Books. Carbondale: Southern Illinois University Press, 1964.

_____. The Wrestle of Religion with Truth. New York: Macmillan, 1927.

_____, and Horton, Walter Marshall. The Growth of Religion. Chicago: Willett, Clark & Co., 1938.

_____; Macintosh, Douglas Clyde; and Otto, Max Carl. Is There a God? A Conversation. Chicago: Willett, Clark & Co., 1932.

_____, and Meland, Bernard Eugene. American Philosophies of Religion. Chicago: Willett, Clark & Co., 1936.

_____, and Wieman, Regina Westcott. Normative Psychology of Religion. New York: Thomas Y. Crowell, 1935.

Williams, Daniel Day. The Spirit and the Forms of Love. New York: Harper & Rowe, 1968.

ARTICLES

Aubrey, Edwin Ewart. "Is John Dewey a Theist?" The Christian Century, LI (December 5, 1934), 1550.

Dewey, John. "Dr. Dewey Replies." The Christian Century, L (March 22, 1933), 394-395.

_____. "A God or The God." The Christian Century, L (February 8, 1933), 193-196.

_____. "Is John Dewey a Theist?" The Christian Century, LI (December 5, 1934), 1551-1552.

_____. "The Present Position of Logical Theory." The Monist, II (October, 1891), 1-17.

Jacobson, N. P. "Marxism and Religious Naturalism." The Journal of Religion, XXIX (April, 1949), 95-113.

Meland, Bernard Eugene. "Is God Many or One?" The Christian Century, L (May 31, 1933), 725-726.

Parsons, Howard L. "God and Man's Achievement of Identity: Religion in the Thought of Alfred North Whitehead." Educational Theory, XI (October, 1961), 228-254.

Perry, Ralph Barton. "Contemporary Philosophies of Religion." The Harvard Theological Review, VII (July 1, 1914), 378-395.

_____. "The Definition of Value." The Journal of Philosophy, Psychology, and Scientific Methods, XI (March 12, 1914), 141-162.

Wieman, Henry Nelson. "Is God Many or One?" The Christian Century, L (May 31, 1933), 726-727.

_____. "Is John Dewey a Theist?" The Christian Century, LI (December 5, 1934), 1550-1551.

_____. "John Dewey's Common Faith." The Christian Century, LI (November 14, 1934), 1450-1452.

_____. "Mr. Wieman and Mr. Macintosh 'Converse' with Mr. Dewey." The Christian Century, L (March 1, 1933), 299-300.

_____. "Mr. Wieman Replies to Mr. Dewey." The Christian Century, L (April 5, 1933), 466-467.

_____. "Perception and Cognition." The Journal of Philosophy, XL (February 4, 1943), 73-77.

_____. "Philosophers' Dean: The Dual Dewey." The Christian Register, CXXVIII (November, 1949), 22-24.

_____. "Professor Whitehead's Concept of God." The Hibbard Journal, XXV (1926-1927), 623-630.

_____. "Religion in Dewey's Experience and Nature." The Journal of Religion, V (September, 1925), 519-542.

UNPUBLISHED MATERIAL*

Application and Record of Work of Henry Nelson Wieman as a Student in Park College. Southern Illinois University Archives.

Brooks, Deems M. "Toward a Synthesis of Creative Communication in the Philosophy of Henry Nelson Wieman." Unpub. Ph.D. dissert., Southern Illinois University, 1968.

Cobb, Larry Russell. "Creativity in Politics: the Political Thought of Henry Nelson Wieman." Unpub. Ph.D. dissert., Southern Illinois University, 1967.

Conversation and Correspondence with Charles Hartshorne. American Philosophical Assoc., Western Division Meeting, May 9, 1970. Letter, May 11, 1970.

Dewey, John. Letters to N. P. Jacobson, May 25, June 13, July 16, 1949. Southern Illinois University Archives.

Hocking, William Ernest. "The Elementary Experience of Other Conscious Being in Its Relations to the Elementary Experience of Physical and Reflexive Objects." Unpub. Ph.D. dissert., Harvard University, 1904.

Howie, John. "Creativity in the Thought of William Ernest Hocking and Henry Nelson Wieman." Unpub. Ph.D. dissert., Boston University, 1965.

---

*All Southern Illinois University citations listed here refer to Carbondale.

Bibliography / 223

Jacobson, N. P. Letters to John Dewey, June 8, July 9, 1949. Southern Illinois University Archives.

King, Martin Luther. "A Comparison of the Conceptions of God in the Thinking of Paul Tillich and Henry Nelson Wieman." Unpub. Ph. D. dissert., Boston University, 1955.

Meland, Bernard Eugene. "Creativity in William James." Paper presented at meeting of Society for Philosophy of Creativity with the Western Division of the American Philosophical Assoc., Chicago, May 4, 1967.

Miller, David Lee. "The Significance of the Aesthetic in Whitehead's Metaphysics and Philosophy of Education." Unpub. M. A. thesis, Southern Illinois University, 1965.

_____. "Value and Some Key but Unfinished Doctrines in Whitehead's Philosophy." Unpub. Ph. D. dissert., Southern Illinois University, 1969.

Minor, William Sherman. "Humility in Religion According to Saint Augustine." Unpub. B. D. dissert., University of Chicago, 1931.

_____. Notes from Courses and Conferences with Henry Nelson Wieman. 1929--

Papers presented in the National Conference for Philosophy of Creativity, Southern Illinois University, Carbondale, October 16-18, 1969. Foundation for Creative Philosophy, Carbondale, Ill.

Research Programs of the Society for Philosophy of Creativity. Papers presented in meetings with the American Philosophical Assoc., 1963- . "Creativity in Henri Bergson, John Dewey, Charles Hartshorne, * William Ernest Hocking, William James, Charles Sanders Peirce, Josiah Royce, Paul Tillich, Alfred North Whitehead, and Henry Nelson Wieman.*" Foundation for Creative Philosophy, Carbondale, Ill. (*See Philosophy of Creativity Monograph Series, Vol. 1.)

Rich, Charles Mark. "Henry Nelson Wieman's Functional Theism as Transcending Event." Unpub. Ph. D. dissert., University of Chicago, 1962.

Wieman, Henry Nelson. "Intellectual Autobiography" (mimeographed). Carbondale: Southern Illinois University Archives, 1957. (Abstract in The Empirical Theology of Henry Nelson Wieman, ed. by Robert W. Bretall [New York: Macmillan, 1963].)

_____. "My Misinterpretation of Dewey's Religious Faith." Unpub. paper. Southern Illinois University Archives, June 15, 1970.

_____. "The Organization of Interests." Unpub. Ph. D. dissert.,

Harvard University, 1917. Southern Illinois University Archives (microfilm).

―――――. "Summation of Whitehead's Philosophy." Unpub. essay. Southern Illinois University Archives, n.d.

INDEX

the Absolute: 22, 24, 41, 55, 59; and empirical and conceptual metaphysical interpretation 55-57
Absolute goal 56
Abstract time 72
Abstraction(s): 97, 106-107; and intellectual knowledge 36; and prehensive feeling 105
Act 127
Action: phases of, philosophical, psycho-physical, scientific 120-121; and intellect 81
Acts of God 29
the Actual 150f, 154, 156, 168
Actual entity/entities: 90, 100-101, 104, 110; and atomism 96-98; and feelings 105; as locus of creativity 97; and particulars 102; relations of 97; and subjective immediacy 96
Actual occasions 97
Actuality: as aesthetic 106-107
Alexander, S. 91
American Philosophies of Religion (Meland and Wieman) 71
Analytical knowledge: and mystical awareness 34
Analytical understanding of God 188f
Anti-intellectual metaphysics 73
Appearance and Reality (Bradley) 24
Art: 108; as experience 177-178
Art as Experience (Dewey) 174, 183
Atomic events 115

Aubrey, Edwin Ewart 153ff
Awareness, open: in tension with scientific method 19-21

Beauty 108
Becoming: 74, 88, 94, 96, 189; metaphysics of 78; and process philosophy 94; and subjectivity 101
Being 88
Bergson, Henri 4-6, 70-86, 88, 91, 94f, 97f, 117, 148, 186, 188
Boulding, Kenneth 6

Causal efficacy 102-103
Causal relations 84
Civilization: contrasted with culture 52
Coherence 56
Comedy 109
A Common Faith (Dewey) 148, 152ff, 158f, 162, 167, 169, 177, 183
Communication: 75f, 84, 165f, 168, 173f; philosophy of 27
Community: 50, 97, 157; of creative interaction 161; human 84; and persons 88
The Concept of Nature (Whitehead) 92
Conceptual: feelings 112; knowledge 93; prehensions 104, 117
Conceptualistic metaphysics 55, 58
Concrescence 88, 97, 106
Concrete time 72
Concretion: and God 93; principle of 93; and societism 93

225

Conflict: 73, 105; human 14, 27
Consciousness: 75-77, 82f, 84, 97, 104, 130f; defined 82; and reflection 82; and theory and fact 104-105
Contemplation 41
"Contemporary Philosophies of Religion" (Perry) 11
Cooley, C. H. 6
Cosmic consciousness 114-117
Created goods 36
Creation: and continuity 79, 84; and duration 79
Creative: activity 125; acts of God 187; advance of nature 95; communication 23, 27, 29-30, 50; community 51, 166f; energy 112, 116; event 29, 30, 37-42, 53, 188--and divine creation 40, four-fold 89, and known creative structure 51, and subevents 41, 46-48, 50, 88-89, and two level commitment to 84; evolution 75, 85f, 88, 97, 109; good 36; interchange 53, 116, 169, 174--and community 54, and human conflict 54, a kind of communication 1-2, knowable aspect of God 1; interest 10, 36--and conflicting interests 14; organicism 148; power 89; unity 152
Creative Evolution (Bergson) 51, 70, 71, 86, 186
Creativity: 23, 37, 40, 53, 72, 79, 83, 85-86, 87, 96, 109, 113, 122-123, 125, 147, 164, 189; as abstraction from creative event 40; centered in the interaction of minds in society 14; and coherence 56; commitment to 2, 13; and continuity 75; empirical nature of 55; as an empirical process 88; experiental view of value as xviii; and fine arts 107; and God 105-117; and greatest possible value 161; ground of 30; human and divine 27;

and human experience 84; and the infinite 57; locus of, in actual entities 97; more than a datum of human experience xviii; in philosophy xvii, 6; philosophy of 26; principle of greatest good 35; and principle of organization of human interests 8, 10; and process 94; and quality 80; of religion 29; and right conditions for 89; structured creativity, and creative event 110

Datum: and subject 101-103
"The Definition of Value" (Perry) 8-9
Degrees of Experience 126
Determinate order 112
Development and Purpose (Hobhouse) 11
Dewey, John 99, 117, 118ff, 188, 190
Diversity 97
Drucker, Peter 6
Dualism: of movement and inertia 75
Duration: 72, 74, 76, 82, 94; and creation 79

Eachness 181
Ecological sciences 53
Ecology: 126; of nature and creativity 53
"The Elementary Experience of Other Conscious Being in Its Relations to the Elementary Experiences of Physical and Reflexive Objects" (Hocking) 27
Elwood, C. A. 6
Empirical: knowledge 28-29; metaphysics 55-57; method of inquiry 6, 118; philosophy 91
Empiricism: 29, 99, 100, 119f; and thought 98ff
End of history 182
Energy 79, 112
Enjoyment: in value 17

Eternal objects: 110; and universals 102
Eucken, Rudolf 3
Event(s) 90ff, 180
Evil 59ff
Evolution: 88; creative 75; philosophy of 94
Experience: 26ff, 102, 118, 125ff, and subjectivism 100-103
Experience and Nature (Dewey) 128, 133, 134, 162, 165
Experimental investigations 144

Fact 98
Faith 191
Feeling: 41, 81-82; awareness 30, 33, 34, 106; and prehension 103-105; and togetherness 105; in value 17
Felt quality: 105; flow of, 78-80; and religions of the world 80
Form: and novelty 84
Freedom 41-42

The General Theory of Value (Perry) 5, 8
God: 162, 167f, 189; "absolute mind" of 58; abstract nature of 31; and all reality 58; and concretion 93; consequent nature of 112ff; and creativity 105-117; creativity of 29; denotative and descriptive definitions of 32ff; and experienceable event xviii; as finite 57; idea of 32; immediate sense of 34; knowledge of 36, 51-52, 80; meaning of, in human experience xviii; nature of 136ff; primordial nature of 110ff; sovereignty of 183; use of the word 1
"God and Value" (Wieman) 143
Good: 9, 59; greatest 8, 35; three categories of 52
Goods 137-138
Grace 33

Growth of meaning 130-131, 134, 149

Haldane, J. B. S. 91
Harmonious happiness: 12-13, 54; defined 11; as an ideal 14
Hartshorne, Charles 114
History 29, 49-50, 108
Hobhouse, L. T. 6, 91
Hocking, William Ernest 5, 11, 21, 22-70, 78, 97, 98, 141, 148, 179, 182, 186, 188
Holt, E. B. 6
the Holy: experience of 117
Human: conduct 157; conflict 30; creativity 41-42; interests, classification of 13; need 161
Human Nature and Conduct (Dewey) 134
Humanism 138, 153
"Humanist Manifesto" 135, 136
Humility 123-124, 132
Humor 109

Ideal(s) 150ff, 154, 156, 168, 170ff
Idealism: defined 22
Imagination: 133, 154f, 157, 159, 174; and creative interaction, 177; and the imaginative 176; locus of, in communication 173f
Immediate awareness 36
Individual: 97, 98; and society 88, 90
Inertia 75
Infinite, the 24, 134
Instinct: 78, 81, 187; and activity 83; and knowledge 81, 83; and sympathy 82
Instrumentalism 122
Intellect: 73, 74, 77, 78, 81, 84, 85, 87, 97, 187; and action 81; and physical causality 82
Intellectual: analysis 36; experience 127f
"Intellectual Autobiography" (Wieman) 1, 79, 118-119

228 / Index

Intellectual Foundation of Faith (Wieman) 163, 167, 169, 190
Intelligence 76
Interest: classifications of 13, 187; defined 9, 78; conflicting 14, 18-19; creative 14, 18-19
Introduction to Philosophy: Syllabus to Course 5 (Dewey) 119
Intuition: 73, 76-78, 81, 84, 85, 87, 187; defined 82; and knowledge 74, 83
Is There a God? (Wieman, Macintosh and Otto) 34, 136, 141
Isolation 90

Jacobson, Nolan P. 161ff, 190
James, William 26, 27, 86, 91, 98, 99, 117, 118-122, 178-184
Joy: in creative interchange 54
Judgment 129
Justice 115

Knowledge: 51, 109, 189; basic and derivative 12; conceptual 93; instinctive 81; scientific 83; and theory and inference 84

Liberal harmony 15-18
Love 115
Lure of aspirations 116

Mach, E. 91
Macintosh, D. C. 141
Man's Ultimate Commitment (Wieman) 14, 89
the Many: 76, 87; as the nature of God 142ff; and process 94
Materialism: 95; metaphysics of 92, 95; mechanistic 95
Meaning: 52; and meaningful experience 129-130; and meaningless experience 130f

The Meaning of God in Human Experience (Hocking) 4, 5, 11, 22, 25, 28, 29, 187, 188
Meland, Bernard E. 141-147
Mentality 121
Metaphysics: 75; of creative evolution 77, 81; and science 73-74
Mind 74, 92
Molecules 115
Moore, G. E. 8, 9, 35, 36
Morgan, Lloyd 91
Movement 75
"My Misinterpretation of Dewey's Religious Faith" (Wieman) 167
the Mystic: and revelation 30; and worship 32
Mystic certainty 31
Mystic knowledge 35
Mystical awareness: and analytical knowledge 34; of God 188f
Mysticism 22, 26, 179f

Naturalism 125
Naturalistic philosophy of religion 161f
Nature: 34, 75, 92-93; and creative advance 95; forces of 172; and human nature 161; monistic interpretation of 161; and process philosophy 94
Negative prehensions 104
Neo-realism: 45, 146; and empiricism 147; epistemology of 31, 34, 51, 55, 96, 102, 118, 190
Newtonian physics 86
Nexus 94, 96
Nihilism 40
Novel togetherness 88, 89, 94
Novelty: 93, 95, 97, 98; emergence of 37; and form 84

Object: 95; and sensation 35
Objectification 97
Objective immortality of events 96

Objective realism 27
the One: 76, 87; as nature of God 142ff; and process 94
Order 97
Organic: connectedness 147; evolution 87; unity 138
Organismic: metaphysics 84, 87, 88, 95; philosophy 71, 81
"The Organization of Interests" (Wieman) 2, 6, 77
Originality 131-132

Particulars 102
Peirce, Charles Sanders 3, 6, 21, 23, 24
Perceived object 103
Perception 101-103
Perceptual event 102, 103
Perry, Ralph Barton 5, 8-21, 23, 35, 54, 78, 91, 99, 186, 190
Persons: and community 88
"Philosophers' Dean: The Dual Dewey" (Wieman) 128
Philosophy: 119-121; as problem-solving process 123; of creativity 88, 94
Physical: feelings 112; causality and intellect 82; prehensions 104, 117
Physics 91-92
Pluralistic metaphysics 146
Positive prehensions 104
Power: 43ff; creative and transforming 89
Practice: and thought 99f
Pragmatism 22, 26
Prehension(s): 90, 93, 96-97; and abstraction 105; defined as "concrete facts of relatedness" 104; and feeling 103-105
Presentational immediacy 102
Primordial: order 112; structure 109-110
Principles of Natural Knowledge (Whitehead) 91
The Principles of Psychology (James) 24, 98, 99, 121, 171
Process: 88, 98; defined 94;

metaphysics 57, 58, 95; philosophy 86, 95, 122; and becoming 94
Process and Reality (Whitehead) 71, 72, 86, 87, 88, 96, 189
Progressive integration 156
Prophetic consciousness 29, 42-48
Propositions 102
Providence 29, 48-70
Psycho-physical event 102
Purpose 92

Qualitative meaning 162
Qualities 180
Quality: 52, 79; and creativity 80; felt, flow of 78ff; measured 73; metaphysics of 79; undifferentiated 73

Radical empiricism 179
Radical idealism 22
Rational speculation 99
the Real 74
Real time 72
Realism 22, 27, 29
Reality: 142f, 145f; concreteness of 13; richness of 104; two approaches to 144f
Realms of Value (Perry) 5, 8, 11
Reason 97f
Reflection: 41; and consciousness 82
Reflex action, arc 122
Reformed subjectivist principle 101
Relations: of actual entities 96; metaphysics of 91; of qualities in events 180
Relativity: 86, 91-92, 93, 106; principle of 101; and process philosophy 94; and societism 90-93
Religion: 134, 149ff; and speculation 93
Religion in the Making (Whitehead) 93, 95, 106, 189
Religious commitment: 113; to creativity 88
Religious datum 31

230 / Index

Religious experience: object of 31
Religious Experience and Scientific Method (Wieman) 85, 91, 95, 128, 134, 185
Religious inquiry: 2, 36, 50-52, 105-106; and cosmological and theological discussions xvii; and problem of value xvii
Religious Inquiry; Some Explorations (Wieman) 41, 85, 100, 113, 185, 190
Religious Realism (Macintosh et al.) 143
Revelation 29-37
Royce, Josiah 3, 4, 6, 21, 23, 24, 27f, 31, 78, 97, 99, 186

Science: 91, 119-121; and metaphysics 73-74
Science and the Modern World (Whitehead) 92, 93, 95, 98, 189
Scientific: knowledge 34, 74; method 19-21, 33ff
Sensation: and object 35
Sensationalist view of experience 102
Shared responsibility 134-135
Social environment 29
Social sciences 91
Societism: 94; and concretion and prehension 93; and relativity 90-93
Society: 14, 94, 96; and the individual 88
Solipsism 25
The Source of Human Good (Wieman) 27, 37, 107, 188
Speculation: rational 99, 100; and religion 93; and speculative philosophy 96
Structure: 40, 79, 103, 109-110, 112; and quality 80; structured creativity, and the creative event 110
Subject: and its datum 101, 103; experience of 100
Subjective immediacy: and actual entity 96

Subjectivism: 27, 45; and experience 100-103
Subjectivity: and becoming 101
Substance: metaphysics of 91
Suffering: in creative interchange 54
Sullivan, Harry Stack 6
"Summation of Whitehead's Philosophy" (Wieman) 106
Supernaturalism 153
Symbolic reference 102
Sympathy: and instinct 82; as primitive mode of feeling 104

Tension: in Wieman's religious philosophy, centered in the immediate awareness of the qualitative richness of reality and the intellectual analysis of this qualitative richness xviii, 19-21, 105-106, 117, 128, 153, 179, 182, 185, 191
Theism 140
Theology: and tragic art 109
Theoretical investigations 144
Theory of Valuation (Dewey) 183
Thought: and empiricism 98-100; and practice 99-100
Time 72, 74
Togetherness: 93; and feeling 105
Transcendence 76, 84-85
Transformation: 73; and power 89; in value 17
Troeltsch, Ernst 3
Truth 109

Ugliness 108
Ultimate concern/commitment: for creativity 89; commitment and worship 64-70
Unity: 97; in growth of child 160
Universals 102
Universe: 72, 75, 93, 146, 157; as aesthetic 105

Valuation 110-111

Value: 9, 15-18, 52, 138, 162;
   cognition of 8; definition of
   9; empirical analysis of 11-12;
   experiental view of xviii; increase and organization of 11;
   and interest theory 6, 8;
   more than a datum of human
   experience xviii; and religious inquiry xvii
Values: 112-113, 155, 157;
   and material universe 114
Valuing 83
The Varieties of Religious Experience (James) 25, 26
Vector feeling 104
Vision: inner and outer, in art
   175

Whitehead, Alfred North 71,
   86-117, 148, 189f
Whole idea 56, 59
Windelband, Wilhelm 3
World and the Individual, The
   (Royce) 3, 24, 28
Worship: 32, 37, 41, 131, 144;
   and ultimate commitment
   64-70; and work 61-62
The Wrestle of Religion with
   Truth (Wieman) 100, 106

LIBRARY OF DAVIDSON COLLEGE

Books on regular loan may be checked out for **two weeks**. Books must be presented at the Circulation Desk in order to be renewed.

A fine is charged after date due.

Special books are subject to special regulations at the discretion of the library staff.